The Effort–Net Return Model
of Employee Motivation

Recent Titles from Quorum Books

Real Interest Rates and Investment Borrowing Strategy
Peter S. Spiro

The Political Limits of Environmental Regulation: Tracking the Unicorn
Bruce Yandle

Summary Judgment and Other Preclusive Devices
Warren Freedman

Distinction Between Measurement and Interpretation in Accounting: A Living
Systems Theory Approach
G. A. Swanson and James Grier Miller

Strict Liability: Legal and Economic Analysis
Frank J. Vandall

Security Program Design and Management: A Guide for Security-Conscious
Managers
Donald B. Tweedy

The Improvement of Corporate Financial Performance: A Manager's Guide
to Evaluating Selected Opportunities
Sherman L. Lewis

The Director's and Officer's Guide to Advisory Boards
Robert K. Mueller

Present Value Applications for Accountants and Financial Planners
G. Eddy Birrer and Jean L. Carrica

Software, Copyright, and Competition: The "Look and Feel" of the Law
Anthony L. Clapes

Regulating Utilities with Management Incentives: A Strategy for
Improved Performance
Kurt A. Strasser and Mark F. Kohler

THE EFFORT–NET RETURN MODEL
OF EMPLOYEE MOTIVATION
Principles,
Propositions, and
Prescriptions

PHILIP C. GRANT

Quorum Books
New York • Westport, Connecticut • London

Library of Congress Cataloging-in-Publication Data

Grant, Philip C.
    The effort-net return model of employee motivation : principles,
propositions, and prescriptions / Philip C. Grant.
        p.   cm.
    Bibliography: p.
    Includes index.
    ISBN 0-89930-495-8 (lib. bdg. : alk. paper)
    1. Employee motivation.   2. Employee motivation—Case studies.
I. Title.
HF5549.5.M63G72   1990
658.3'14—dc20   89-10481

British Library Cataloguing in Publication Data is available.

Library of Congress Catalog Card Number: 89-10481
ISBN: 0-89930-495-8

First published in 1990 by Quorum Books

Greenwood Press, Inc.
88 Post Road West, Westport, Connecticut 06881

Printed in the United States of America

The paper used in this book complies with the
Permanent Paper Standard issued by the National
Information Standards Organization (Z39.48-1984).

10 9 8 7 6 5 4 3 2 1

Copyright Acknowledgments

The author and publisher gratefully acknowledge permission to use material from the following:

Thomas O. Kirkpatrick, *Supervision,* pp. 335, 367-68. © by Wadsworth, Inc. Reprinted by permission of PWS-KENT Publishing Company, a division of Wadsworth, Inc.

Adapted from Gray and Starke, *Organizational Behavior: Concepts and Applications,* Exercise 2-1.
© by Merrill Publishing Company, 1977.

Dr. Michael Jucius, *Personnel Management,* Sixth Edition, 1967, pp. 550-51. © by Richard D.
Irwin, Inc.

Andrew DuBrin, *Human Relations: A Job Oriented Approach,* © 1978, pp. 39, 125. Reprinted by
permission of Prentice-Hall, Inc.

Douglas T. Hall et al., *Experience in Management and Organizational Behavior,* © 1976, pp.
25-27. Reprinted by permission of John Wiley & Sons, Inc.

Contents

List of Figures vii

Preface ix

Acknowledgments xiii

1. The Effort-Net Return Model 1

2. Principle 1: Employees Will Be Motivated When They
   Perceive that Effort Leads to Performance 15

   Proposition 1.1: Employees must perceive that they have, or
   can easily acquire, the ability (traits, knowledge, and skills
   included) to perform. 15

   Proposition 1.2: Employees must perceive that the job design
   facilitates performance. 32

3. Principle 2: Employees Will Be Motivated When They Perceive
   that Performance Leads to Reward 47

   Proposition 2.1: Employees must perceive that rewards are
   contingent on performance. 47

   Proposition 2.2: Employees must value rewards. 67

4. Principle 3: Employees Will Be Motivated When They Perceive
   a Performance-Supportive Cost Structure 87

   Proposition 3.1: Employees must perceive that the costs associated
   with high effort are low. 87

   Proposition 3.2: Employees must perceive that the costs associated
   with low effort are high. 104

5. Principle 4: Employees Will Be Motivated When They Perceive
   Little "Pull" from Alternative Goal Systems   123

   Proposition 4.1: Employees must perceive that noncompatible,
   away-from-work pursuits are not too attractive.   124

   Proposition 4.2: Employees must perceive that at-work, nonjob,
   semi-work, antiwork, and low priority task activities are not
   too attractive.   139

6. Application Aids: Cases, Exercises, and Instrumentation   157

Bibliography   233

Index   235

List of Figures

1. The Effort-Net Return Model   2

2. Multiple Goal Systems   5

3. Noncontingent Rewards   6

4. Contingent Rewards   7

5. Reward Curve Height vs. Slope   8

6. Effort Short of Capacity   9

7. The Utility of Penalties   11

8. Changes in the Contingency Relation   49

9. Sample Performance-Reward Schedule   52

10. The Effect of Penalty Function "Location" on Motivation   106

11. Degree of Penalty Contingency   117

12. Degree of Contingency vs. Absolute Level   126

13. Noncontingent Rewards   141

14. Motivation with Penalties   142

Preface

The purpose of this book is to provide insight into the variety of avenues, suggested by the effort-net return model of employee motivation, that management can pursue to help build employee motivation. Classical thinking in the field of motivation is far too narrow and restrictive. Of course, employee motivation is not entirely within the control of management, but great opportunities to heighten employee motivation are missed when one relies for guidance on the overly simplistic theories of human motivation that have been popularized by the literature over the last few decades.

Though over 200 prescriptions for motivating employees are provided in chapters 2, 3, 4, and 5 of this book, this inventory should be regarded as a sampling—a list of courses of action, which is far from exhaustive but nonetheless representative of the avenues managers can pursue to enhance employee motivation. It is hoped that the inventory will stimulate the reader's thinking about additional ways to heighten employee motivation.

In Chapter 6 a number of real-life case problems are presented with analyses and suggested prescriptive packages. This presentation is provided to help the reader "move" from reading to using the material presented here. Chapter 6 also provides numerous instruments and exercises which should add considerably to the reader's ability and motivation to implement this material.

The reader should keep in mind throughout the book that a given prescription may well have a different motivational impact on different people. This is because of individual differences and perceptions, which are highly personalized. Different employees will perceive the nature of a given prescription in different ways. Likewise, a given prescription may affect a given employee in different ways at different points in time because conditions, needs, moods, and personal goals, for example, change over time.

A given prescription applied to an employee may aid motivation in multiple ways, too, by attacking a number of different determinants of motivation. This book acknowledges this fact by discussing a few prescriptions in multiple places in the book—under a number of different motivational propositions. Also a given prescription may increase motivation in some ways and diminish it in others. You must look for the *net* effect of an implemented prescription.

Further, the reader should appreciate the point that a number of prescriptions applied to a given individual may conflict, or negate one another, or interfere with one another causing a lowering of motivation, just as too many medicines taken by the medical patient may result in a chemical reaction causing more damage than good.

Finally, let the reader be most sensitive to the fact that how well a prescription works depends heavily on how, when, under what conditions, and so forth, that prescription is communicated to the employee. You can have great motivational plans, but they can all fall apart because of breakdowns in communication. What good is a bonus system, for example, that no one knows about? How effective is the threat of penalty in stimulating effort if no one knows what the penalty is?

The inventory of prescriptions for motivating identified in this book should make clear that a great many management actions or practices can have an impact on motivation. Employee motivation is entwined with so much of what a manager does. Perhaps a majority of the actions taken by a manager, either directly or indirectly, somehow affects employee perception of positive and negative outcomes experienced in either the short or long run.

Actually this book relates to so much of what managers must give attention to in fulfilling their responsibilities that it is an extremely valuable reference for those interested in management in general. If managers can "shape up" their knowledge and skills in the area of employee motivation, they are likely to increase their performances across a wide range of general managerial functions and specific duties and responsibilities.

The number and variety of prescriptions available for motivating is large indeed. You are likely to ask, "Which ones should I use?" To be sure, "working up" a total motivational plan and implementing it will take considerable thought, patience, time, effort, and, sometimes, money. You generally should select a battery of prescriptions for a given problem situation. To select an appropriate package of prescriptions, look at whom you are trying to motivate, the circumstances, the resources you have available, and so on. One thing is certain: Implementing just a few of the motivational techniques suggested in the upcoming pages probably will not accomplish as much as you would like. You will need a multi-pronged, broad-based attack.

But you have to draw a line somewhere. You cannot let the costs of developing and implementing a motivational system exceed the benefits. The most effective motivational system may cost too much, so you will have to accept a suboptimal plan in terms of effectiveness.

One further point for the reader is that as much time should be spent properly diagnosing motivational problems and opportunities as in planning and implementing prescriptions for heightening motivation. Often it is possible to excessively motivate a person. Excessive motivation can mean "football-like fumblitis." The employee makes a host of mistakes that would not be made at a lower level of motivation. And it does no good, of course, to implement a prescription or solution for a nonexistent problem. Accurate diagnosis is a critical first step in managing employee motivation.

Acknowledgments

Students in my organizational behavior class over the last few years deserve considerable thanks for their contributions of specific prescriptions contained in the pages that follow. Professors Charles Sullivan and William Read receive my sincere gratitude for their informal discussions with me—discussions that have sharpened my grasp of numerous concepts and techniques. My wife, Kathy, deserves considerable recognition for her help with various aspects of organizing and proofing the manuscript. Finally, I wish to thank Sue McLaughlin for her professionalism in preparing the various drafts of this work.

1

The Effort–Net Return Model

The number of different models of human motivation is many—too many. Unfortunately, few of these models adequately define and describe the components and component relationships which constitute their structure. The list continues to grow without periodic refinement and consolidation and without attempts to synthesize motivation concepts with other segments of behavioral science and, for that matter, with the domains of science outside the behavioral area. But the various models of motivation can be integrated. They are not in significant conflict with one another.

This chapter introduces a construct that stresses conceptual clarification and the integration of theory. Analysis of the construct leads to identification and explanation of some phenomena previously avoided, or neglected, by motivation theory and to identification of a considerable number of practical means to pursue in attempting to motivate the human being.

A. DEFINING AND RELATING THE VARIABLES

Motivation is a psychological force—analogous to a physical force in that it is a vector quantity possessing both magnitude and direction. Motivation is the amount of effort that one desires to expend in a given direction (toward a goal). The amount of effort one does expend to reach a goal is assumed, in the absence of the imposition of constraints on effort expenditure, to be in direct proportion to the amount of effort one *desires* to expend. Alternatively stated, and again neglecting constraints, the amount of effort (energy) one actually expends in pursuit of a goal is in direct proportion to the magnitude of the force that causes the expenditure.

One acquires a desire to exert effort from the anticipated receipt of satisfaction from the exertion. That is, humans are willing to exert energy because they believe such behavior will relieve a need (tension state).

The strength of one's desire to expend energy is a function of one's perception of the expected rewards to be received and the expected costs to be incurred as a consequence of effort expenditure. The amount of energy one actually does expend depends upon this perception. If one is striving to achieve a goal, he or she will exert an amount of effort perceived to yield the maximum possible difference between expected rewards and expected costs. Since satisfaction is defined here as rewards minus costs (net return), an individual will, then, select an effort level believed to maximize expected satisfaction.

Figure 1 helps isolate and relate the variables in the construct. The rewards (positively valued outcomes) received by an employee in an organization such as wages, promotions, recognition, power, competency development, and personal growth generally increase at a declining rate with increased effort expenditure. Costs (negatively valued outcomes) such as fatigue, boredom, stress, fear, others' jealously toward you, early burnout, frustration, stimulation of "opposing" competitive forces, and interference with someone else's accomplishments, for example, generally increase at an increasing rate with increased effort expenditure. At some effort level, point X in Figure 1, the

Figure 1
The Effort–Net Return Model

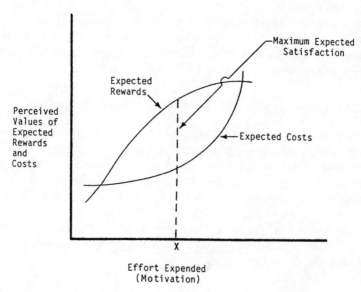

individual perceives a maximum expected net return—maximum expected satisfaction. This is the effort level one selects in striving to attain a goal.

B. SOME UNIQUE INSIGHTS

A number of unique insights and important points concerning motivation are illuminated by Figure 1. First, the model shows how positive and negative outcomes combine to affect motivation. At low effort levels, rewards generally rise faster than costs, thus moving the point of maximum satisfaction to a higher effort level. At high effort levels, costs generally increase faster than rewards so the employee is stimulated to keep effort expenditure below these levels.

Second, the model suggests what can be done to increase the energy expenditure of employees. Management must find ways to "bend upward" employees' perceived expected reward curves and to "bend downward" their expected cost curves. Such "bending" makes a difference by shifting the point at which maximum satisfaction is experienced to the right—to a greater level of effort. Upward bending at higher effort levels might be achieved, for example, by simply increasing the employee's perception of the likelihood of reward (such as a promotion) at higher effort expenditure. This could be done by bestowing rewards more frequently for higher effort levels. Also, upward bending could be achieved by noting when the employee begins to sense a decline in the utility of additional units of a reward and then shifting the rewards given the employee to other kinds of rewards which will better meet the employee's more predominant needs. Downward bending of the cost curve could be achieved by such means as increasing the quality of the work environment or the quality of the employee's tools and equipment to reduce the stress and fatigue perceived to be associated with high effort.

Third, the model clearly distinguishes and relates the concepts of motivation and satisfaction which were heretofore inadequately accomplished in the literature. Note that motivation does not depend upon the magnitude of expected satisfaction but rather upon the magnitude of effort that yields maximum expected satisfaction. One will exert that amount of effort that provides more satisfaction than any other effort level. Whether that amount of satisfaction is high or low in absoluse terms makes no difference. This relationship between motivation and satisfaction is further explored later.

Fourth, the model goes beyond other theories by incorporating expectancy notions, by recognizing an effort capacity (discussed later), and by distinguishing and relating the concepts of expended effort and costs. Some theories have been particularly negligent in failing to distinguish effort expended from the costs incurred by that effort. Certainly they are not the same thing. It is conceivable that in some situations—an employee watching for breaks in a conveyer belt in a cold storage facility, for example—low effort could be accompanied by high costs. High effort could well be accompanied by low costs in other situations.

C. MULTIPLE GOAL SYSTEMS

This effort–net return (ENR model) provides revelations of particular utility when it is recognized that in practice each individual strives to reach multiple goals. An employee must distribute his or her limited energy among a variety of goal systems.

The classical approach to the study of employee motivation has been to isolate for analysis the on-the-job system. On-the-job motivation has been considered a function of on-the-job forces. But employee motivation is a function not only of the job goal system. Off-the-job goal systems play an equally important role. Failure to recognize the impact of these "competing" systems may be the major weakness in contemporary motivation theory.

All employees are members of at-work social groups and various away-from-work groups and organizations, for example. All employees pursue interests, at work and away from work, that are not job related. A portion of an employee's limited effort supply will be allocated to these other systems.

Individuals actually strive to maximize their aggregate satisfaction—in other words, the total of satisfactions received from all goal systems in which they participate. To achieve total system optimization of satisfaction, with a limited capacity for motivation, one may have to devote an amount of effort to the job that suboptimizes job satisfaction. That is, one may find it desirable to exert less effort on the job than that amount which yields maximum on-the-job satisfaction! So doing will allow for greater satisfactions to be realized in other goal systems.

Figure 2 helps explain the phenomenon. Suppose an individual's effort expenditure is measured by time spent. Suppose, for one reason or another, that one has only eight hours of time available each day. Suppose, further, that the individual participates in just two goal systems—one is the on-the-job system, the other an off-the-job system such as a social club or hobby. This person will seek to distribute his or her limited supply of time between the two goal systems such that overall satisfaction is maximized. Actually overall (total) satisfaction is maximized, borrowing a concept from economics, when the marginal (or incremental) satisfaction of the last unit of effort exerted in the on-the-job system equals the marginal satisfaction of the last unit of effort exerted in the off-the-job system. One will distribute effort so that the marginal satisfactions of the last unit of effort exerted in the various systems in which he or she participates are equal.

In Figure 2, four effort (time) distribution options are indicated with the corresponding amounts of satisfaction experienced as determined from the reward-cost differences at the four effort levels in each of the two goal systems. Note that for distribution option III—the option that maximizes total satisfaction—the amount of effort spent in the on-the-job goal system is less than the amount of effort that maximizes satisfaction for that goal system. This phenomenon is commonplace. Since effort must be distributed among competing goal systems, employees often lack high—or even moderate—job motivation.

Figure 2
Multiple Goal Systems

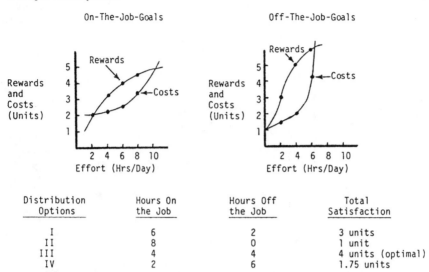

On-The-Job-Goals   Off-The-Job-Goals

Distribution Options	Hours On the Job	Hours Off the Job	Total Satisfaction
I	6	2	3 units
II	8	0	1 unit
III	4	4	4 units (optimal)
IV	2	6	1.75 units

The employee's motivation to perform depends very much on off-the-job pursuits.

To motivate employees, management must examine the incentive structure of off-the-job goal systems as well as the job incentive structure. To cause workers to exert less effort in other systems and more on the job, management must make sure that employees receive high job satisfaction *only* at high effort levels.

The analysis here also suggests that management might control employee motivation by using applicant screening techniques that distinguish candidates on the basis of intensity of extracurricular interests. Those who are likely to derive the majority of their satisfactions from the job incentive structure are likely to expend most of their efforts in the on-the-job goal system. Those who have strong outside interests must reduce job-oriented effort to achieve satisfaction of those other interests. It, therefore, often makes sense to hire those individuals whose primary source of satisfaction will be the job.

Complicating the management of motivation is the fact that rewards and costs experienced in off-the-job goal systems can affect perceptions of on-the-job rewards and costs, and vice versa. The interdependence of on-the-job and off-the-job systems must be fully appreciated.

D. THE PERFORMANCE/SATISFACTION RELATIONSHIP

Researchers continue to try to establish the correlation between employee job performance and employee job satisfaction. Some hypothesize that satisfaction

Figure 3
Noncontingent Rewards

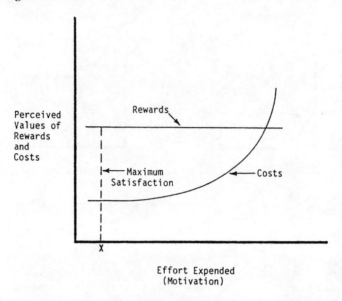

Effort Expended
(Motivation)

leads to performance; some say performance leads to satisfaction. Others, recognizing the failure of studies to demonstrate a significant correlation, conclude there is no relationship between the two. And on goes the debate with little progress toward resolution.

ENR helps resolve the issue by showing *how* performance and satisfaction are related, thus demonstrating *why* they are not positively correlated. Consider Figure 3 which is drawn from the ENR construct. The horizontal line illustrates a common situation in which the value of all rewards (both intrinsic and extrinsic) rHceived by an employee is perceived by that employee as essentially guaranteed (fixed). Rewards are seen as independent of the amount of effort expended. The tenured, 60-year-old full professor may be a case in point. Also, unionized employees often operate under such a reward function.

The positively sloped curve in Figure 3 illustrates that as an employee increases on-the-job- effort expenditure, the costs (stress, fatigue, boredom, and so on) associated with the effort are perceived by that employee to rise. The exact shape of this curve, of course, may differ from one situation to the next.

As mentioned previously, the distance between the reward and cost curves at any given level of expended effort represents net perceived value (net return) which is nothing more, or less, than employee satisfaction at that level. According to ENR, an employee will strive—sometimes subconsciously—to exert the amount of effort that provides maximum satisfaction. In Figure 3 it is obvious that maximum satisfaction is achieved at a very low level (point X) of

Figure 4
Contingent Rewards

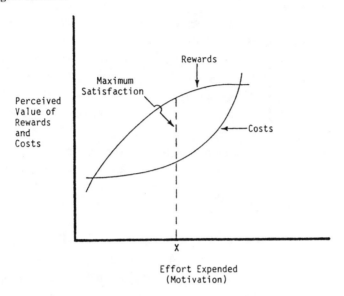

Effort Expended
(Motivation)

motivation. Indeed, motivation and satisfaction in this figure are inversely associated!

Since performance is a function of motivation, and these two variables show high positive correlation (few argue with this), it is clear that, in the previous example, the *lower* the performance, the *higher* the satisfaction!

Now consider Figure 4, which shows a different but nonetheless common situation. In this case, both rewards and costs are seen by the employee as contingent on effort expended. A piece-rate worker, for instance, faces such a reward-cost structure. Managerial employees under a merit reward system also perceive contingent reward and cost functions.

Again the employee seeks to maximize satisfaction. Maximization is now achieved at a relatively high level of motivation (point X). But the maximum amount of satisfaction experienced is small compared with the employee in Figure 3. This is a case of high performance and low satisfaction.

So what is happening? Are performance and satisfaction negatively correlated? No, not at all. Many workers experience low satisfaction and exhibit low performance simultaneously. Many also experience high satisfaction and exhibit high performance simultaneously. Any combination of satisfaction and performance levels can readily be found among employees because satisfaction and motivation are, to a great extent, each determined by different and independent attributes of a reward function (curve).

Consider Figure 5. If reward curve R is shifted to R'—a vertical translation—

Figure 5
Reward Curve Height vs. Slope

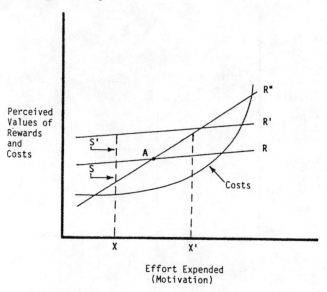

Effort Expended
(Motivation)

satisfaction is increased from S to S plus S'. But motivation remains the same since maximum satisfaction is still achieved at point X. Satisfaction changes; performance does not. The absolute level of rewards has nothing to do with motivation and performance. Changes in the "height" of the reward curve affect only the level of worker satisfaction. If an employee's wages are increased independent of performance, for example, that employee's satisfaction will increase, but motivation will remain unchanged.

If reward curve R is rotated about point A to position R''—a change in slope—motivation *will* be changed—increased from X to X'. It is the slope of the perceived reward curve that determines motivation. The greater the slope (the greater the contingency relation between effort and reward), the greater motivation and performance. This is because the point of maximum satisfaction is forced to the right—to a higher effort level—with an increase in slope. According to ENR, to make rewards more motivational, a manager must increase the dependency of rewards on effort.

In this illustration the maximum amount of satisfaction possible is not appreciably changed by the angular transposition (R to R'') of the reward curve. Generally, however, the maximum amount of satisfaction possible will increase or decrease depending on the point about which the reward curve is rotated and on the degree of rotation. An in-depth analysis of this phenomenon is beyond the scope of this book. It should be appreciated here, though, that even for an extremely "steep" reward function, satisfaction can well be low providing the function is sufficiently "close" to the cost curve.

Because, in practice, reward curves take on various slope-height combinations, various satisfaction-performance combinations must be expected. Satisfaction and performance are related: One's motivation level depends on the level of effort at which one perceives maximum satisfaction to be obtained. This level can be high or low (or in-between). It depends on the slope of the reward curve. The absolute amount of satisfaction at maximization will be high or low (or in-between) depending on the height of the reward curve.

Thus, high satisfaction does not lead to high performance, nor does high performance lead to high satisfaction. Performance and satisfaction are not positively correlated, each being principally linked to different and independent dimensions of a reward structure.

E. EFFORT SHORT OF CAPACITY

Most managers are only too aware of how difficult it is to achieve full utilization of human resource capacity. Regardless of the type of job, employees will exert amounts of effort short of their capacities for effort expenditure—frequently, far short. Even when an organization's reward system is of outstanding quality, no employee can be expected to produce at potential. From the employee's view, to do so would make no sense. The ENR model of motivation explains why.

Figure 6 illustrates a common situation in which an employee perceives that rewards (both intrinsic and extrinsic) generally rise with increases in expended

Figure 6
Effort Short of Capacity

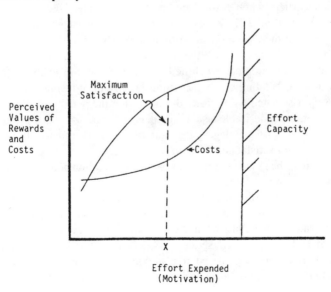

Effort Expended
(Motivation)

effort (motivation). As is typical, the rate of increase of rewards is shown to taper off at high levels of effort. With increases in effort, the employee also perceives the costs associated with that effort to rise. Costs will increase rapidly as one becomes highly mytivated and approaches effort capacity.

As stated earlier, the difference between rewards and costs at any given level of effort represents employee satisfaction (net return) at that level, and an employee will seek to exert an amount of effort that maximizes satisfaction. In Figure 6, point X marks the effort level that yields this maximization. Note, this effort level is considerably short of capacity. It is not in the employee's best interest to exert a higher amount of effort because of the fact that as one moves to the right of point X, costs increase faster than rewards. Costs tend to accelerate rapidly as effort capacity is approached. The positively sloped cost curve forces the point of maximum satisfaction to the left of one's effort capacity.

Because of the costs, or negatively valued outcomes, associated with high effort, employees will not work to potential. Indeed, motivating employees to just moderate levels of effort requires that management give considerable attention to the design of cost structures as well as to reward design—a point often neglected in contemporary discourse on the subject.

F. THE UTILITY OF PENALTIES

In recent years numerous psychologists and managers have discounted the value of penalties as a motivational tool. Citing the undesirable consequences of penalty, psychologists frequently recommend abandonment of this type of incentive as a component in the manager's motivational arsenal. But penalties can and do play a useful and strategic role in motivating. ENR illustrates the point.

As noted earlier, when reward curves are horizontal, such as curve A in Figure 7, motivation will be low—that is, unless management takes action. Management can increase motivation by manipulating the costs experienced by the employee. By "bending up" the cost curve at low levels of effort, the point of maximum satisfaction can be shifted to the right—in this example from X to X'. This upward bending can be accomplished by introducing penalties which are inversely associated with effort. By increasing the penalty (criticism, points toward demotion, undesirable task assignment, poor performance evaluation for the record, or loss of privileges, for example) as performance drops off, the point of maximum satisfaction is realized at a higher effort level. A negatively sloped cost curve has much the same impact on motivation and performance as a positively sloped reward curve.

Of course some costs (penalties) rise automatically with declining effort levels. Management does not have to impose them. Such things as disrespect from peers and the boss, loss of influence ability, and peer group ostracism are penalties that often spontaneously emerge as one's effort level declines.

The point must be emphasized that although penalties can motivate, they reduce satisfaction (see Figure 7). To cite an extreme example, chain gang

Figure 7
The Utility of Penalties

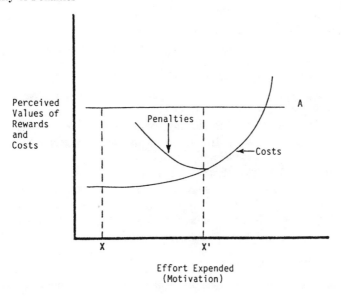

Effort Expended
(Motivation)

workers are usually highly motivated but perceive little satisfaction! But, importantly, in order to motivate, penalties must be exercised, even though satisfaction is sacrificed, when rewards are fixed as in Figure 7.

G. STRATEGIES AND SUBSTRATEGIES EMERGING FROM ENR

The effort–net return construct, as presented here, suggests numerous avenues for management to pursue in attempting to increase the efforts of employees to achieve organizational goals. Generally, to increase an employee's motivation, management must get employees to perceive that they will achieve higher satisfaction at higher effort levels. To do this, management must assure that employees perceive greater differences between expected rewards and expected costs at higher effort levels than at lower levels. To generate such employee perception, rewards must clearly be contingent upon effort expenditure. Also the cost (such as fatigue, stress, or boredom) increase that occurs with an increase in effort expenditure must be at a slower rate than the reward increase.

ENR indicates that how satisfied employees are with their jobs has nothing to do with motivation except as indicated earlier during the discussion of multiple goals. Whether or not one perceives greater satisfaction at higher effort levels is what is important. This explains why many highly touted job enrichment programs implemented by organizations during the last two decades have not succeeded. Enriched jobs, with high salaries, status, good working conditions, fringe benefits, and so on, will not motivate unless the enrichment is granted (or experienced) as a result of higher employee effort expenditure rather than irrespective of it.

It must be appreciated, however, that though the absolute level of employee satisfaction has little to do with motivation, it is an important determinant of the volume of employee turnover, employee gripes, absenteeism, alcoholism, and related variables. High employee satisfaction as well as high motivation must be developed for an organization to succeed.

ENR treats motivation as a function of the difference between perceived rewards and perceived costs. If costs rise with increased effort expenditure, so must rewards. If one is to be highly motivated, the reward function must have a positive slope sufficient to offset the accelerating costs encountered at high effort levels and to force the point of maximum satisfaction far to the right on the effort (motivation) axis. If the reward function cannot be adequately sloped, then motivation can be achieved through cost function design by reducing the stress, fatigue, boredom, and the like, one experiences at high effort levels or by making costs an inverse function of effort (using penalties) at low effort levels.

But operating on the at-work reward/cost structure will usually not be enough. Influencing of rewards and costs in off-the-job systems is typically needed to properly motivate the employee. Remember the earlier discussion of multiple goal systems.

Thus, from the ENR model of motivation four distinct general strategies for improving employee motivation emerge. ENR tells us that for high motivation one must perceive that effort *leads* to reward—that a strong contingent relation exists between effort and reward. But the linkage between effort and reward is seldom direct. One will seldom sense that effort leads (converts) directly to rewards. One is not rewarded for simply expending effort—for effort alone. Instead one is rewarded for performance (which, we hope, results from that effort). Therefore, we must break the effort-reward linkage into two components: (1) an effort-performance (effort leading to performance) linkage, and (2) a performance-reward (performance leading to reward) linkage.

Strategy one for improving motivation then becomes improving the perceived strength of the relationship between effort and performance (i.e., getting employees to sense a stronger link between their efforts and the performance which results from that effort). Strategy two becomes improving the perceived strength of the relationship between performance and reward (i.e., getting employees to sense a stronger link between their performance and the rewards that result from that performance).

The third strategy management can adopt for improving motivation involves operating on the employee's perceived cost structure. Instead of influencing perceived rewards, management can influence perceived costs, or negative outcomes, which have just as much to do with motivation as rewards, or positive outcomes. The fourth general strategy management can adopt for improving motivation involves reducing "pulls" from alternative goal systems (i.e., affecting employees' distribution of effort by getting them to put more energy into relevant job dimensions and less into off-the-job pursuits that "use up" effort and time).

Each of these four general strategies has at least two key substrategies, which can be readily inferred from the general strategies. For improving the effort-performance link management must (1) assure that employees see that they have sufficient ability to perform—that effort will pay off because ability is fully adequate; and (2) assure that employees see that their jobs are well designed—that their jobs will "allow" for performance. Ability and job design are the two key variables in addition to motivation that affect employee job performance. These are the two variables that moderate the conversion of effort to performance. If ability is weak and the job is not well designed, effort will not "readily" convert to (result in) performance.

For improving the perceived performance-reward linkage, management must (1) assure that employees perceive rewards to be received on a highly contingent basis—that they sense that the only way to "get more" is to perform better; and (2) assure that employees value the rewards they receive. One cannot possibly perceive that performance leads to "real" reward if what is received is not valued. Getting "more" means nothing if what you get is not valued.

In operating on one's cost structure, management must (1) assure that employees perceive costs to rise at a relatively slow rate at high effort levels; and (2) assure that employees perceive the costs of low effort to be high. Either or both actions help keep the effort level, at which employees sense maximum satisfaction, relatively high.

To reduce "pull" from other goal systems, management must (1) assure that away-from-work goal systems—such as family, outside clubs, or hobbies—do not siphon off too much effort; and (2) assure that at-work, competing goal systems—such as informal social gatherings or organizational politics—do not draw too much effort from priority tasks.

In the following chapters you will look at numerous techniques, or prescriptions, for implementing each of these substrategies. The major, general strategies are forthwith formulated as principles deduced from the effort–net return model. The substrategies are stated as propositions derived from these principles. Numerous prescriptions are given under each proposition. In a few cases a given prescription is discussed under more than one proposition indicating that the particular course of action affects motivation in more than one way.

The reader may want to refer back to this chapter on strategies and substrategies. This material is critical in bridging the gap between theory and practice.

2

Principle 1: Employees Will Be Motivated When They Perceive that Effort Leads to Performance

For employees to exert high effort, they must see that it makes a difference in their performance. Employees must sense that effort will pay off in terms of performance—that it is highly correlated with performance and that higher effort will yield better performance. The stronger the perceived correlation, the stronger the motivation.

Employee-job performance is a function of ability, job design, and motivation. If the employee has adequate ability and the job is designed well, then performance is solely dependent on the level of motivation. Assuming ability and job design are in order, high motivation becomes a necessary and sufficient condition for high performance. If employees know their ability is high and the design of their job is "top notch," then high performance is perceived as indeed possible and perceived to depend on their efforts. On the other hand, low ability and faulty job design limit the effect of effort on performance. They reduce the perceived correlation between effort and performance and, thus, the slope of the effort-reward function. When the slope of the reward curve decreases, motivation decreases.

PROPOSITION 1.1: EMPLOYEES MUST PERCEIVE THAT THEY HAVE, OR CAN EASILY ACQUIRE, THE ABILITY (TRAITS, KNOWLEDGE, AND SKILLS INCLUDED) TO PERFORM.

To sense a strong effort-performance correlation, one must sense that other variables are not interfering with effort—constraining or negating the results of effort. Ability is a key determining variable of employee-job performance, as mentioned before. This moderating variable affects to what degree effort results in performance. If ability is high, the employee perceives that effort has a good chance to yield success. If ability is low, the employee senses that no matter how hard he or she tries, accomplishment will not result. Deficient ability constrains performance, making good performance seem unlikely if not impossible. Perceived high ability is a necessary condition for one to perceive a strong correlation between effort and performance—that effort will definitely lead to performance.

You may be thinking that ability is important in its direct effect on employee-job performance. You are right. Obviously employees cannot perform without it. But it is the *indirect* effect of *perceived* ability on employee-job performance, and its effect on motivation, that is the focus of attention in the ensuing discussion of prescriptions.

The classical view is that ability and motivation both affect job performance but that these two determining variables are essentially independent of one another. The fact is, however, that perceived ability (note, perceived not actual) has a lot to do with one's motivation and vice versa, to some degree.

The following are ways to get employees to see that they have or can easily acquire the abilities, traits, knowledge, and skills necessary to perform well.

1. Make sure quality help, or guidance, is readily available.

For employees to perceive that effort will in fact result in performance, they must sense they either have the ability or can easily get it. Providing readily available help, or guidance, makes them feel they can easily gain the required skills and knowledge, if they do not already possess it. They must know that when they run into difficulties because of a skill or knowledge deficiency, they have ready access to a source that can resolve the deficiency. Accessible help allows them to sense that the lacking ability is not a "block" to performance.

A supervisor, available to willingly provide help when such is needed, is one key source. Supervisors should let employees know that one of their major functions as supervisors is to provide help when it is really needed. Perhaps too often supervisors make themselves unavailable either by not being around or by giving the impression subordinates should not "bother" them with problems. If supervisors cannot make themselves available, lead workers or workers long on experience, or recognized expertise, can be assigned the responsibility of providing help to other workers when needed.

Making useful job-related literature available is another good way to stimulate an employee's sense that answers can be obtained when needed. Having employees regularly meet to ask questions and deal with job performance problems is also a good means for letting them know they have access to mechanisms that provide them with needed guidance on their jobs. Further, employees can be encouraged to join professional clubs and associations which can provide significant information and sources of expertise on various problems they may encounter.

2. Help employees build their self-confidence.

Employees may actually have ability but not perceive it as such. They do not believe in themselves. They lack self-confidence. Persons who have high confidence in their abilities will calculate a higher probability of their efforts leading to performance than persons who lack faith in what they can do. Therefore, it is important to assure that employees have sufficient confidence.

Many avenues can be pursued to help employees build self-confidence. Praise for good work not only helps satisfy the esteem and status needs, it also serves to enhance employees' sense of confidence in their abilities. Praise tells workers they are doing things properly. And most workers realize they do not do things properly without the requisite ability.

Giving workers job-related tests they can pass with flying colors, and feeding the results of these tests back to them, can also go far toward convincing them they have the basic skills and knowledge required. Workers may not think they have what it takes to do good work, but management can help prove to them they do by designing and administering job-related tests, and feeding back good scores.

Assertiveness-type training can help build workers' confidence in their abilities. With such training, people are taught that their ideas and values are just as good as anyone else's. They are taught how to avoid feelings of inferiority and how to stand up for what they believe in. Such training coupled with other self-image, or self-worth building, almost invariably helps increase one's confidence level.

Self-image building can come in various forms—most of which are beyond the scope of this book—but may involve something relatively simple like getting workers to improve their physical appearance through better dress and grooming. People feel better about themselves when they look better, when they know it, and when they know others know it.

You can also help workers see that they do have required abilities by entrusting authority to them and letting them make key decisions. Perhaps nothing builds confidence quicker than when the boss shows his or her confidence in you by giving you some autonomy and self-determination in the workplace.

3. Put new employees through quality job orientation programs.

New employees are likely to sense they have the requisite abilities, skills, and knowledge to do the job if the organization puts them through well-designed and executed employee orientation programs. No new employee, no matter what the extent of previous experience and training, can be expected to perform well on a new job without considerable preparation. Workers must sense that they have been fully prepared to do the full job for which they have been hired. Orientation

programs can provide this sense of preparedness if they provide sufficient time
for worker start-up.

Quality job orientation programs should provide workers with a complete
body of information on the company as a whole—its philosophy, objectives,
products, profitability, history, physical layout, and so forth. Such information
helps any employee see the "big picture" and better "mesh" his or her efforts
with the efforts of others throughout the organization.

Orientations should help the new employee become quickly integrated into the
organization's social system. New employees should be introduced to fellow
workers and should be given ample opportunity to get to know those with whom
they must regularly interact in executing regular duties. Proper integration into
the social system helps workers feel they can get things done relatively easily
through others.

Also, orientations should deal in depth with the specific work obligations for
which the new person is hired. Passing out job descriptions and encouraging
discussion about their content is helpful. Giving the new worker an actual
opportunity to try out the work while under the watchful eye of a supervisor is
essential. Close guidance must be provided to the worker while the job is being
learned. Through such orientations workers' abilities can be properly developed.
Employees will feel well prepared. They come away from the orientation
believing they have the ability needed for effort to yield real results.

4. Show employees that their skills, abilities, and traits are compatible with job requirements.

Perhaps there is no quicker way of enhancing employees' belief in their
abilities than by simply telling them they have the ability. But you can go a step
beyond simple telling. You can help persuade them they have the ability by
pointing out that they were selected from among pools of candidates by using
valid, job-related selection techniques. You can inform them that they were
hired because their specific knowledge and skills are well matched to the job
requirements or person specifications for the job. You can show them that the
data you gleaned from their application forms indicate a solid match with the
kinds of skills and knowledge listed in their job descriptions. You can point out
to them the results of any in-depth tests given during employee selection
procedures and show how these results demonstrate they are fully qualified for
the job.

Usually when you can demonstrate to employees that they were selected with a
disciplined procedure that evaluated their strengths and weaknesses carefully,
they will be convinced that you think they can do the job. When they think you
believe they can do the job, they are more apt to believe it too.

It is important to convey information on how compatible employees' abilities
are with job requirements early in their employment—soon after they are hired.
Waiting too long on this can blur one's sense of what went on during selection

procedures and will have less impact as other matters come to dominate the new person's consciousness.

5. Provide periodic opportunities for employees to participate in skills and knowledge upgrading programs.

Employees will be convinced they are maintaining or improving their competencies to perform if they have periodic opportunities to participate in formal training programs. Having employees frequently upgrade their skills through training increases performance directly, of course, because employee ability, affected through training, along with motivation and job design are the primary determinants of the quality and level of their performance. But the training also boosts performance through its indirect effect on motivation. When people are trained well, they believe their efforts can pay off. Ability is not perceived as a barrier. A strong contingent relationship is seen between effort and performance.

Periodic quality training opportunities help workers know they are keeping up, keeping pace, keeping current—not slipping. These opportunities convince them that needed ability acquisition, maintenance, and improvement are possible. Without such training opportunities employees may soon feel that they are falling behind their "competition" in other organizations. They may feel that they do not have what it takes in the way of the latest skills and knowledge to compete with their rivals. This is often stimulus enough to generate a lack of willingness-to-try posture and a who-cares attitude. The same phenomenon occurs as workers compare their training opportunities with the training opportunities of fellow workers in their own company. If workers think fellow workers are getting better training, they are likely to calculate that they will not have the abilities needed to perform up to expectations.

6. Make sure employees have adequate technical knowledge and skill.

For most workers to perceive that they have the ability, skill, and knowledge necessary to perform, they must actually have that ability, skill, and knowledge. There are certain kinds of abilities, skills, and knowledge that all employees need. An organization must make sure workers have them. Neglecting just one of these is enough for workers to feel they lack what it takes for effort to yield performance.

One type of ability required on the job is technical ability. Technical knowledge and skill refers to ability in a specific area. Someone with high technical knowledge and/or skill has expertise in a particular discipline, or competence to perform a specific kind of task. It is generally regarded as an ability to use information, methods, techniques, or equipment in the execution of specific responsibilities. It may be mental or physical. Further, technical skill tends to involve working with "things"—processes and physical objects.

All kinds of jobs require technical knowledge and skills. Accountants need technical knowledge concerning how to prepare financial statements. Carpenters need technical knowledge and skill in home construction techniques. Nuclear engineers must possess technical knowledge in mathematics and physics. Typists need technical skill that allows them to prepare the printed page. A gymnast needs highly polished physical, technical skills.

All jobs, from top to bottom, in an organization require technical ability. Presidents and vice presidents need to know how to interpret financial data and how to design organizations. Mid-level managers need to know such things as how to read computer printouts and how to conform with equal-employment legislation. Lower-level workers must know how to read blueprints and how to run their machines.

Trade schools, colleges, and universities generally offer extensive opportunities for development of technical knowledge and skills. In existence are schools for practically every type of technical training imaginable. But companies cannot afford to ignore this area because schools can never provide the exact knowledge and skills required on a particular job. The specific content of any given type of job will vary from one company to the next. In most organizations, employees will often have to undergo at least some technical training to learn the conditions particular to the organization. Also, schools—even specialized trade and professional schools—tend to emphasize development of the trainee's theoretical perspective. It is up to the organization to fully develop the employee's applied orientation.

7. Make sure employees have needed conceptual skills.

All employees need conceptual skills too. Without it, they will find it difficult to overcome various hurdles involving the relationship of their work to the larger system of which they are a part. Without it, employees will not likely see how their efforts lead to truly worthy performance.

Conceptual skill is the ability to think in systems terms—to perceive relationships among variables and entities. Employees with conceptual skills are able to understand how various functions of the organization complement one another, how the organization relates to its environment, and how changes in one part of the organization affect the rest of the organization. Persons with strong conceptual skills appreciate the complexities of the aggregate organizational system. They also are able to put issues in perspective and to establish proper priorities for issues. They are "big picture" thinkers.

It is vital for top-level employees to possess well-developed conceptual skills. They must coordinate the efforts of many subsections of the organization. Lower-level people also need some of this skill. In fact, numerous intra-organizational conflicts can be traced to a lack of conceptual skill on the part of mid- and lower-level managers. Possession of conceptual skill helps persons better understand and appreciate the roles of other departments and personnel, and thus to overcome interdepartmental and interpersonal conflicts.

Schools probably do little to develop conceptual skill. In fact, they may foster the opposite. One with conceptual skill tends to be a generalist. Much education tends to develop specialists—people with expertise in particular areas. Some liberal arts programs and advanced courses in business administration attempt to develop conceptual thinking, but such training simply is not present in the schooling of most of us who end up as employees in organizations. The organization must assume most of the burden of providing conceptual skill training.

8. Make sure employees have needed interpersonal relations skills.

All employees need these skills. Interpersonal relations skill (IRS) is the ability to effectively interact with other people. It is the ability to work with and through others. With high IRS, employees will be able to properly coordinate their efforts with the efforts of others in the organization. Possession of IRS contributes to one's effectiveness as a real team player.

Persons with strong interpersonal relations skills tend to be excellent two-way communicators. They are able to express themselves verbally and in writing so that others easily understand them. They are sensitive listeners and able to readily interpret messages sent to them.

IRS includes leadership skill and the ability to influence others. In order to accomplish assignments in an organization, one must frequently persuade others to pursue certain courses of action. Without being able to win the support of others, one cannot long survive. Employees cannot function on their own, apart from the cooperation of others.

Development of leadership and the ability to influence depends significantly on how well one learns to play organizational politics. Organizational politics involves establishing internal political alliances, building friendship networks, constructing informal power coalitions, and nurturing YOM (you owe me) relations. You can have all the technical skill in the world, but technical skill without political savvy will prevent you from maximizing your contributions to the organization.

All employees require interpersonal relations skills, because all employees must interact with other people. Though these skills are probably most important for supervisors and mid-level managers who must regularly interact with bosses and subordinates as well as peers, at various levels and in various departments, they are also vital for employees dealing with customers, chairing committees, serving as receptionists, doing interviewing, working in public relations, and performing similar tasks. In short, from top to bottom and from side to side in an organization, IRS is useful.

Though colleges and universities typically offer courses in written communications and speech, this is where formal training usually stops. Some schools do provide courses in human relations, leadership, and organizational behavior, but these offerings are usually limited to business schools. Thus, the majority of employees miss out. The skill one does pick up in this area is largely a product of informal social activity and the interpersonal relationships developed during one's maturing years. Experience relating with family and friends, though extremely valuable, is often the sole source of interpersonal relations skill development. Consequently, organizations must assume a substantial role in developing employee IRS.

9. Make sure employees have requisite problem-solving skills.

All employees need an ability to solve problems. Problem-solving skill is the ability to identify, define, and resolve difficulties. One with this skill has an inquisitive mind, an ability to reason, and a desire to search for truth. These employees know how to investigate and analyze a problem situation and to diagnose sources of trouble. This skill also involves creative ability—ability to generate novel ideas and to derive multiple ways of attacking a problem.

Problem-solving skill is in part manifested in one's capacity for critically evaluating potential solutions to problems and for making decisions. Many employees simply do not understand how to make a quality decision. Indeed, many fear making decisions because of the risk of choosing the wrong course of action. The quality decision maker knows how and does not shy away from the task. He or she has likely mastered the scientific method as applied to problem solving and, because of this, likely has a high measure of self-confidence relative to decision making.

Problem-solving skill is critical for every employee at every level in an organization. Every employee faces problems daily. Machine operators need to diagnose causes of breakdown and then get their machines fixed. Department managers may need to diagnose why customers may be disgruntled and then attempt resolution. Top-level managers have to diagnose such things as the causes of declining sales, poor employee performance, and flaws in organizational communications systems.

Colleges and universities generally provide ample opportunity for students to develop problem-solving skills. The scientific method is taught and practiced in numerous curricula. But organizations will usually find it necessary to supplement the academic contribution with some in-house training.

10. Make sure employees know how to manage their time.

Every employee requires organizing skills and the ability to manage time. Many technically competent managers, professionals, and operative employees have failed because they lack a sense of how to allocate time in the workday to the various duties for which they are held responsible.

Employees often have trouble setting priorities. When they are pressured to get many things done at once, they find it difficult to sort out the various tasks and to distinguish those tasks that are most important from those of lesser import. They wind up spending too much time on relatively insignificant assignments and neglecting significant ones.

Workers often allow interruptions to get the best of them. Interruptions become the norm. Workers find themselves moving from processing one interruption to another. Instead of planning the workday and setting up "buffering" mechanisms to "inventory" potential interruptions until they are freed up to deal with them, workers are continually caught in a reactive mode with unplanned work dominating their workdays and planned work being given secondary treatment.

Time management experts have identified dozens of ways to save time and free more time for getting priority work items done. These techniques need to be taught to workers so that they can see how their efforts will yield the maximum possible results. Without such knowledge, high effort may well be perceived as yielding less than high performance.

11. Select employees who have a personality type compatible with job requirements.

Personality type refers to an aggregation of associated traits or personality characteristics. For example, the traits of competitiveness, impatience, and high activity tend to be lumped together in certain individuals. These individuals have been classed as Type A personalities. People with an ectomorphic body type have been found to have a personality type characterized by a desire for privacy, social inhibition, and quick reaction to events and circumstances. Femininity is a personality type characterized by sensitivity and friendliness toward others. Masculinity is a personality type characterized by competitiveness and independence. Numerous classifications have been derived.

No particular personality type is best for all employees. The personality one needs depends on the nature of one's job. Management must study the different jobs in an organization to discover what personality type best fits each. Employees should then be selected so that their personalities match the demands of the jobs. When workers see that their personalities are well suited to the job, they sense their chances of success are greater and, therefore, are encouraged to work harder.

Schools do little directly, or as a matter of design, to develop personality. It may not be feasible for them to try. There are simply too many jobs requiring too many different types of personalities. Besides, changing or molding personality is time-consuming and expensive. Also, personality development is, to a great degree, determined by a host of powerful out-of-the-classroom factors such as physical health, social interactions, and heredity.

Organizations must generally try to select people with personalities already well suited for the job. Where this cannot be done, the organization would be well advised to consider at least moderate investment in training designed to shift employee personality to meet job requirements. For productive behavior, one's personality, as well as other abilities and skills, must meet the demands of the job.

12. Be sure employees have the physical and emotional health needed to perform.

In any job, good physical and emotional health are critical for high-level performance. It is not just the manual laborer who needs physical health, and it is not just the person doing a stressful job, or mentally demanding job, that needs emotional health. All workers do better when they feel physically and emotionally fit. They have more stamina. They can stick to a task longer and exert a higher sustained energy level. Many, if not most, workers realize this. It is important, therefore, to assure they are fit and that they know they are fit in order to prevent them from perceiving lack of fitness to be a constraint on performance.

High effort exerted, without the health to support it, or without the health required to convert that effort to an efficient usage of energy, will not, over time, result in high performance. High effort without good health will result, in a fairly short time, in loss of control of behavior. Wasted motions, irrelevant thinking, physical or mental breakdown, for example, tend to be the outcomes. The individual usually senses how a lack of fitness prevents effort from leading to performance. Employees may not admit it, but many have experienced performance problems that result from high energy exertion in the absence of fitness. High effort does not pay off in the absence of fitness.

13. Assure employees have the necessary motor skills.

All jobs require some degree of motor skills too. Abilities to coordinate the movements of one hand with the movements of the other, to coordinate finger movements, to coordinate hand movements with foot maneuvers, and to coordinate hand, foot, and body movements with what the eye sees and with what the ear hears are important abilities whether the person is driving a truck, typing, working on an assembly line, working on a science research project, or serving in the role of a manager. Of course, on some jobs such skills are far more important than on others. The airplane pilot needs an extremely high level of such skills. Someone shoveling dirt may not need high levels of motor skills.

There may not be a lot the organization can do to help people develop this skill. Much of this type of ability seems to be a product of inherited traits and of early childhood development. But there are some eye and hearing exercises and some physical rhythm training programs that can help. If workers sense any problems with motor skill development, management should have physical examinations set up to rule out medical problems. Once this is done, workers can be put in motor skill improvement programs that may help. Again, what is important for motivation purposes is that the worker perceive no reason for motor skill deficiency to prevent effort from yielding performance.

14. Select employees with the required aptitudes, if not ability, and be sure they know their aptitudes will be converted to ability.

Some employees may not have developed certain talents or abilities when hired. Perhaps the organization just cannot locate already trained, or appropriately experienced, people. But if the organization cannot find people for jobs with the needed abilities already developed, it should be sure to hire people with the aptitude, or potential, for development. In fact, often it makes sense to give candidates who have the aptitude, but not the developed ability, first consideration in hiring because it frequently costs the company less to hire and then train than to hire the already trained.

If employees with sufficient aptitude, but undeveloped skill, are hired, they should be made aware that the company knows this and that the company fully intends to provide them with ample opportunity to engage in the training needed to perform required job duties proficiently. If employees know they have the potential to perform and they know the organization is going to work with them to develop that potential, they are likely to calculate that initial lack of ability will not interfere with their efforts toward performance. But the key is to assure employees that they have the aptitude and to then convince them that these aptitudes will, in fact, be converted to actual skills as needed on their jobs.

15. Select employees with adequate prior experience.

Perhaps one of the best ways to make sure employees perceive that they have the ability to do the work is to hire employees with plenty of prior, successful experience at the kind of work which they will be doing for you. Employees with the proper kind and length of experience are likely to have more confidence in being able to handle the jobs you have hired them for.

The word *successful* is a key here. One may have had years of relevant experience, but if that experience was not a satisfying and productive one, it is not likely to contribute to a perception of high ability. Too often when organizations hire people, the focus is on checking candidates' types of past work experience and lengths of service on past work assignments. Rigorous assessment of past work satisfaction and performance is neglected. Rather casual checking of references is the normal practice. This is, almost without exception, extremely inadequate as a way of validly assessing past performance and satisfaction. Companies should spend more time obtaining records of past performance (absenteeism or grievance filing, for example) which better show the success of past experiences. If workers have not had successful past experiences and you are hiring them for work very similar to work they have done before, they may not perceive that effort will lead to performance in your organization.

16. Encourage, and provide opportunity for, regular self-development activity.

Much ability and skill improvement can come from self-initiated activities. Employees do not have to wait for formal training programs to be offered by the company. If formal training is not offered, employees must be given ample time to engage in self-development activities.

Employees who get into routines of continually engaging in activities designed to improve ability are more likely to sense that they are keeping pace with the ever-increasing demands made of workers in today's constantly changing technological and economic environments. They are likely to have more confidence that they are keeping current in their knowledge and skills. This leads to the perception that their efforts will yield performance. They do not see that ability will be a constraining factor.

Workers should be encouraged to read publications related to their work, to seek out self-paced programmed learning experiences, and to engage in hobbies and outside activities that facilitate on-the-job skill development. Workers who do not do this often wake up one morning realizing, suddenly, that they no longer have the talents needed to perform at the high level their organization requires. Organizational life demands continual learning. A successful life on the job is impossible without it.

No organization is able to devise all the formal training sessions employees will need to keep up. Workers, themselves, must adopt a positive attitude toward the need for self-development and get into the habit of regularly initiating developmental routines. Management, however, can help by encouraging and showing them the way.

17. Provide practice laboratories.

Many types of jobs do not keep employees busy 100 percent of the time. When workers are not engaged in actual production, they may practice their skills with simulations if such opportunities are made available. Good simulations can be developed for almost any type of job—factory labor, office, managerial, and so forth. Off-line machine mock-ups for factory workers, typing labs for secretaries, computer simulations for truck drivers and managers, and target practice labs for police officers are examples of systems designed to provide workers with the opportunity to practice their skills.

Well-designed practice labs which provide workers with rapid, accurate feedback on how they are doing and on what they need to do to correct deficiencies can lead to high levels of proficiency as exercises are repeated over and over again. Repetition leads to perfection, and if the simulations are realistic, the worker will sense a high transferability of skills—developed in the lab—to the actual job situation. Such perception of transferability means workers will believe in themselves. They will perceive that they have whatever ability it takes to do good work on the actual job.

Apprenticeships and understudy training programs that allow workers to observe the performance of an expert and, from time to time, "try out" the work themselves, with the expert present for guidance, is another excellent way to build workers' belief that they have the ability to perform. Such kinds of training are among the best for developing employee competence and confidence.

18. Conduct periodic, formal training needs assessments and regularly address any deficiencies identified.

The organization that has in place a system for regularly assessing training needs and addressing those needs is an organization which is likely to have employees who are convinced their abilities are being kept at a level sufficient for high performance. Most organizations can, at relatively little expense, conduct semi-annual or annual evaluations of skill and ability deficiencies. These evaluations may be tied in with regular performance evaluations and reviews or may be implemented somewhat independent of the regular performance evaluations and reviews.

It is generally best to coordinate training needs assessment with the performance evaluation and review (PER), using the PER as a means of detecting the task areas in which performance needs improvement and as a means of diagnosing just what the sources of performance deficiency are. Ability may be the problem, but a flawed work design or a problem in the organization's reward structure may be the source of deficient performance. If ability is identified as the problem, then a follow-up, detailed training needs assessment can be implemented to spot the exact kinds of abilities that need attention as well as the exact degree to which abilities need upgrading. A quality system will convince employees that the organization wishes to assure adequate ability and that ability will, therefore, not serve to interfere with payoffs from effort.

19. Persuade workers of the quality of the organization's training programs.

Employees will believe they have the requisite ability to do the job if they believe the organization has provided them with the best of training. You have to provide employees with convincing evidence here, though. There is much you can do. For one, you can point out to employees that your company invests substantial dollars in training compared to the competition, or you can show employees that the organization invests as much, or more, in upgrading the human resource than it does in upgrading other kinds of resources.

A second approach to convincing employees of the quality of the organization's training is to promote the credentials of those who design and conduct the training. If employees know, for example, that their trainers are experts or have long experience in the same kind of work they do, they are likely to respect those trainers more and value the training experience more highly.

A third approach to convince workers of the quality of the training is to be sure you use state-of-the-art technology and methodology in training. Employees who think that the typewriter they are training on is ten years out of date certainly will question the validity of the training.

Fourth, the quality of a training program can be substantiated by showing films of workers in identical types of training in other highly reputable firms. Seeing workers in the industry's or community's most successful companies who are involved in the same kind of training helps persuade workers that they are getting the best training available and that once completed their abilities will be as fully developed as anybody's.

Fifth, management can persuade employees that training is high quality by engaging in training program quality assessment. When employees see that management is making valid evaluations of the quality of training, they likely will feel that management is trying hard to assure the best training available.

20. Design the job so that it is not overly complex and confusing.

The design of the work directly affects employee-job performance. It also indirectly affects performance and does so in numerous ways. One way has to do with its impact on employees' perceptions of their ability to perform. Employees are not likely to see that they have sufficient ability to perform if the work is unduly complex, too rapidly changing in content, too uncertain in content, or too dependent in content on someone else's whims. Employees will feel, under such conditions, that performance requires exceptional capacity for adaptation, which they just do not possess.

To avoid such a situation, managers must design jobs that are perceived to require a reasonable level of ability—not a superhuman talent. Quite often jobs become overly confusing and complex because they evolve informally over time without periodic review and refinement to assure they do not become unreasonable in scope and depth. Jobs must be matched to employee ability levels and must not be allowed to change at a pace in considerable excess of the employee's rate of ability growth.

One can be highly trained and have maximum ability, but confusing jobs make employees wonder if they know enough. There is no way employees will calculate a high correlation between effort and performance if they see the job as requiring far more ability than is within the capacity of the normal human being. Excessive ability requirements destroy employees' desires to exert high effort because they see the effort will be fruitless.

21. Let employees participate in formulating their jobs and performance evaluation criteria.

Often companies will want to let employees "build" their own jobs to some degree. This helps assure employees get involved in work that interests them and work that their skills and abilities are well suited for. Employees are not likely to design tasks requiring types and levels of abilities they do not possess.

When employees formulate their own jobs, they are quite likely to develop a fuller understanding of the nature of their jobs and of how those jobs fit into the organization. Employees' knowlege of what they are responsible for is critical in determining whether they will be successful. Employees often cannot get excited about exerting effort because they do not know the direction in which they are supposed to exert effort. This lack of knowledge is seen as a constraint on what effort can accomplish.

Employee knowledge of task priorities and knowledge of the ways in which performance will be assessed is also crucial. Without such knowledge, employees will calculate a relatively high probability that effort will not yield performance. By allowing employees to take part in designing the tasks, priorities, and performance measurement schemes, management is assuring the employee will have substantial knowledge about factors that affect performance. Such knowledge helps the employee feel more sure that effort will convert to performance. Of course if employees do not get involved in designing their own jobs, management must still take pains to convey to them what the job is like. But this is more appropriately reserved for discussion in the next chapter under job input design.

22. Be sure employees experience real on-the-job successes.

Starting employees out properly is important. When new workers come on the job, they should be given relatively simple assignments first—assignments you know they can handle well. As they grow, so should their task obligations. But early success is essential to convince them they have the wherewithal to perform.

Some companies use the sink-or-swim philosophy with new people. Such a philosophy assures a certain percentage of new workers will fail. Many of these workers would turn out to be top performers if given a chance. Even if the company is willing to keep them on after an initial period of failure, many of these employees are likely to lose motivation because they perceive the company is holding them back from acquiring needed skills and knowledge.

Perhaps the greatest real proof of ability is actual performance—success. Management must, therefore, assure that employees experience success—not only the praise or rewards that are provided in return for good performance but also the sense of real personal achievement. They must know, in their own hearts and minds, that they are able to do the job and do it well. Such knowlege can be derived if employees are taught to self-assess performance—to monitor and control their own work behavior. Clear goals are one simple way of facilitating self-assessment. Assuring employees have clear, realistic goals can help employees experience success and, thus, confirm their personal abilities.

23. Give employees an opportunity to prepare for new assignments.

Whenever possible, advanced warning should be given to employees concerning new assignments to be delegated to them. If workers have little or no opportunity to properly prepare for a new assignment, they are likely to perceive a knowledge or ability deficiency and, therefore, that their efforts may not yield performance.

Start-up time is essential for any assignment. You cannot instantaneously launch into full and proficient execution of something new or different. Information needs to be assembled. Skills need to be honed if they have not been used recently. Time must be allowed for a general assimilation of the nature of the assignment. Without allowing preparatory, or start-up times, management is forcing the employee to develop a hurried attack—to barge forth without a feeling of having the proper ability in hand. This, of course, makes any effort exertion seem significantly less than maximally worthwhile.

Generally, an organization should help workers with preparation and, indeed, test their level of preparation before immersing them in new assignments. Not doing this can negatively impact on motivation and can also result in very costly mistakes for the company. It is like the sink-or-swim philosophy, mentioned earlier, used with new employees. Such an approach may cause fine employees to lose so much motivation that they disengage from the organization altogether. They quit.

24. Use employees to train others.

You can show your faith in employee ability by asking the employee to help someone else on the job. Perhaps there is no finer form of recognition for quality performance. This shows those persons requested to provide help in training that you believe they have the right kind and level of ability and that you respect their talents so much you are willing to use them as role models and to entrust the development of others to them.

When persons realize that they are instructing others in how to do the job, they are likely to perceive their own ability levels to be high. This helps them feel that their own efforts are highly likely to pay off in terms of high performance.

Also, the person being trained will often identify with a fellow worker more readily than with the boss. This can mean that he or she will believe more strongly that ability acquisition is possible. Often managers or professional trainers exhibit an extremely high level of task proficiency. This can be discouraging to the worker. A fellow worker, on the other hand, can frequently relate better to the trainee and better assure the trainee that skill development will come with proper attention, given a reasonable time. This peer training can reduce tensions, stimulate more open discussion of problems during the training, and, in the process, provide the trainee with greater certainty that the appropriate skills will be developed.

This prescription thus works for both employees—the trainer and the trainee. Both may well sense higher abilities because of the peer training experience. This sense of higher ability leads both to conclude that their job-directed efforts will yield quality results.

25. Be sure employees have compatible attitudes and values.

In the broad sense, attitudes and values are a dimension of personality and, therefore, constitute a portion of one's ability profile. Attitudes are predispositions toward something. They tend to be either positive or negative. For example, a positive attitude toward the federal government would mean support for the government and belief in the worthwhileness of its activities. A negative attitude toward the same might mean a dislike, nonacceptance, or sense that official government is generally useless to society.

For employees to be productive in an organization, they need to hold positive attitudes toward the elements of organizational life. For example, one should view such factors as work, authority, taking risks in decision making, the need for control, and the need for change in a positive way. A negative attitudinal posture toward these factors will keep one's job satisfaction continually low as well as stimulate considerable resistance to many normal organizational processes and activities. Someone with the wrong attitudes shies away from high effort because the performance it yields is not perceived as worthy. It is not "real" performance from the viewpoint of the employee.

Values are beliefs about the way things should or should not be. G. W. Allport has identified six different value orientations people hold: aesthetic values, religious values, scientific values, economic values, political values, and social values. If, for example, people hold strong social values, they think socializing with others is desirable behavior, and they derive satisfaction from such behavior. They think that "good" people engage in such behavior. If persons hold strong religious values, they think being religious is proper and the right way to be. They derive satisfaction from pursuit of religious experiences.

Value orientations encompass ethics. One's ethical posture refers to one's views of what is right or wrong—proper or improper behavior. Personal ethical standards can be powerful forces channeling employee behavior. Often they are more powerful than the organization's formal rules and regulations.

Employees need to hold values compatible with organizational life. Strong economic, social, and scientific value orientations will contribute to one's satisfaction and performance. Organizations require high levels of economic, social, and scientifically oriented behavior. Someone without these values, or having opposing values, sees this as constraining the degree to which effort can yield "real" performance. When the results of effort are not deemed worthy, one, in essence, perceives little or no correlation between effort and real performance. Both negative attitudes and inappropriate values dampen the perceived impact of effort on performance.

PROPOSITION 1.2: EMPLOYEES MUST PERCEIVE THAT THE JOB DESIGN FACILITATES PERFORMANCE.

To sense a strong effort-performance correlation, employees must sense that other variables are not interfering with effort—constraining or negating the results of effort. A key determinant of employee-job performance is job design. Like ability, discussed in the previous section, this moderating variable affects to what degree effort results in performance. If the job is well designed, the employee perceives that high effort can yield high success. But if the job is poorly designed, the employee sees the job as interfering with opportunity for real accomplishment. Performance is blocked by a faulty job design. No matter how hard the employee tries, there will be little significant payoff. The job does not allow for high performance. A perceived quality job design, in addition to the ability discussed under Proposition 1.1, is a necessary condition for one to perceive a strong correlation between effort and performance—that effort will definitely lead to performance.

Special cases of flawed job designs are those that purposefully make performance largely independent of effort and those that "slap" an absolute maximum on the amount of effort possible. For example, machines that run at a set pace and are almost entirely responsible for the quality of output leave little room for varying levels of human effort to have an impact. And the job that does not provide the worker with enough resource "inputs," such as materials and information, forces the worker to be idle. Such designs do not take advantage of the human's capacity to exert effort. They do not utilize the potential of the human resource.

You may recognize here that, as with ability, job design is important in its direct effect on employee job performance. Obviously performance is impossible if the job is faulty in "set up." But it is the indirect effect of perceived job design on employee job performance—its effect on motivation—that is the focus of attention in the following discussion.

Probably no other single variable impacts as much on motivation as job design. Job design affects motivation in a variety of significant ways. Its impact on the perceived correlation between effort and performance is developed in the following prescriptions. In ensuing chapters, job design appears again as a major factor affecting the perceived linkage between performance and reward, affecting the perceived costs associated with effort, and affecting the distribution of effort among alternative uses for effort.

The following are ways to get employees to see that they operate under a quality work or job design—one that will facilitate high performance.

1. Design inputs of the right quantity, quality, and type.

When designing jobs for employees, attention must be given to the design, or planning, of the resources that will "flow" to the workers. In order to perform, workers need inputs (resources) such as materials, information, and money. They use or transform these inputs into products, or services, or into portions of products or services.

If workers are to be productive in their endeavors, they need to receive inputs that are sufficient in quantity. Obviously, if workers run out of raw materials, they are not going to be able to finish their jobs. A limited supply of resources leads workers to perceive that sustained high levels of effort are not possible. The limited availability of resources prevents any opportunity to exert that full measure of effort needed for full accomplishment. Limited resources are a direct constraint on motivation. Even if the worker wants to exert high effort, there is no opportunity to do so!

An inferior quality of input prevents effort from yielding quality output. If workers think that the materials they use are flawed, or that the information they receive is inaccurate, they are not likely to calculate a very high probability of effort yielding quality performance. The faulty inputs will prevent good performance. No matter how much effort is exerted, high performance is seen to be impossible.

Input of the wrong type can prevent employees from seeing a strong correlation between effort and performance too. If a market researcher, for example, needs information on net sales to "work up" a forecasting model, information on gross sales will not suffice and will not allow the researcher to perform at a high level no matter how hard he or she tries.

2. Time inputs properly.

Resource inputs can be of the proper quality, quantity, and type but still not be right for facilitating performance. Timing is all important too. To perform, workers need resources when they are ready for them—not too early, not too late. When information and materials arrive too early, workers have to take the time to store these resources until they are ready to use them, or they have to alter their routines to somehow absorb the inputs at the pace with which the inputs are received. Such alterations are usually relatively hasty, inefficient adaptations that may result in the workers' keeping up but having to lower the quality of their performance. Too early input arrivals interfere with effort yielding performance.

When inputs arrive too late, workers obviously cannot perform to a maximum either. They are idle while waiting for the resources. You cannot exert effort with no resources to work with. They may receive adequate quantities, qualities, and kinds of inputs to do the job, but not receive them when needed. Motivation is thus constrained. High effort and performance are seen as impossible.

Giving workers control over the timing of the inputs can help alleviate the problem of timing. For example, workers may be given keys to the raw materials inventories or access to a computer terminal to pull out information when they are ready for it. When workers must depend on others for input, timing can be a problem. Without the best of communications and without the motivation and ability of other individuals to provide resources as requested, the worker is likely to encounter frequent problems of timing and to sense that high performance is impossible.

3. Provide employees with sufficient authority.

How much authority to build into the job is a critical job design decision. Often how much authority is built in will be a function of who it is that occupies the job. Some workers—those who are more responsible and more capable— should have more authority than others, even though they are doing the same kind of work.

When employees have authority, they have a right to command others or to make key decisions regarding the use of organizational resources. Insufficient authority granted to workers will constrain them in getting the job done. A machine operator, for example, a man who has twenty years of service with the company, who is not given the authority to requisition simple replacement parts from the factory supply parts room when his machine breaks down, is faced with a job design problem which prevents him from being productive. He may know how to fix the machine, can fix it in just a few minutes, and can get the machine back on line, but his lack of authority prevents this. Instead of getting the replacement parts himself and getting the machine back into production immediately, he has to clear it with the boss. The boss, in turn, has to get authorization from the head of plant maintenance. The head of maintenance has to call the supply parts room to have the parts delivered to the machine site. Then the worker has to wait for "official" maintenance people to arrive to fix the machine. The worker waits half the day before becoming productive again. Under such conditions, workers see a lack of authority as constraining what they can produce. The perception of a strong effort-performance linkage is weakened because effort and time are spent going through channels rather than running the machine.

4. Keep equipment, tools, and facilities in good repair.

When workers' equipment, tools, and facilities are continually breaking down, workers will not sense that effort leads to performance. If high effort is exerted for a period of time—while systems are working properly—high performance may result during that time. But workers see that sustained performance is not possible because of equipment, tool, and facility failures. Their energy is spent addressing failures. Employees soon say to themselves, "Exerting high effort is senseless, because the design of the tools, equipment, and facilities is preventing us from being productive. What's the sense of busting our guts when as soon as we get going our equipment fails? We spend all of our time and energy fixing things."

A good preventive maintenance program in an organization not only directly influences productivity by cutting downtime, but indirectly affects productivity through its impact on employee motivation. With regular maintenance at intervals adjusted to reflect the pace at which workers work, workers are likely to see that increasing their efforts will not result in frequent breakdowns. Higher effort is seen as possible and as leading to performance.

When management is trying to decide on an optimum preventive maintenance schedule, the indirect effect of maintenance on motivation must be considered. Typically this effect is neglected. Most companies simply attempt to find a maintenance interval that balances direct downtime costs from equipment failure with direct repair costs. This, however, is an oversimplification because of failure to recognize the behavioral factor.

5. Provide employees with state-of-the-art equipment and tools.

Will effort yield performance? Not if workers have to use out-of-date equipment. This perception is highly intensified if the worker knows that workers on other similar jobs do have the latest equipment or that workers on similar jobs in other companies have more up-to-date equipment. Employees' performance may be measured against objective standards which recognize the limitations of their equipment, but, even so, workers' perceptions of how well they can do will invariably be influenced by what they know other workers have for equipment.

Most workers will assess the quality of their equipment in terms of their levels of ability. If their ability will allow them to work faster and better than their equipment permits, they see a job design constraint on performance. Higher effort is impossible because the rate at which the equipment operates will not allow it. Workers say, "What's the use?" They see relatively little correlation between effort and performance.

Workers must see a strong correlation between effort and performance—if effort goes up, so must performance and *significantly*. Putting a boundary on the maximum effort possible as well as permitting performance to increase at only a negligible rate with effort increase destroys motivation.

6. Develop streamlined procedures, methods, and workstation layouts.

The work procedures and methods employees follow, and their workstation layouts, are other moderating job-design variables between effort and performance. With inefficiently designed procedures, methods, and station layouts, workers are likely to see that a lot of effort can be spent accomplishing very little. They exert much energy going through the motions but do not produce much. They may well see that lower effort yields almost the same results as higher effort. Production is constrained by the work design.

For high motivation, workers must see that effort makes a difference in terms of performance. It is important to design procedures, methods, and layouts that do not make performance relatively independent of effort. Making performance independent of effort means not only that high effort makes no difference in performance but also that the capacity of the human resource is not going to be fully utilized.

You may say, "Who cares if workers are not exerting high effort as long as the systems and procedures are designed to yield high output?" Good point. But a work design that makes performance independent of effort is a work design that is forcing waste of the human resource. Companies still pay big bucks for that resource, but they are dollars largely wasted. Can organizations afford this approach? Is it not possible to develop advanced technologies that allow high worker involvement and effort expenditure to pay off?

7. Do not overload workers with too much (too little) to do or too great (too small) a variety of tasks.

Determining how much workers will do and how great a variety of tasks they will perform is a critical decision in designing their jobs. If employees are underloaded with too little work to keep them busy, effort is being constrained. Workers cannot realize high performance because the job does not permit high effort. They complete their assignments, but accomplishment is short of what could be accomplished. The job prevents high effort expenditure because its content is not sufficient to match the effort capacities of the worker.

If employees are overloaded with work—too much to do in a given period of time, or too many different tasks to do—they sense that effort may yield quantity but not quality, which is as important a performance criterion as quantity in most cases and more important in other cases. The overloading causes the employee to feel that doing the job right is next to impossible. He or she can exert high effort but does not see that such energy expenditure will yield top results. Quality will be deficient.

Management must optimally load jobs in such a way that employees know they are achieving, with high effort, the right balance between quantity and quality. If this is not done, employees perceive that good aggregate performance is not going to be realized with high amounts of effort exerted so the tendency is to diminish the effort exerted.

8. Provide regular and accurate feedback on performance.

If employees are to do well at work, they need to know how they are doing. Mechanisms must be established to provide employees with information on whether they are achieving what they are supposed to. Such information—called feedback—tells workers when things are going right or going wrong. When they know things are going well, they can continue performing the way they have been. When they discover things are not up to par, they then have a chance to make it right. Feedback makes proper performance possible. Without it, workers do not know whether effort is paying off. They do not see a clear high correlation between effort and performance because they sense that their efforts may be yielding the wrong results.

Whenever possible, it is useful to build self-generated feedback mechanisms into jobs so the worker does not have to wait for feedback from somebody else or rely on somebody else's measurements of performance. Self-generated, direct feedback is usually more rapid and less biased. Workers can usually be taught the essential performance criteria for their jobs and be trained to assess performance levels along these criteria. Doing this lets employees know that they will have the information they need to cue redirected efforts if necessary.

9. Make task designs and performance standards clear.

Job designs must be clear. What workers are supposed to do, and what they are supposed to accomplish for outcomes, must be well defined and properly communicated to them. Workers cannot see that high effort leads to high performance if they do not know what high performance qs! Good job descriptions can help here. These written documents should spell out in succinct language the various duties one is supposed to spend time and effort pursuing. Written documents detailing performance criteria and desired levels of performance are also extremely helpful. Such documents show precisely toward what, and toward what level of performance, one's energies should be directed.

It does not hurt to review tasks, performance criteria, and performance standards with employees rather frequently. Certainly this is an appropriate activity to pursue during the annual performance review. Sometimes workers think their jobs have changed or may "lose touch" with certain infrequently performed parts of their jobs. Periodic refocusing helps keep "what they are there for" in clear sight. When workers lose sight of what constitutes performance, they can hardly perceive a high likelihood that high effort will yield high performance. For such workers, the perceived effort, or performance curve, is too low in slope to see that high effort pays off.

10. Set realistic goals.

The importance of setting challenging work goals will be discussed in a later chapter. Challenging goals tend to be more highly valued than routine goals; therefore, their accomplishment is more rewarding and therefore more motivational. But challenging goals must never be unrealistic. Workers must know that their efforts have a chance of leading to success. People will muster the effort to do something if they know that, with reasonable effort, they can, in fact, do it.

To assure goal realism, it is important to adjust goals to match individual personalities and abilities. One way to do this is to encourage workers to participate in goal formulation. When individuals have a voice in what they are supposed to accomplish, what level of accomplishment is expected, and when accomplishment is expected, they usually develop something that is in line with their capabilities. When goals are in line with capabilities, employees perceive that high effort will succeed—in other words, will yield performance.

Another approach to establishing realistic goals is to base goals on past performance. People learn from experience. They learn what is sensible and what is not. Often new goals can be set a little higher than those of the past because people grow from their experiences. Of course in setting performance goals, attention must be given to many variables which will affect levels of achievement, but assuming other factors constant, the goals in successive time periods can generally be set increasingly higher—at least up to a point. There is, of course, a limit as to how much can be accomplished in a given time period with given resources.

11. Do not judge performance by comparing one persons's performance with another person's.

Feedback systems, as discussed earlier, are part of the design of a job. Designing a job involves specifying what the worker does, when, where, how, with what resources, and in what kind of environment as well as specifying what feedback means will be used for informing the worker of his or her performance.

A feedback system must incorporate performance standards. These should be developed for each worker to reflect each worker's unique situation. Each worker's performance must then be measured against those standards and the results fed back to the worker.

Often organizations measure performance by comparing what the worker achieves with what others achieve. Such systems should be avoided. These systems guarantee that a certain percentage of the workers will be "flunkies." It is like the college professor who informs the class on the first day of the semester that the students should expect there will be so many A's, so many B's, and so on in that class. A person can actually do well in terms of job demands but be rated low because the system grades by comparison. Under such conditions, employees are likely to perceive that exerting high effort may not be recognized. Even though their performance is in fact good, it may not be seen as good when compared with others.

It should be possible for all workers to get A's if their performance merits such. Forget about comparing one worker to the other. Instead, compare real accomplishment with predetermined plans for accomplishment established for each individual worker. Allow any person who properly realizes those plans to be judged successful.

12. Be sure job goals do not excessively conflict with one another.

Workers are not likely to see that high effort yields high performance when different job goals interfere, or conflict, with one another. When high effort exerted in accomplishing one goal makes it more difficult to achieve another goal, employees are likely to see their various efforts as self-defeating. For example, one may increase effort to increase the quantity of production, but an increase in quantity may exceed the capacities of quality control to monitor results so an increase in defective product occurs. Quality objectives are not realized; thus the overall impact of increased effort is not a real improvement in total performance. Similarly, an increased effort to upgrade quality may result in a downturn in quantity. The two objectives, quantity and quality, are not independent. The effort put into quality can cause a quantity deficiency, and vice versa. Aggregate performance may not be positively impacted by increased effort toward one goal.

The same phenomenon occurs with workers on the assembly line. If one increases effort, up goes his or her production, but a bottleneck occurs at the next workstation because the next worker in line does not increase his or her rate of production. The worker sees that an increase in effort results in higher production at his or her station but causes problems at another. How positive the overall impact is, is questionable.

Whenever workers have jobs with multiple task dimensions, the kotential for goal conflict exists. An improvement along one task dimension may hurt accomplishment of another. This phenomenon is familiar in the field of medicine. You take an aspirin to relieve the headache and develop severe stomach upset. The net improvement in health is questionable. Higher effort in one area does not lead to a significant *net* increase in performance.

13. Minimize interruptions to employee work flow.

Employees see a relatively low correlation between effort and performance when they are constantly interrupted in their work. Too many interruptions make it impossible to get into a smooth, efficient work routine. Interruptions mean you are forever spending your energies "starting up" and "shutting down" on tasks. This problem is probably at its worst when workers are engaged in "think work" or planning activities. Interruptions spoil a worker's train of thought.

Management must design jobs to screen workers from too many noncontrollable, interrupting factors. Once you start a job, you should be allowed to finish it unless other exceptional demands must be given attention. Buffering mechanisms can be established to "store" potential interruptions until employees have time to deal with them. For example, secretaries can hold calls or take messages for supervisors instead of interrupting their supervisors every time someone wishes to talk to them. Employees wishing face-to-face encounters with their supervisors can line up in the secretaries' offices until their supervisors are free. Similarly, space for storing various types of materials can be provided so that employees will not have to stop working to process unexpected deliveries.

With constant interruptions, you perceive that much effort is spent processing those interruptions instead of addressing your main assignments. It is difficult to see how high effort really leads to high performance under such conditions.

14. Minimize inter-station travel.

Workers need well-designed workstation layouts as mentioned earlier. But few workers spend all their time at a given workstation. A worker may operate at numerous workstations or carry materials, tools, or information among workstations. However, very little true productive work is done during inter-station travel. Management must give attention, therefore, to designing a proper network of jobs and workstations. If your travel time among stations is too high due to excessive distance among stations or too difficult due to such factors as wall barriers or hazardous equipment, you will be using up a significant portion of your energy in simple semi-productive travel activity instead of in truly productive work.

Paths among stations should be straight, barrier free, and short. If at 8:00 in the morning you must work in the northeast corner of a 300,000 square foot plant, at 10:00 A.M. you have to be in the southwest corner, and at 11:30 A.M. you have to be over in the northeast corner, you will be spending much of your time traveling. The job should keep you in one general area to minimize effort devoted to inter-station travel. The same situation applies if you are a field sales representative. It is important to plan your routes so that inter-city travel distance, time, cost, and effort are minimized. When you see that a lot of your effort must be spent on simply getting from "here to there" you will likely see that high effort does not have that large a performance payoff.

15. Design supportive social environments.

When designing jobs, attention must be given to the environments in which tasks are executed. The social environment is one key type of environment that significantly affects performance. Workers produce best when they have a supportive social environment. A supportive social environment exists when you have a chance to interact with others while at work, when you enjoy the interaction you have with others, and when that interaction is helpful to you. Having others to work with gives you a chance to ask questions and to obtain ready help. Having friendly others to work with tends to cause effort spent in interpersonal interaction to be more productive as well as more satisfying. When the social system is supportive, you do not have to exert as much energy dealing with such matters as a fellow employee who refuses to take needed action or intentional stumbling blocks thrust in your way by an excessively competitive peer. You are much more likely to see a strong correlation between the effort you put out and what you are able to accomplish.

Management must carefully consider dimensions of the social system when constructing jobs. Do not isolate employees. Hire people who can work together well as a team. Hire people who have like personalities—or at least compatible personalities. And avoid casting the worker into an environment that involves excessive daily interpersonal encounters because too much social exchange can evolve in place of productive work.

16. Provide a healthy, safe, and pleasant physical work environment.

Another key type of environment that affects performance is the physical workplace. If workers are to be productive, they need a physical environment that allows for high effort to pay off. When designing the physical environment, management must give attention to such factors as the quality of lighting, room temperature, humidity, the noise level in the work area, the quality of the air employees breathe, and the colors and decor in the work situation. Attention must be given to keeping the work system free from hazards and as physically pleasant as possible.

When work systems are not hazard free, you spend too much time and energy trying to protect yourself—for example, strapping on protective helmets and goggles, carefully tiptoeing around fast-moving blades, or adjusting your face mask or clean air conversion device. When work systems are not pleasant, you spend an inordqnate amount of time grumbling and complaining or trying, often without results, various ways to improve the pleasantness of the system. In other words, effort is spent in nonproductive ways. You see that instead of all your effort going toward performance, a significant percentage is spent on responding to the unhealthy, unsafe, or unpleasant work system. Not only does a quality physical environment tend to keep worker satisfaction up, but it also stimulates greater effort expenditure.

17. Avoid having task sets change at too rapid a pace.

If the content of your job is changed too often, you find yourself forever in a trying-to-learn-the-job situation, and, as with excessive task variety in a job, you find that a high percentage of your time and energy is spent on start-up and shut-down activities. You are always having to get ready for new tasks and to close out old work.

A good example is the general-purpose laborer who, during the first week, serves as plant janitor, during the second week serves as a carpenter repairing facilities, and during the third week works in the yard organizing materials being inventoried there. When he or she starts the janitor's portion of the job, it takes a half day or more to locate cleaning supplies and tools and to get instructions on just what areas need cleaning and when. At least the first two days are spent "spinning wheels" and making mistakes. At the end of the week, a half day must be spent shutting down the job—getting all supplies and tools back into the closet, informing purchasing of new supplies to order, and so forth. The following week the same worker goes through the same kind of routine with the carpenter's job: assembling tools, getting information, and making mistakes the first part of the week, then cleaning up, storing the tools, and informing management of completed tasks the last part of the week. The third week it is more of the same. The worker never has time to develop an efficient, smooth-flowing work pattern. He or she calculates that effort, under such circumstances, does not have too high a real payoff.

18. Avoid excessive task uncertainty.

Work tasks and standards may be clear (when they are communicated), and task variety and the rate of task set change may not be excessive, but task uncertainty is something a little different. And we are not talking about interruptions. A job exhibits content uncertainty when you do not know ahead of time what type of work you are going to be confronted with. Executive jobs are like this. You may not know from one day to the next just what problems and issues you are going to be confronted with. You are always "tasting" surprise. This is the nature of the job. These uncertainties are not interruptions of regular routines. They are the norm and fully expected.

When you face high task uncertainty, however, it is next to impossible to prepare for tasks. Forget planning. You have to deal with issues as they come up. The problem is that you do not know what is coming or when. Under these conditions you cannot ready yourself to deal efficiently with issues. You cannot think through the best way to respond. You often wind up with inefficient expenditures of effort, pursuing trial-and-error solutions and making unreasonable snap decisions that create frequent need for a repeated effort to cover your mistakes the first time around.

When you face such uncertainty, it is hard to perceive that high effort really leads to high performance. A large portion of your time and energy is wasted because of the lack of opportunity to plan proper means for task execution. Management must be careful not to allow excessive uncertainty to creep into the jobs in its organization.

19. Clearly prioritize tasks/responsibilities.

If you do not know which of your job duties are really important and which are not so important, it is difficult to sense that a given amount of effort will have maximum payoff in terms of performance. You will feel that you may be exerting a high level of effort on tasks that do not count that much in any measure of aggregate performance.

Employees must be clearly instructed on the relative priorities of the different task assignments they are given. They must understand on what their efforts should be concentrated. They must be highly sensitized to what tasks must be performed without error and what tasks must be performed exactly on time. They must be able to distinguish critical duties from the not-so-critical. If the workday is excessively loaded with interruptions and the worker cannot get to all tasks assigned for the day, it should be clear to the worker what *must* be done and what can be left until tomorrow. When you do not know these things, you calculate a relatively high probability that your efforts may not yield what management really wants, which is maximum overall performance.

Task priorities often do change. During one week, planning the budget may take priority over quality control issues. The next week quality control issues may be more important to deal with than budget items. Management must adjust priorities as conditions change and time passes. This is an adjustment in a crucial aspect of job design. Employees need to be regularly informed of these changes in order to perceive a high effort-performance correlation.

20. Properly integrate and sequence tasks.

For efficient, quality performance, your tasks should be arranged such that transitions from one to the other can be made smoothly and without time loss. This means tasks should be integrated. Integration is helped by building tasks into the job which require similar types and levels of knowledge and skills. All tasks should be related to one another, for example, in terms of similarity of function or in terms of all being required to produce the same given product or service.

Also tasks should be properly sequenced so that accomplishment of one leads naturally to the next. Perhaps the output from one task can serve as input for the next. Sequencing should recognize the need to minimize inter-task disruptions— such as excessive start-up and shut-down activities. Sequencing should recognize physical task positioning or spacing too. For example, you should not have to reach to the far left for a part to put on your assembly, then have to reach to the far right for the next part. In one smooth, fluid motion it should be possible to grab both parts quickly. Work tasks that move the worker *from* relatively simple, repetitive activities *to* more complicated, less routine activities should also be considered in planning task sequences.

When you see a lack of proper task integration and sequencing, you see that much effort is nonproductive—that is, the performance resulting from effort exertion is relatively low. A quality job design stimulates worker perception that efforts are not wasted and that effort clearly translates to performance.

21. Avoid making performance on a job too dependent on results from other jobs.

When you make performance on one job a function of performance on another job, you may be severely restricting what the worker can do. You may be directly limiting the amount of effort expenditure possible. If one worker cannot do his or her job until someone else has finished a job, that worker may be idle a good percentage of the workday.

Often employees will have to wait for information from others, delivery of materials from others, or help from others. If the other employees get behind, the problem snowballs because the worker depending on output from those others will also get behind. Sometimes workers have to wait for others to turn on the electricity, wait for others to give instructions, wait for others to check the quality of their production, wait for phone calls, or wait for others to finish with certain tools. Sometimes organizations do not realize the high level of inter-job dependency they build into their work systems. Because of this, workers may not be able to exert the effort they are capable of exerting because they are constrained by the performance of others.

Making a job independent from others may allow the worker to expend as much effort as he or she chooses and, therefore, to perceive that high performance is possible. Employees sense that performance can be realized because effort expenditure is not blocked or bounded by problems or slowdowns on other jobs. It is up to them.

22. Provide input/output buffering devices.

It was mentioned earlier that job input buffering devices are useful for minimizing interruptions. Such input buffers can also be useful for controlling differences in work pace from one station (office) to the next. Workstation cycle time will fluctuate as workers' moods change, as fatigue sets in, or as technical problems develop, for example. One workstation in a line may slow down while the one preceding it in line may speed up. A storage space (buffer) to house the excess production from the first workstation during its rapid production rate cycle can be used as a buffer device for input going to a second, "slower" workstation. The storage space allows for a buildup of in-process inventory— keeping it on hold until the next worker can attend to it or get some help in processing it.

Buffering devices should be provided to hold a worker's output until others are ready to process it. The worker should not have to slow his or her production rate to accommodate the input capability of another worker. One worker should not have to produce a unit then "hold" that unit until somebody else finds time to "absorb" it.

These concepts apply to jobs of every type in the organization—managerial as well as operative. Buffering devices are needed for information like paperwork and computer information flows too. When employees see no buffering systems, they see that much time and effort is wastefully spent regulating flow rates so that they will be equal from one station to the next.

23. Specify when the work is to be done and what is to be done.

This is basic but a point often neglected. Many times workers have to spend energy redoing tasks, storing the results of completed tasks, or expending excessive energy on a task (while neglecting others) trying to catch up or to get it done on time. The reason such things happen is often because management forgets to specify when the task is supposed to be done. The assignment is clearly delegated with respect to what the worker is supposed to do, but the time line is not made clear. A prime example is the case of the employee who spends all afternoon preparing that requested written report and then finds out management really does not want it until six months from now. Similarly an employee may perform a task such as cleaning the shop for inspection only to find out inspection is next week so the worker has to redo the cleaning job just prior to the inspection, when normally it would be done only once every three weeks. Or an employee fixes a piece of equipment in the repair shop only to find out the company does not need it for a while. Now the employee has to find storage space for the piece of equipment while waiting for the plant supervisor to request reinstallation on the factory floor.

Not knowing when work should be done results in effort being wasted. The employee sees a weakened correlation between effort and performance when there exists a question about timing. Specifying an accurate completion time on tasks is often as critical as specifying what must be done. Too often delegators do not specify required timing precisely enough, causing a perception of likely wasted effort and, thus, decreased motivation.

24. Be sure equipment and tools recognize human limitations.

The field of ergonomics has alerted us to the fact that man and machine must be tied together into one integrated, productive unit. Machines must not be designed to "force" wasted effort or effort that leads to error. For example, cockpit instrument panels in aircraft must be laid out to permit ease of eye focus on critical instruments at the right time. Dials that must be read in sequence should be positioned side by side in the order they must be read. Dials should not all look alike, because a reading on one may be mistaken for a reading on another. Absolutely critical dials or "alert" dials should be centrally located on the panel to assure the pilot sees them and reads them correctly. Not giving attention to such factors in the workplace means error and wasted effort—a situation not conducive to perception of a high effort-performance correlation.

As a further example, levers and buttons should be located on shop floor machines so they can be pulled and pushed with sufficient ease, but not pulled and pushed by mistake. Every machine should ideally have an abort (safety) system built in to quickly alert the worker if a mistake has been made in "setting the machine" or if some other problem with equipment operation is imminent. This kind of equipment convinces the operator that his or her efforts will not be in vain—that the payoff from effort will be performance.

25. Break goals into subgoals.

Goals motivate in different ways. They can help employees perceive that performance leads to reward, and they can help employees see that effort leads to performance. Breaking broad goals into subgoals can be particularly helpful in stimulating one's sense that effort leads to performance. Subgoals serve as checkpoints. Their accomplishment helps verify that effort is on track and that continued effort will result in full accomplishment.

Establishing subgoals provides one with a mechanism for self-evaluation of performance on an assessment-as-you-go basis. The feedback that comes from subgoal achievement or nonachievement helps workers continue or redirect their efforts as necessary. Subgoals can, therefore, significantly aid performance.

When you add the benefits of goals in aiding workers experience satisfaction from accomplishment, and in aiding workers see that rewards are contingent on performance, to the benefits of subgoals in aiding workers see that performance is contingent on effort, you have a powerful case for establishing clear, realistic goals and subgoals for people in the workplace. Goals help motivation in so many ways that management's focus on them is absolutely essential. Participative goal and subgoal setting, with management involvement to assure organizationally relevant and nonconflicting goals among different employees, is worthy of considerable attention as a prescriptive motivational agenda.

3

Principle 2: Employees Will Be Motivated When They Perceive that Performance Leads to Reward

In order for employees to exert high effort, they must see a good reason for it and know that there are benefits to it. Employees must sense that performance pays off—that it will yield desired positive outcomes. The stronger the perceived correlation between performance and desired rewards (positive outcomes), the stronger the motivation.

PROPOSITION 2.1: EMPLOYEES MUST PERCEIVE THAT REWARDS ARE CONTINGENT ON PERFORMANCE.

To sense a strong performance-reward correlation, one must sense that rewards are received on a performance contingent basis. One must get high rewards for high performance and low rewards for low performance. One must not feel that rewards are experienced independent of performance.

One of the overriding conclusions of the effort–net return model of motivation is that you do not just simply provide the employee with valued rewards—rewards matched to his or her needs—to motivate. You must be sure those rewards are experienced contingent on performance. And it is the degree of contingency (the slope of the reward function) that is particularly important.

The following are ways to get employees to see that the rewards they receive from the organization are highly contingent on their level of performance.

1. "Talk up" any contingent relations between performance and rewards.

If rewards are contingent on performance, employees have to know it in order for the rewards to be motivational. And casual awareness is not enough. They should be acutely sensitive to the fact. To build this sensitivity, managers can frequently and enthusiastically talk about how performance is the *only* means for employees to realize successes and enjoy satisfaction. Managers must emphasize that the only way you get ahead in the company is to produce; the only way you get your income up is to produce; the only way you gain real job security is to produce.

Managers have to make it crystal clear to employees that in their organization performance does make a difference. Without it, there is nothing. With it, there is everything. Frequent discussions informally, in meetings, and in written communiqués will sensitize employees to the fact that performance counts for something.

Managers would do well to emphasize the dependency of specific rewards on performance. They should point out, for example, how end-of-year bonuses are tied to individual performance, how promotions are largely a function of performance and not a function of length of service or friendship with supervisors, how improved job assignments will be forthcoming if performance is good, and how annual awards will be given to top performers. The dependence of rewards on performance must not be kept secret or camouflaged.

2. Assure that the degree of performance-reward contingency is sufficiently high.

Just having rewards dependent on performance is not enough, however. Critical is the degree to which rewards are contingent on performance. Rewards must not only rise with improvements in performance, they must rise substantially. The greater the reward increase for a given change in performance, the greater the motivational impact of the reward.

If an organization's rewards are only slightly or moderately contingent on performance, it may not be enough to make the employee fully realize that performance does make a difference. Every employee has an awareness threshold, and the rewards one experiences must be highly enough dependent on performance to break through this threshold. In the eyes of the employee, the rewards associated with high performance must be significantly greater than the rewards associated with low performance.

The increase in rewards for given units of increase in performance must be sufficient over all ranges of performance too. For example, simply providing relatively high reward increases for changes in performance over medium to high ranges of performance may not motivate if relatively small reward increases are provided over low ranges of performance. See Figure 8 for an illustration. The highly contingent rewards over Range 2 are inconsequential. The employee sees greater satisfaction possible within Range 1.

3. Assure that a significant portion of the rewards employees receive are contingent on performance.

Not all rewards employees receive can or should be made contingent on performance. For example, most sound compensation systems include

Figure 8
Changes in the Contingency Relation

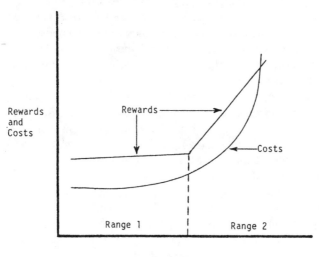

components of pay based on length of service and on the value of the work performed. Such pay is important for assuring that employees sense fairness in pay and, for assuring sufficiently high employee satisfaction with compensation. Fair systems and satisfying systems do, among other things, ease the organization's efforts at recruiting and retaining a work force. And this is important.

But rewards will not motivate unless a relatively large percentage of the total reward package—of the different kinds of rewards offered by the organization— is made dependent on performance. Certainly many of the rewards which will serve to satisfy employees' most intense needs should be made contingent on performance. There should be at least some performance-contingent rewards for each of the five types of basic human needs—physiological, safety and security, social and belongingness, esteem and status, and self-actualization.

No single reward, be it recognition, compensation, promotion, or whatever, will likely have a large impact on employee motivation no matter how contingent it is on performance. "Man does not live by bread alone," someone once said. A few rewards may be highly contingent on performance, but these will not motivate unless these rewards, taken together, constitute a substantial portion of the reward package. Basically the employee must sense that "almost everything around here" in one way or another depends on performance. Sensing that only a few things are dependent on performance is generally not enough to generate a strong perceived performance-*total* reward correlation.

4. Set clear goals or divide work into distinct units.

A key type of reward that employees experience is the intrinsic reward—the satisfaction that comes from engaging in the work itself. A key type of intrinsic job satisfaction is the satisfaction that comes from accomplishing or achieving something. Achievement means progress. It means success. Achievement means your efforts have been fruitful. Your investment of skill, time, and energy has paid off. It is, therefore, rewarding.

The sense of achievement is highly enhanced by providing benchmarks for measuring achievement. One simple way to do this is to assure the worker has clear work goals, or work end points. Reaching such goals clearly signals accomplishment. It vividly shows performance has paid off and generated a concrete outcome. It makes the worker more aware that performance has, in fact, yielded accomplishment.

Similarly, dividing work into distinct units helps one see that performance leads to accomplishment. When a unit of work is completed, it is clear that effort has succeeded. When workers simply perform one or a few tasks, repetitively, in the ongoing production of a product, they never really sense any completion point which gives that fulfilling sense of having really accomplished. Nothing ever seems finished. They do not see real results for their efforts. If workers do not know whether or not, or when, the product is finished, it is difficult for them to see a strong correlation between their performance and real accomplishment. Completing a distinct, whole unit of product clearly signals accomplishment and triggers the satisfaction that accompanies accomplishment.

The clearer a goal or end point, or the more distinctive the work unit, the more easily measured the degree of progress and the greater the impact of accomplishment on satisfaction. Establishing multiple criteria or goals to signal a given stage of accomplishment can make achievement and success even more vivid and contribute to heightened intrinsic satisfaction.

5. Make sure the organization has the capacity to reward.

Rewards promised in return for performance are great. But the employee will ask, "Does this organization have the wherewithal to back up its intentions to reward for performance?" Many companies have fine contingent reward plans but seldom seem to be able to fulfill those plans. They have honest intentions, but various events and circumstances interfere with the organization's ability to actually deliver the promised rewards.

When the employee feels the company may not be able to make good on a promised reward, the reward is rendered relatively impotent as a motivator. The higher the worker's calculation of the probability that the reward cannot be delivered, the greater the impotence of the reward. If one thinks the organization may not be able to provide the reward, one does not see a very strong correlation between performance and reward.

One good example of this is the case of a company promising $1,000 end-of-year bonuses to managers whose departments reach production quotas. But at year's end, the company has to renege because sales have been down and profits are too low. If employees know ahead of time there is a good chance of such happening, the promised bonus has little effect in spurring effort.

Another example is the case of the company which promises promotions for good work. But every employee cannot be promoted. There are too few upper-level positions for all good performers to be moved up. Employees know this. They know the company does not have the capacity or resources to always come through on such promises. The chances one perceives of actually receiving the reward may be quite low. If so, the strength of the perceived performance-reward linkage is diminished. It is the actual ability of the company to reward that is often paramount in affecting one's perception of the chances of receiving a reward.

6. Be sure reward agents are trusted.

Rewards may be well communicated, valued, highly contingent on performance, and so on, and the company may have the capacity to "pay," but employees will look at another factor when assessing the probability of reward receipt. That factor is the trust level of those who deliver rewards. A manager may promise an employee a wonderful, all-expenses-paid vacation in return for good performance, but will the employee believe the manager? Are such promises from the reward agent (manager, here) to be taken seriously? Perhaps the employee is aware of past broken promises by the manager. If so, the employee will calculate a probability of reward receipt considerably less than one. The employee senses a weak link here between performance and reward and may think there is a good chance that performance will not result in the reward being bestowed.

Building a relationship of trust between boss and subordinate, or between reward agent and employee, is basic for successful motivation. Only through trust will any contingent reward system, verbalized or written, be believed. To build trust, though, usually takes time. Employees have to see that reward agents mean what they say. Reward agents have to demonstrate, through their consistent behavior over time, that they are honest and will actually follow through on what they say they will. There is really no other way for trust to be developed. All it takes are a few errors, and a relationship of trust can be ruined. One mistake among a thousand can destroy the trust. Reward agents, therefore, must work hard at not faltering in honesty or in the fulfillment of promises.

7. Develop and communicate performance-reward schedules.

Written, published, and distributed performance-reward schedules can make highly vivid the fact that rewards are contingent on performance, and they make clear the precise nature of contingent relations between performance and rewards. Such schedules aid communication of rewards by spelling out, in rather

Figure 9
Sample Performance-Reward Schedule

Performance Dimension & Level	Reward
a. $5,000-10,000 monthly sales	$1,000 commission
b. $10,001-15,000 monthly sales	$1,200 commission plus 3 weeks vacation with all expenses paid
c. $15,001-20,000 monthly sales	$1,400 commission plus 4 weeks vacation, plus 2 points toward 10 required for promotion
d. 1 to 3 new recruits	$100 per recruit
e. 4 to 6 new recruits	$200 per recruit

certain terms, what rewards can be expected for different levels of performance. These schedules serve as a reference for employees who may wonder about a performance-reward relationship or who may have forgotten about certain performance-reward linkages. They serve as a means of reinforcing other communications about rewards versus performance.

Figure 9 illustrates a portion of a sample performance-reward schedule for a salesperson. This schedule informs the reader in precise terms just how rewards depend on performance. Such schedules are extremely valuable when a job involves many different and distinct performance dimensions with different kinds and amounts of rewards being issued for different levels of performance on different dimensions. These schedules are probably more easily utilized for description of extrinsic rewards but can be developed, with a little ingenuity, to cover intrinsic rewards as well.

One of the key points to keep in mind in developing a schedule is to establish rewards for different levels of performance. One should not have to reach a single overall goal before receiving any reward at all. If one falls a bit short of the ultimate goal, one should still be recognized for the level of accomplishment. Rewards should go up as performance goes up—not all or nothing.

8. Design and implement a performance evaluation and control system.

It is very hard for employees to ever see a contingent relationship between rewards and real performance if performance is not measured. If a company is going to reward on the basis of performance, it must in fact assess or measure performance. This means the organization must develop a means of measurement and use that means. Employees often point out that management says they reward for performance, but the employees do not see any evidence of how and when evaluations of performance are made. If you do not see performance being measured, it is hard to accept that rewards can ever legitimately depend on performance.

Management must develop means of relatively frequent performance assessment and communicate these means to employees to assure employee sensitivity to the fact that performance is measured. Full-blown semi-annual evaluations of the employee's total performance should be coupled with weekly, if not daily, observations and feedback on performance. This lets the employee know that management is serious about performance assessment and leads to the realization that rewards can, in fact, be tied to performance.

More than just the evaluation is needed though. Results of evaluations should be fully communicated to workers so they can see for themselves how their performance and the rewards they receive relate. What is communicated is what is really important here. If the worker has an erroneous understanding of his or her performance, the performance-reward linkage is weakened. Sometimes self-assessment systems can be coupled with other evaluative mechanisms to help minimize defective communications of results between evaluators and those being evaluated.

9. Assure that performance evaluations are valid.

It may have been implied before, but the point must be emphasized that evaluations of performance, even though done regularly and fed back to workers, are rather useless if employees perceive those evaluations to be invalid. Rewards granted contingent on invalid assessments of performance can quickly destroy motivation and be a total waste of resources for the company. If employees think that high performance has a good chance of not being recognized because of lack of assessment validity, they are likely to say, "What's the use?" They will not sense a strong relationship between their performance and rewards.

To be valid, evaluations must be as objective as possible. Personal bias cannot play a role here. Whenever possible, measurements should involve "counts"—quantification of the variable under study. Whenever subjective descriptions of performance are used, too many sources of error can creep in.

To be valid, evaluations must cover the right areas too. They should focus on assessment of how well the worker fulfills his or her assigned duties and respon-sibilities. Assessments must not be made of how well the employee does on nontask or ill-communicated task dimensions. Avoid evaluating the employee on personality traits, habits, customs, and similar items, which do not constitute duties or responsibilities.

To be valid, evaluations must also recognize high and low priority tasks. Good performance on an important task should far overshadow poor performance on a relatively unimportant task. All measurements of performance must not be identically weighted if evaluations are to be valid.

Further, to assure validity in evaluations and to assure employees that true performance will be measured, it is important to have highly trained and motivated evaluators. And the fact that evaluators are well trained and motivated must be communicated to employees. When employees think evaluators know what they are doing, and are trying hard, the employees calculate a higher probability that true performance will be recognized and, therefore, that the proper rewards for performance have a chance of being forthcoming.

10. Develop a historical record of reward for performance.

Perhaps nothing will enhance one's perception of a strong contingent relationship between performance and rewards any more than a clear record of the organization actually granting rewards to workers who have earned them by way of top performance. Confirming performance through consistent bestowance of rewards through time can create such a high expectation that rewards will, in fact, be received for high performance, that other factors like lack of trust of reward agents or perceived insufficiency of company resources can be overshadowed.

Of course, as with other prescriptions discussed here, communication is a key. A simple history of rewards for performance does little for motivation unless that history is communicated to employees. This can be done in a variety of ways. Managers can mention in conversation specific examples of past rewards given for performance and point out that the company has a long-term record of such rewarding. Old company newsletters and bulletins that recognize employees who have received rewards can be put on display. Adhering to a company policy of promotion from within can help. Filling a wall with awards (plaques, certificates) received through the years by top performers makes quite vivid that the company has followed, historically, a policy of rewarding for performance. Also, bringing past top performers to employee meetings which focus on productivity and performance can help. Be sure to point out at these meetings how these top performers were rewarded for their successes.

11. Provide reward agents with the power to control rewards.

If those who issue, or provide rewards, to employees are not in control of their reward inventories, employees may well calculate that even if their performance is deserving, they may miss getting rewarded. The worker will calculate that the likelihood of getting a deserved reward is relatively low if the control over issuance of that reward is unclear, diffused, or forever changing.

Supervisors should do most of the motivating in a company, and to do this they must be able to administer rewards as they see fit. They should not have to get the okay from their bosses. They should not have to get a majority vote from some reward committee. They should not have to receive authorization from the personnel department or from the controller.

Reward budgets should be set. Supervisors should develop, and have authorized, a reward inventory that they can draw on throughout the year as they think appropriate. Reward agents should be able to control, by themselves, how rewards are to be used as well as if and when they will be used. Reward agents must be delegated authority to flexibly apply rewards. Without such authority, agents may be unable to grant rewards as earned.

The greater the social power of supervisors and other reward agents, the greater the chances they will be successful in acquiring rewards to bestow and in controlling the application of those rewards. Whenever these people boost their abilities to influence through such avenues as gaining valuable information, developing their expertise, or improving their personalities, they acquire, as perceived by the employee, a greater capacity to reward. Reward agents with high ability to influence others in the organization have a greater capability to build reward inventories and to control the flow of rewards to employees. Nonpowerful agents are relatively hard pressed to affect the acquisition and application of rewards.

12. Avoid excessive use of group rewards.

For rewards to motivate, the individual must see how they relate to his or her individual performance. Group rewards are used to reward an entire group, or members of that group, for the group's performance. When such rewards are used, the individual cannot see a direct strong relationship between his or her own performance and the reward he or she receives. The individual may perform well, but if the group does not perform well, as a whole, then the individual does not get the deserved reward. Similarly, the individual can perform poorly and receive a large reward because the group as a whole did well. In either case the individual sees a relatively weak tie between his or her level of performance and a reward.

If group rewards are to be used, a modified group reward system usually works better. The group can receive its reward—money, recognition, better project assignments, or whatever. Subsequent to this, the reward should be allocated among individual members dependent upon individuals' relative contributions. This requires that the group develop and use, internally, some valid system of assessing individual contribution.

Such development and use of an internal evaluation system need not be that great a burden. If done properly, it need not destroy cooperation and sharing among team members. Critics of individual contribution assessment within teams claim that the whole spirit of teamwork is destroyed when moving from pure group evaluation and reward to this modified approach. There is some truth in this, but further analysis reveals that mature, responsible group members are not likely to be happy or productive if individual differences in performance go unrecognized. When people's performance levels are different, few argue that the same reward should go to each person.

13. Hire personnel who have a strong work ethic.

This may be one of the easiest and most practical of all the techniques for assuring that the worker sees a high correlation between performance and reward. Employees with a strong work ethic receive reward automatically from performance. Performance itself is the reward. Indeed, to many of these folks, effort itself is the reward. Whether performance results from that effort is not really important. The worker experiences satisfaction simply from knowing that he or she has worked hard. We have a case here of effort leading directly to reward rather than indirectly by first impacting on performance.

People with a strong work ethic believe that the mark of a quality person is his or her engagement in lifelong hard work. They believe all that is good will eventually come to one who labors long and hard. The valued outcome here is as much the toil itself as it is the product produced, the service rendered, or the goal achieved. The toil itself yields a satisfying sense of self-worth, dignity, and pride.

If organizations can assemble work forces of operatives and managers who incorporate in their philosophies a strong work ethic, most of the organizations' problems of motivation will be resolved. But such is not entirely possible and seems less and less likely to be possible as time goes by. Evidence abounds that as a society's standard of living increases, there is diminished value placed on hard work as the mark of a good or a successful person. No longer is the measure of a quality human being necessarily a hard-working, effort-exerting person.

14. Build employee loyalty to the organization and its goals.

Employees who are loyal to their organizations believe in their organizations. They accept the values of their organizations and believe their organizations fulfill a worthwhile role in society. They are strongly supportive of the philosophy and goals of their organization. They are committed to the organization—to what it stands for and to fulfillment of their individual roles within it.

Loyal employees see performance as the means of fulfilling or realizing their commitments. They see performance as an obligation. They see performance as a means of helping the organization succeed. Organizational success is translated to personal success and, thereby, causes personal satisfaction. Loyal employees derive automatic satisfaction from performance because they see performance as a key means of helping the organization, and providing such help is a rewarding and satisfying experience.

Loyalty can be instilled in employees only over time. When the organization demonstrates real usefulness to the community coupled with unwavering fairness in the treatment of the employee, loyalty eventually evolves. Strong loyalty is often developed when organizations demonstrate a sincere willingness to help out employees who may need financial help, good advice, time off for personal reasons, etc. Strong loyalty is also enhanced when organizations are fortunate enough to have, over the long run, competent, charismatic leaders. Employee attachment to those exhibiting such leadership translates into attachment and commitment to the organization.

15. Do not socially isolate employees.

When you socially isolate workers on the job, you are removing a great source of reward for performance. Many rewards experienced by the employee come from other employees. If employees are socially isolated by their jobs, opportunity to receive these rewards is significantly diminished.

When employees work with others they have an opportunity to experience compliments, expressions of gratitude and praise for their good work or for providing help to others. When employees do not work with others, nobody else knows what they do and, therefore, nobody else is in a position to offer recognition-type rewards. Making one part of a well-integrated social system increases one's perceptions of the chances that performance will be recognized and lead to rewards.

A number of courses of action can be pursued to develop the social system in an organization and to assure workers are not isolated. Even if workers are physically isolated while *at* work, after work parties, company-sponsored recreation events, etc., can provide these employees with an opportunity to convey to others their achievements and to receive some positive reinforcement in return. On the job, open, wall-free work areas and offices with chest-high walls can permit ease of social- and work-related interaction. Establishing labor pools can foster interaction too. Excessive departmentalizing—both physically and administratively—poses a severe barrier to the development of interpersonal reward exchanges because the departmentalization interferes with the formation of cohesive work teams. Hiring workers who tend to have similar personalities, likes and dislikes can also stimulate interaction which can lead to peer-generated recognition-type rewards.

16. Coach and counsel on performance.

This is a powerful vehicle for providing rewards contingent on performance. Coaching and counseling focus heavily on helping employees develop skills and abilities, and in the process provide the supervisor with an excellent opportunity to recognize workers for improved performance.

If managers are to really succeed at coaching and counseling, they must be in close working relationships with their employees. The managing coach and counselor will almost continuously monitor employee performance in order to help the employee make appropriate performance adjustments. When workers see the nature of this relationship with the coach/counselor, they sense that performance is going to be measured and likely measured precisely. They perceive that rewards for improvement will likely be granted as deserved. They can expect praise for learning (performing) well, an upgrading in task assignments as the coach/counselor spots improvement, and eventual freedom, or autonomy, at work as they prove themselves. The existence of a quality person serving in a coach/counselor role relative to the worker helps convince the worker that performance improvement will not go unrecognized and, therefore, unrewarded.

Coaching and counseling can be used at any stage in an employee's development. It is not just for new employees. Even the most experienced employees will need to keep up with changing technologies and new work assignments. Coaching and counseling should be used whenever the company requires employees to change behaviors or to upgrade performance. It not only helps assure that ability will be upgraded but also provides opportunity for motivation by serving as a framework for introducing certain kinds of desirable rewards on a strictly performance-contingent basis.

17. Design work so that greater learning and growth will come from higher performance.

This prescription will be discussed in a succeeding chapter but in a different context. It is mentioned here to emphasize that certain motivation techniques can motivate in multiple ways.

Much work can be designed so that with increased performance the worker learns more. Learning and personal growth are two key intrinsic rewards that naturally flow from performance if the work is structured properly. For example, if you design work such that when one project is accomplished successfully a new assignment will be confronted, you provide the worker with a reward for performance—a learning opportunity on a new assignment. The reward is for having performed well on the preceding assignment. Similarly, you can design work that requires considerable search-and-find activity or problem-solving activity. When good performance occurs, the problem gets solved and a considerable amount of learning occurs in the process.

When performance is seen as leading to new experiences, employees will likely perceive a contingent relationship between performance and learning. The greater a salesperson's performance, for example, the more new clients or customers he or she likely encounters. Each new customer means a different experience and learning opportunity. Likewise, the quicker musicians learn one piece, the sooner they can get on to others. When performance leads to such additional learning opportunities—a reward—employees are likely to be motivated. Learning, as a contingent reward for performance, is nearly nonexistent in the highly repetitive, routine job, however. On such jobs, the greater one's performance, the more one repeats the same, rather than the more one confronts the new.

18. Convince employees that their jobs and their organization's survival depend on how well they perform.

Employees should always clearly understand that they live in a competitive world. They have to earn their positions in the organization, and the organization has to earn its place in the community of organizations. Job security really depends on employee performance, not on length of service or length of employment contract, for example. If employees and the organization are not productive, success for the organization will not be realized.

Employees can be sensitized to the contingency relation between performance and organization survival by pointing out the numerous dramatic cases of organizations that have failed to boost worker productivity and performance, in light of growing competition, and have subsequently had to close their doors. Emphasis can be placed on the performance-job security link by granting long-term employment contracts, or such things as guaranteed annual income, only to those whose performance deserves these arrangements. Such rewards must not be assured forever, regardless of future changes in the worker's performance, however. The security must be assured only in return for high performance. An organization might assure security over the period of time, say, between performance reviews.

Job security has been found to be one of the most valued types of rewards employees experience. Tying job security to performance, therefore, has potentially high possibilities for motivating. This is something too few companies regularly do.

19. Instill the notion that a fair day's pay deserves a fair day's work.

Even though the amount of pay one earns may not be directly contingent on one's level of performance—even though the amount of pay may be assured regardless of one's level of performance—that pay can still motivate providing the employee perceives it as a fair day's pay for high performance. Management may have to do some influencing here to convince workers that a given pay amount is an appropriate level for high performance. But fortunately most people are reasonable and rational and have a sense of fair play. Employees do not expect to go through life taking more out than they put in. If they see the organization using them ethically and equitably, they are likely to do the same for the organization.

If employee pay is set at a high level, workers are likely to feel that the organization deserves high performance in return. If pay is perceived as inappropriately low, the organization is likely to get low performance in return. Many organizations have not fully appreciated this phenomenon and have suffered the consequences. In one case, an organization was faced with stiff competition and its profit margin was declining. The firm decided to address the problem by not giving any pay raises to its employees. These employees had already been receiving pay lower than the community average. Their wages and salaries were also significantly below what the competition was paying. The result of no pay raise was a pronounced reduction in worker performance. Workers left their jobs earlier in the day. Absenteeism went up. Workers cut back on internal voluntary assignments. And grievance filing increased. This is exactly what the company did not need in the face of the rising competition. It happened because employees will only give a level of performance that they perceive is deserved—in other words, that matches the level of rewards they receive.

20. Be careful not to reward for nonperformance.

Remember this chapter is about the need to make the experiencing of satisfaction from rewards dependent on the level of one's performance. One must sense greater reward at higher levels of performance. This means we do not want workers to experience high reward for nonperformance. But, in practice, organizations allow this to happen frequently. They guarantee high wages and substantial fringes to workers regardless of performance levels. The annual salary or fixed hourly wage rate is all too common. With such systems workers see that performance really makes little difference in terms of what they are able to earn to sustain a given standard of living. When workers function apart from little valid assessment of performance, coupled with this fixed level of monetary payments and benefits, the problem can be severe. Organizations must generally not provide high rewards regardless of performance because one may well perceive nonperformance more satisfying than high performance. This is due to the costs (discussed in a later chapter) associated with performance. Organizations will end up motivating low performance if they do.

This phenomenon occurs in other ways too. Two examples: First, there is the case of the draftsman who was good at his work and could produce fine work nearly 100 percent of the time without getting help from anybody else. But this draftsman had a habit of frequently bringing partially completed work to the boss for approval. Obviously the draftsman needed recognition. And recognition is what he got. The boss would invariably say it was fine, well-done work.

But the boss was overburdened by these constant interruptions by the draftsman. From the boss's point of view, the draftsman's behavior (regularly bringing work in for approval) was not what was desired. The boss wanted the draftsman to complete the work, then bring it in. The boss did not know how to stop the problem. He had often told the draftsman not to bring in partially completed work, but the practice continued. Why? Because the practice— undesirable performance—was being rewarded with the recognition given the draftsman each time he came to his superior's office.

In a second case, an employee was often called to the supervisor's office and "chewed out" by his supervisor for not following standard operating procedures. But the employee kept violating those procedures. In fact, a high frequency of criticism resulted in an increased frequency of violations. Why? Because after each time the employee was criticized, he would go back to his work group and get applauded for standing up to the supervisor and asserting his independence. The other workers thought he was a hero. So much recognition came from his peers that this reward far overshadowed the penalty (criticism) received from the supervisor. Again, the worker was, in effect, receiving a net increase in satisfaction for inappropriate behavior.

21. Subdivide goals into clear intermediate completion points.

By breaking work down into individual segments to be completed in some sequence, you make vivid to the worker how performance leads to accomplishment. Remember, the sense of satisfaction that comes from accomplishment is a key intrinsic reward. Clear intermediate completion points provide relatively frequent experiences of accomplishment and resultant satisfaction to workers. Intermediate completion points help them avoid losing sight of the fact that performance is paying off. Subdividing goals not only leads to greater aggregate satisfaction, as stated later on, but also helps one see the contingency relationship between performance and the special intrinsic reward, accomplishment.

When just one overall goal is established with no, or ill-defined, intermediate stages for completion, it is often difficult for the worker to sense—during work on the goal—that performance is really yielding achievement. Without intermediate completion points, workers not only sense relatively little reward from accomplishment, but may also get discouraged because of lack of feedback provided on progress. Intermediate goals, or clearly defined stages for completion, help in providing feedback which shows the worker whether or not he or she is on track. Such information helps the worker take corrective action as needed and thus helps convince the worker that total accomplishment will be realized.

In writing this book, I found it highly motivational to subdivide the writing into clear segments—headings, subheadings, and so on. Completion of each segment sent a clear signal of achievement, and the sense of achievement was satisfying. The perception of a strong linkage between performance and the reward of accomplishment was made more acute. Not dividing goals into subgoals reduces the satisfaction which can potentially be derived from performance.

22. Build employee respect for the institution of authority and for those in positions of authority.

An employee who has respect for authority sees performance as a fulfilling, rewarding experience. Performing means meeting the desires and expectations of those in authority. Performing at a high level is seen as the right thing to do (assuming that respected authority has expressed a desire for such high performance). When one respects authority, one tends to sense that responding properly to the directives of those in authority is a means of gaining acceptance into the organization. Such acceptance is often of great value to workers.

When workers do not respect authority, it means they have relatively little need to please the supervisor. One gets relatively little satisfaction from fulfilling prescribed obligations when one lacks respect for the office which made the prescriptions. One may even question the value of what he or she is doing or the legitimacy of what he or she is called on to do. Such attitudes lead to low performance.

Perhaps more serious than lack of respect for the authority of position is lack of respect for the person in the position. If a supervisor commands respect from others, the supervisor's ability to elicit performance is extremely high. Employees who respect a supervisor will perform at request because they believe such is in their best interest and in the best interest of the supervisor and organization. It is satisfying to fulfill the wishes of someone you respect because you feel you are doing the right thing and that you will please the person.

23. Assure certainty in the organization's reward schedules.

A key underlying point in assuring that employees see rewards as strongly contingent on performance is to make sure that reward receipt is seen as a certainty given the desired performance. As mentioned earlier, if reward agents are not trusted, or if the organization is seen as unlikely to have the capacity to reward, or if reward agents do not really have full power to control rewards, it is hard to calculate a high probability that performance will actually lead to reward.

But many other factors can affect one's perception of the probability of reward receipt. For example, one may anticipate not being around at the time rewards are issued or may expect his or her job assignment to change in the near future and that eligibility for rewards earned now will not transfer. Or one may feel that the company's reward schedules are more ideals, guidelines, or maximum amounts rather than contracts for actual rewards. Further, employees may feel that if their organization is changing rapidly, any reward schedules published for the present may be altered in the future, before implementation of the present schedule is complete. Any number of factors can reduce one's sense of the likelihood of planned rewards actually being received. These factors can render otherwise quality contingent reward plans rather ineffective.

As conditions within and outside an organization change, employees are likely to see changes in the probability of reward schedules being fulfilled. Perceived changes in this probability can lead to variability in employee performance. Such variability can lead to further uncertainties about the company's ability or desire to "come through" according to published reward schedules. It can become a disastrous and demotivating cycle unless management builds some stability and permanency into its reward plans—unless these plans are insulated from forces that constantly encourage change.

24. Reward for specific acts.

It is, perhaps, axiomatic that in order for employees to see that rewards are contingent on performance they must know what specific aspects of performance bring the reward—what specific dimensions of performance or what specific acts are responsible for eliciting rewards. It is quite common for employees to receive rewards for good performance as measured by some mechanism but for those same employees to not be sure of what specific actions, behaviors, or results were really responsible for the good assessment of performance. Praising the employee for doing good work does not enlighten the employee on what specifically must be done to assure continued reward (praise) in the future. It is much better to tie the reward to something specific. Praise the employee, for example, for getting fifty crates loaded by 2:00 P.M. Such rewards make clear for just what performance one is being rewarded. A clear contingency relation between a specific act and a specific reward intensifies employee awareness of how performance leads to reward.

Without rewards for specific acts, employees are not sure what kind or level of performance generates rewards. This results in employees' allocating efforts to inappropriate behaviors. Whatever the reward—end-of-year bonuses, promotions, or new work assignments, for example—be sure you clarify for what or why the reward is given. Without this, employees may exert effort in the wrong direction.

25. Broadcast or post high-performance results.

Employees soon get the message that performance is recognized if management makes high performance public. Posting high performance scores on bulletin boards, publishing high performance scores in company newsletters, and broadcasting high performance scores at employee assemblies and depart-ment meetings is a good way to help satisfy employee ego needs, and it clearly shows that recognition is contingent on performance.

Of course, poor scores can be published too. Doing this can enhance one's perception of the contingency relationship between reward and performance. The key here is to make sure those reading the scores recognize that the low scores do reflect significant differences in performance from the high scores.

Many companies shy away from broadcasting and posting performance results because they feel that doing so creates excessively fierce interpersonal competi-tion and can actually result in some good performance being covered up. As stated in an earlier chapter, employee performance should not be measured against the performance of others. Rather, objective standards tailored to each job should be established and performance measured against those standards. It should be possible for all employees to succeed! If not done properly, broadcasting and posting can put emphasis on comparison and ranking of employees. Those on top are the winners. And those on the bottom are the losers even though they may have done well in relation to standards. This may be a good argument for not posting all scores. Posting only the high scores may be best in many situations. Doing this should not generate too strong a sense of win-lose but at the same time should create a sense of the performance-reward contingency. You have to be careful here.

26. Clearly delegate tasks and follow up.

For employees to see a strong performance-reward contingency, they must be aware that performance is being assessed and assessed validly. This was mentioned earlier. Clearly delegating tasks, specifying just when those tasks should be accomplished, and regularly following up to check on progress quickly convinces employees that performance is being carefully monitored. If performance is, in fact, monitored, then employees see it as very possible for the company to grant rewards contingent on performance. Without monitoring, rewards would necessarily have to be granted independent of performance, or arbitrarily.

Managers often fail to do a good job at delegating. Assignments are frequently not clear and complete. Managers tell what to do without too much trouble but neglect to inform about how, with what resources, where, why, and, most important, when. If they do happen to spell these things out, they frequently neglect to follow up on assignments. This neglect often occurs because they fail to record what assignments they have given out, to whom, when and when completion is desired. Without recording, they forget. A typical manager may dish out thirty or forty major nonroutine tasks per week. Without follow-up the manager not only loses control of progress on the assignment, but also diminishes employee motivation by weakening the perceived performance-reward linkage.

27. Let employees participate in formulating performance-reward plans.

One of the best ways to assure that employees understand and accept plans is to have them participate in the formulation of those plans. When employees participate in the formulation of performance-reward plans, the result is likely to be a highly relevant plan that is adapted to employee needs as well as a plan which is fully understood and appreciated. You can publish performance-reward schedules and talk about them forever, but for really sensing the nature of the performance-reward contingencies there is no substitute for being involved in their design.

Numerous organizations encourage employee participation in designing their own jobs or the task demands made on the employee. But less attention has been given to encouraging employees to provide significant input in the design of the reward systems they work under.

Employees have been given choices on rewards. For example, cafeteria-style reward packages allow employees to choose those rewards that best fit their needs. But these option packages are typically not formulated by the employees themselves or even with input from the employees. Perhaps organizations could make substantial advances in sensitizing workers to the rewards available to them and to how those rewards work. Companies could involve them in the design of the reward system—particularly in contingent reward design because it is the exact nature of the dependency of rewards on performance that employees most frequently fail to understand and appreciate. Also, in designing the contingent reward system they work under, employees can develop clearer understanding of just what constitutes performance and of how performance is best measured. All this helps strengthen the perceived performance-reward linkage.

28. Respond to performance increases quickly.

Letting time pass between when performance occurs and when the reward for that performance is bestowed not only tends to result in devaluation of the reward, as mentioned in the next chapter, but also blurs the dependency relationship between performance and rewards. With an application of rewards immediately following the performance, one vividly senses that the rewards are experienced because of the performance. Not rewarding for an extended period of time—particularly for an uncertain or arbitrarily extended period—makes it difficult for employees to see the nature of the contingency relation and that the reward even depends on the performance at all.

If rewards are given prior to accomplishment, the same phenomenon occurs. You make it difficult for the employee to see a strong performance-reward contingency because the reward is given without the performance being confirmed. It is given in anticipation of the performance, but if the actual performance does not coincide with the anticipated, the reward will be either too large or too small thus interfering with the development of a clear, consistent performance-reward contingency.

If rewards cannot be timed to immediately follow performance, it is a good idea to keep the interval between performance and reward at least as short as possible and to fix that interval. If repeated over time, a fixed interval can be internalized by workers, and the rewards will then be readily interpreted as being received as a result of performance.

29. Parade your role models.

If you really want workers to see that rewards are contingent on performance, find some people who have performed and received rewards for it, and show them off. Show other employees the successes and satisfying experiences these top performers have enjoyed. Let these success stories talk to workers about how their performance has led to rewards. Let the workers see what performance actually has given to others.

Role models can be powerful influences on behavior. They serve as a visual standard for patenting the behavior of others, and they motivate emulations because role models are people generally admired. "Parading" those who have performed and who have enjoyed the rewards of such performance provides living proof of the performance-reward contingency relation. These people are real-life examples of what performance can do for an employee. Actual examples can be far more convincing than the best of plans and promises.

Giving attention to selection of the proper people to serve as role models is critical. Usually employees who have pleasant, dynamic personalities, a record of consistent high performance, a history of ethical behavior, and an ability to articulate how rewards they have received have been related to performance are what you look for. Picking employees who have few personal assets or credentials besides high performance probably will not work. Employees most readily identify with others who are total human beings—complete "specimens" who have a wealth of skills and desirable traits beyond those that lead to good on-the-job performance.

30. Make extrinsic rewards for performance automatic or allow rewards to be self-drawn.

If an organization can arrange for rewards to automatically and directly flow to the employee after a measurement of performance is made, the uncertainty about reward receipt for performance is practically eliminated. For example, it is possible in some companies to simply have the computer process daily employee evaluation forms, derive aggregate performance scores, and print out contingent paychecks for employees to pick up at the end of the day. About the only possible motivation flaw in such a system is the possibility the evaluation was done improperly. But in many cases, evaluations themselves are objective and rather automatic as it is strictly a matter of counting units of output, number of rejects, or similar items. And often evaluations can be rigorously mechanized, thus reducing the error factor present with a human being doing the counting. For example, an employee may be loading materials on trucks. Computerized scales can be set up to record the amount loaded in a given time period and to send a message to a print device which converts that recording to a paycheck.

On occasion it may make sense to have employees draw their own rewards. If the competency, honesty, and trust levels are high in an organization, certain workers may be allowed to self-draw monies and other benefits, proportional to their performance levels, from the organization's asset storage areas once they have officially filed evidence of their performance levels. Such systems convince the employee there is a high likelihood of performance yielding reward.

PROPOSITION 2.2: EMPLOYEES MUST VALUE REWARDS.

To sense a strong performance–real reward correlation, one must place a high value on (strongly desire) the rewards one receives. Unvalued rewards, no matter how large they are or how many there are, do nothing for motivation. Even if rewards are received on a highly performance contingent basis, they fail to motivate when they are deemed worthless. The less valued a reward, the less the positive impact on motivation additional units of that reward will have.

Complicating the issue here is the fact that the value one attaches to one reward is frequently affected by the perceived value of other rewards. The values one places on different rewards received are inter-dependent. When planning and applying multiple rewards, management must not neglect this point in estimating the overall valuation the employee is likely to place on the aggregate reward package. Though it is not discussed later, this phenomenon also applies to the interaction of various perceived costs and to the interaction of rewards with costs. Costs are discussed in the next chapter.

The following are ways management can get employees to place high value (or to avoid placing low value) on the rewards they receive from the organization.

1. Tie rewards to individual needs.

Human beings have needs which can be classified as physiological, safety and security, social, esteem and status, and self-actualization. If any of these needs is unmet, or unsatisfied in a person, the individual can be motivated if provided with an opportunity to satisfy the unmet need or needs. The most motivating opportunities are the most valued. The most valued opportunities are those designed to provide satisfaction of the most intense unmet needs.

What needs are most intense varies from individual to individual. One person's most dominant need may be the safety and security need. If this is the case, such rewards as insurance plans and retirement plans will be the most highly valued. Another person's most dominant need may be esteem and status. This person will value such rewards as praise, promotion and write-ups in the company newsletter. The key is to investigate each employee's individual need profile in order to spot the strongest needs, then to design rewards tailored to those needs.

Some organizations have adopted cafeteria-style reward packages that meet the objective of matching rewards to individual needs by allowing the employees themselves to choose the kinds of rewards they value most. These plans tend to work well as long as employees are permitted to adjust their reward packages. Over time people's needs change, and to assure that the rewards one receives are the most valued, one must have a chance to periodically alter them.

You cannot motivate employees with promotions if their most intense needs are social or if they do not want promotions. It does no good to promise employees end-of-year monetary bonuses if they happen to already be very well-to-do financially (perhaps from an inheritance or the like). Rewards not matched to wants and needs are not valued. Rewards must be matched to one's most dominant needs to be highly valued and thus to highly motivate.

2. Assure that rewards are of the proper magnitude.

For a reward to be valued it must be of the appropriate kind—in other words, be related to one's needs. Appropriateness of kind is what was just discussed. But simple matching of the kind of reward to the type of need is not enough to stimulate a sense of high reward value. The absolute magnitude, or size, of the reward is a critical determinant of the perceived value of the reward too.

All other factors equal, the larger the reward, the greater its perceived value— at least up to a point. It is possible, with many types of rewards, to provide an overabundance of those rewards to a person. An employee may experience such an excess of rewards that disutility is actually attached to a portion of the rewards. For example, employees who receive an excessive amount of space in the company newsletter, devoted to discussion of their excellent performance, may actually feel embarrassed by such attention. Or employees who get too many plaques, for quality service to the company, at an annual banquet may see many of those plaques as just a nuisance.

But excess magnitude is usually not the problem. Insufficient magnitude is by far the most common problem. And the problem posed by insufficient reward magnitude is often compounded by a ripple effect. Not only can a reward be too small to be significantly valued in its own right, but it can be so small that it serves as a "slap in the face." When this effect is sufficiently pronounced, employees often feel they would be better off getting no reward at all. The reward can actually cause a net dissatisfaction if it is too small.

The true perceived magnitude of a reward can only be appreciated by knowing all the different needs that reward may serve to fulfill in a human being. Any given reward may satisfy multiple needs simultaneously. For example, employees may be promised two silver dollars for increasing production by 10 percent in a given month. At first glance, one may say that such a reward would not motivate because it is not large enough to be highly valued. However, this reward may be seen as a large reward in terms of its impact on satisfying ego (esteem and status) needs. Two *silver* dollars may be perceived as a fine form of recognition, though its value in terms of purchasing power is minuscule.

3. Make sure rewards are seen as fair.

Rewards can be large and well matched to needs and still not be perceived as possessing high value. Such a phenomenon occurs when people compare what they receive with what others receive for rewards and conclude that they are not being rewarded appropriately in comparison with others. Even though one receives a reward that is large in absolute terms, if it is not of proper size relative to rewards received by others, the value attached to the reward is diminished.

Executives who make $200,000 a year make plenty to fulfill all their economic requirements, but are often not highly satisfied with their pay when they discover their peers are making more—say $300,000. Such revelation has caused many an executive to become angry, to become dissatisfied with employment, and to resign. Others have turned to drugs or overindulgence in alcohol. Still others have internalized such perceived inequity causing ulcers and heart attacks.

We do not value what we do not perceive as fair. To assure a perception of fairness in rewards, rewards must properly reflect the kind of work one does, the quality of one's performance, one's length of service to the organization, the general reward level in the community, and other dimensions. All other factors being equal, someone doing more difficult work than another person should make more. Someone doing work requiring the same level of difficulty as the work done by another should be paid the same. All other factors being equal, two people having worked for an organization for the same length of time should receive the same pay. All other factors being equal, two people who perform at the same level should be recognized equally with pay, promotion, prizes, and so forth. When rewards are not adapted to the kind of work, length of service, or performance level, they are likely to be seen as unfair. When rewards are not adjusted to a magnitude which is comparable to what others, in the same or very similar situation receive, those rewards are likely to be valued suboptimally.

4. Properly schedule rewards.

For rewards to be valued, they must be properly scheduled. Generally rewards received by an individual soon after accomplishment of a goal, or soon after attainment of a given targeted performance level, are the most valued rewards and the rewards that serve best to instill a desire for further achievement or continued good performance. When the reward is tied to performance in time, that reward is closely associated with the performance. It becomes an extension of the performance. It has real meaning because one can vividly see that it was received for performance.

Rewards received by the employee long after the behavioral act, or acts, for which they are received are devalued. For example, a real estate salesperson will value a $4,000 commission promised and actually received immediately following a sale. When, however, he or she must look forward to a $4,000 commission paid at the end of the year for a sale next week, the perceived value of the reward is relatively low.

Similarly, a reward received too far before the act may not be highly valued because the employee cannot judge if its kind and size are fully appropriate for the behavior that is expected. Rewards that are too little for the effort required and rewards that are too great for the effort required may, as indicated previously, be valued less than optimally. The only way to assure the reward is just right is to measure accomplishment, or performance, and then establish the level of the reward.

Not knowing when a reward will be received also diminishes its perceived value because the employee often translates this uncertainty into an assumption it will be received late or perhaps not at all. Such an assumption causes one to attach less value to the reward.

Generally, for rewards to be perceived as having high value, they should not be scheduled at fixed or arbitrary time intervals. Instead they should be scheduled to coincide with performance. Good practice calls for granting employees different pieces of the total reward at different stages of accomplishment to maximize the aggregate perceived value and to properly reinforce desired behavior.

5. Recognize the impact of group recognition.

Providing a group with recognition for its accomplishments can generate high group cohesion, or a team spirit. When such a spirit develops, group members tend to value membership on the team more highly. When this happens, they tend to develop closer ties with other members which can lead to heightened satisfaction with work and heightened on-the-job social satisfaction. One of the major contributions of group rewards is this indirect effect. The spirit of sharing and camaraderie that develops means the recognition generates higher satisfaction than would exist if the recognition provided only for the direct satisfaction of ego (esteem and status) needs.

The usefulness of group rewards for satisfying esteem and status needs is very limited. Group recognition does not do much for the individual member. Recognition given to a group does not give attention to the unique contributions of each person. One's ego needs—self-esteem, personal identity, self-image, and stature, for example—are not well satisfied with awards, verbal praise, or written recognition given to the group as a whole. The impact of group recognition is diluted or diffused among all group members. Each individual's share of the reward is not perceived as very significant. The recognition-type group reward, therefore, lacks value for satisfying the ego-type need.

Also, group recognition does little to entice interpersonal competition, some of which is extremely healthy for the organization and for the individual. Many employees enjoy a certain level of competition at work. They like the stimulation. They like the thrill of winning. And they learn from their losses. Excessive reliance on group recognition denies many of the elements of a competitive environment because individual effort is not distinguished. The intrinsic rewards and satisfactions that come from competition are not substantially realized because the group reward discourages competition.

6. Adapt rewards to the situation.

For rewards to be highly valued, they must fit the situation. What is a good reward under one set of circumstances may be a poor reward under a different set of circumstances. A given need can usually be addressed by a number of different types of rewards. The selection of a specific reward should depend on various factors such as the time of year, the kind of performance for which it is given, the values placed on rewards by one's peers, the supervisor's preference for rewards, the mood of the employee, demands on the employee's time, and the objectives of the employee, among others. If an employee is striving for a promotion, he or she would likely place much higher value on a written letter of commendation as a form of recognition for good work than upon, say, words of praise or a plaque received at the annual company banquet. The letter has greater utility for persuading others as to one's suitability for promotion.

Snow skis given as a prize would obviously be more highly valued if given in December than if given in July. Water skis would have greater value in July.

Time off at a later date is an appropriate reward for a worker who works overtime. Flowers or a thank-you card would be more appropriate for a worker who does something nice, above and beyond the call of duty.

A worker might highly value oral words of praise more than written praise if that oral praise is given when the worker is physically surrounded by peers. Similarly, management should not give wall plaques for recognition if recipients have no walls to hang them on. Neither should social and recreational activities be arranged as rewards for employees if these activities conflict, time-wise, with other obligations the employees may have.

Give a turkey for performance in November, but in February perhaps roses would be better. Do not post red stars on the performance chart if the worker hates red.

Basic needs can stay fairly constant, but specific wants can vary from situation to situation. The nature of any rewards received by individuals should be adapted to their wants at the time of receipt. This helps assure rewards have high perceived value.

7. Engage employees in value training.

On many an occasion it may make sense to avoid adjusting rewards to meet given needs or wants and instead change the wants to meet given rewards. Instead of designing rewards to fit needs, it may be more practical, through value training, to alter wants (if not needs) to fit available or obtainable rewards. By increasing one's desire for a reward, the reward becomes more valuable and thus a more powerful motivator. A variety of different approaches may have utility here.

Helping employees develop pride in their work helps them place greater value on the results they achieve. They experience greater intrinsic satisfaction. There are various ways to stimulate worker pride in work. One way is to sell them on the value or worth of the work they do. Another way is to give them singular responsibility for the work they do. Whatever the approach, once pride is developed, the intrinsic satisfaction from work accomplishment is enhanced.

Similarly, an organization may have slack times of the year and because of this can easily give employees extended vacations. To make such a reward valued, management can spend time "talking up" the value of vacations, helping employees better use vacation time, and helping assure that employee work loads do not pile up during vacations. The vacation becomes more valued, the greater the employee's desire for it.

A manager may have an old oil painting which he could use as an incentive to get an employee to do a special weekend project. But if the employee has no taste for such art, the painting will not be valued and will not be an effective incentive. Instead of finding some other reward, the manager may attempt to cultivate the employee's desire for the painting. Usually such things cannot be accomplished overnight, but given sufficient lead time, value change of this kind can be accomplished. The manager may use persuasive techniques that show the employee how he or she will experience long-term enjoyment from this type of painting, how valuable the painting will become in time, how well the painting will fit in the employee's living room, or how well others will like it.

8. Use a mix of rewards.

Though employees have certain needs that dominate their need profiles, they usually have many needs and wants that are not fully satisfied. No one reward, no matter how well matched to the employee's most dominant need, and no matter how large, can possibly provide as much satisfaction as a mix of rewards designed to address a variety of unsatisfied needs. People have multiple unfulfilled needs at any given time, therefore, multiple types of rewards are required to provide a perception of maximum reward package value.

Money is a rather unique type of reward that can satisfy a variety of needs—physiological, security, ego, and even social needs. But no company can rely solely on monetary payment and expect to satisfy its workers. Workers need a sense of job security that wages or salaries cannot buy. Also they need recognition and opportunities for self-actualization that money cannot buy.

The employee will require benefits, and noncompensation rewards, as well as compensation-type rewards. Every worker will need to experience intrinsic as well as extrinsic rewards. To maximize the value of the aggregate reward package, a variety of needs must be addressed with a variety of rewards. Distributing the company's investment in rewards across an appropriate reward mix will yield a higher return in terms of total perceived reward value than pumping the same investment into one or two rewards. It is investment in the proper *set* of rewards that counts. This point is often forgotten as companies frequently focus investments in reward upgrading exclusively in the monetary payment area.

9. Switch rewards when utility begins declining.

Earlier it was mentioned that a given reward can be so large that it is valued less than a lesser amount of the reward. The same phenomenon exists as one kind of reward is repeatedly provided the employee over time. As additional units are accumulated, the accumulated value increases, but at some point so much of the reward has accumulated that additional units only provide negative utility. This is the old concept of declining marginal utility from the field of economics. Each additional unit is valued less than the preceding unit because it satisfies a smaller portion of the unmet need. For example, when you perform well, you might highly appreciate a television for an end-of-month prize. If you perform well the following month, another television might be appreciated too (but a little less than the first). When a television is given for good performance in the third month, you value that television somewhat less than the second one and substantially less than the first one. This is your third television! You still value it, but less. If you keep getting televisions, a point will be reached (assuming some restriction on your opportunity to sell them or give them away) at which receipt of additional televisions will be a real problem for you. Where do you put them?

When the utility of additional units of a reward becomes sufficiently low, it is time to switch the type of reward to something else. One can receive too much of a good thing. When the employee has had enough of a given reward, the reward must be changed. It is up to management to monitor the history of reward bestowance and to switch to other rewards when the marginal utility of those other rewards just begins to exceed (cost factors assumed equal here) the marginal utility of the first reward. Ideally, the marginal utilities (utilities of the last units received) of all rewards in the reward mix should be equal if aggregate reward package value for a given investment in rewards is to be maximized.

10. Assure rewards come from proper sources.

The value one attaches to a reward is highly affected by the source of the reward. People value rewards more highly when they come from admired sources, legitimate sources, trusted sources, highly visible sources, high stature sources, respected sources, liked sources, and knowledgeable sources, among others.

Nothing is valued any less than words of praise from someone who knows nothing about your actual performance. He or she has not monitored your performance in any way. The praise is based on a simple assumption of good performance.

What is valued more, a monetary payment from one who has the authority to reward you or a monetary payment (same size payment, now) from a person in the organization who does not have the proper authority to make such a payment? You value the latter so little, you are likely to turn it back. You want nothing to do with embezzled funds!

What do you value most, a job assignment given you by the president of the company or the same assignment given by the assistant to the president?

Often the best sources of recognition—the most valued kind of recognition— for professional employees is recognition from their peers because such recognition is judged to be validly bestowed. You value most those rewards given you by others who know you really deserve it.

Rewards from friends have high value, comparatively. A friend can give you a trinket which you will always cherish. If a person you dislike gives you the same trinket, you will throw it away. The source, thus, has high impact on the value we attach to a reward. Management must assure, therefore, that rewards flow to employees from the proper sources.

11. Do not camouflage rewards.

The impact or full value of a reward can be lost when that reward must compete with a plethora of other demands for the worker's attention. To appreciate rewards—to be sensitized to their full value—one needs time to savor them. Timing in bestowance is critical. Those controlling the release of rewards to employees must choose the right moment to convey rewards to assure the worker will have an opportunity to fully receive and contemplate the significance of the rewards. Releasing rewards when workers are too busy or when other issues occupy their minds will reduce the positive impact of the rewards.

A reward should never be conveyed to an employee along with a deluge of other information. The reward can literally go unnoticed. Such camouflaging renders rewards impotent. The receipt of a reward should be an outstanding event. When conveyed it should take priority as an information "bit" over other types of information. The event should not be covered up.

Sometimes rewards are camouflaged by penalties which are conveyed at the same time. Penalties must be conveyed, but do not allow them to detract from the satisfaction provided by positive outcomes. Sometimes when managers convey criticism early in the conversation, the criticism makes such an impact that any rewards communicated later are not fully appreciated.

Never disguise a reward. If it is a reward, make that fact clear. Let it be known to the recipient. I am aware of a case where an employee's office was moved to a better location as a reward for years of good service. But, astonishingly, the employee was not informed as to the real reason for the move. In fact, the employee thought the move was actually a penalty for some criticism of management that he had recently made.

12. Make rewards public.

No matter what kind of reward one receives, its value is generally heightened when others know about it. We all have ego needs. We all want others to know who we are and to appreciate us. We need others to think well of us. Making rewards public—telling others about the rewards one receives—helps satisfy one's ego needs. The public pronouncement is an extension of the reward itself, which directly satisfies esteem and status needs whether the particular reward offered does or not. For example, a new job assignment may be given as a reward to satisfy one's needs for personal growth. The public announcement of this enhances the value of the new assignment by adding a dimension which satisfies the ego needs.

Announcing rewards in meetings or other employee gatherings is often a good way to publicly acknowledge rewards going to individuals. Posting notices of rewards on bulletin boards can help. Write-ups in newsletters and company newspapers can be particularly effective.

Nine times out of ten, simple words of praise take on greater value if given to a person when others can hear or see. If you come upon an employee in a gathering of his or her peers, this may be a good time to release the praise. Or if you are giving out an award at a banquet, it may be a good idea to assure the employee's spouse is present. Employees like their families to appreciate what they do away from home.

Management should keep in mind that satisfying one's ego needs is essentially a process of letting the person know that others know how well he or she is doing. True recognition is by definition something that is public. When you are recognized, others must know what it is all about. By taking action to assure the word is spread, you broaden the base of the reward and thereby increase its perceived value. Further, public pronouncement leads to others providing additional recognition to the individual.

13. Properly package rewards.

When we talk about packaging a reward, we are talking about the whole reward—the sum total of all that is experienced upon receipt. Critical in the packaging of a reward is not only the reward itself but also how the reward is conveyed or presented. The pleasantness of the environment in which a reward is received is part of this.

If a promotion to a high-level management job is granted in an environment of organizational upheaval and interpersonal hostility, its value is not likely to be perceived as high. One would like to think that he or she enjoys full support and will have a cooperative and stable human resource base to facilitate decision processes.

The value of a prize given out at an awards dinner can be greatly enhanced by packaging the bestowance with friendly words or good humor. Praise is always valued more highly when given with a smile. A letter of appreciation works best if prepared professionally on high-quality paper. An invitation to a golf match is judged more valuable if friends instead of enemies are invited to play with you.

The mode of delivery of the reward is so essential that, if done wrong, it can totally negate the positive value of the core reward. A good example is the case of a prize for good performance being given to an employee in a box that is dirty and torn and has obviously been crushed. Such an experience is enough to make the recipient decide, on the spot, that the item inside is probably used, broken, worn out, or the like. The recipient may well desire that the giver take the item back! The packaging destroys the image or perception of the value of what's inside and can cause a net negative evaluation of the reward.

Another key point here is the powerful effect that excitement can have on one's judgment of the value of a reward. Awards given with an enthusiastic verbal accompaniment can be highly valued. The same rewards accompanied by a dull presentation will likely be less valued.

14. Be sure employees know rewards exist and know what they are.

Employees cannot value rewards they do not know about. Many an organization has had an excellent reward packge for its employees but has failed to communicate it. Motivation comes from rewards only when the employee has clear and full knowledge of what they are. This applies to intrinsic as well as extrinsic rewards.

Managers should "talk up" rewards—point out fairly frequently what they are and how valuable they are. Organizations should develop and distribute in-house publications that spell out the nature of all rewards offered to its employees including the formal rewards (those planned by the company) as well as the informal rewards that the employee is likely to experience. These publications can serve as ready reference for employees unsure about what the company gives them for their efforts. If the descriptions of rewards are written properly, the descriptions themselves can help sell the rewards or persuade employees of the value of the rewards.

Every time new employees are brought into the organization, they should be channeled through a formal employee orientation program. One of the key informational components of such a program should be a full disclosure of the kinds and amounts of rewards available to the employee from the organization. Doing this helps build job satisfaction early in the work life of the new person.

Another time to assure that workers understand their rewards is during the annual performance review. Periodic reiteration does not hurt. The supervisor would do well to reemphasize the great rewards available to employees in the organization and to provide employees with an opportunity to ask questions (and get answers) about their reward packages. It is amazing how frequently, in practice, employees are not aware of key types of rewards such as certain benefits, or learning and growth opportunities available through special project assignments. When organizations take a little time to list on paper all the rewards they offer and distribute this to the employees, it often impresses and helps increase the total value employees attach to their reward packages.

15. Set work goals that are challenging or allow for creative expression.

I have alluded in previous pages to intrinsic rewards, or rewards experienced as a natural outcome of doing the work itself. These types of rewards can be powerful and are a necessary supplement to extrinsic rewards such as prizes, pay, promotion, or recognition.

To assure that employees value their work experiences, goals should be set for the worker to pursue. Achieving a goal is satisfying. It is an indicator of success. The experience of achievement is an intrinsic reward. Setting goals has many benefits, but here it is important to emphasize how to maximize the perceived value of the goal.

The more challenging the goal, the more highly valued is its accomplishment. A challenging goal forces one's energies and talents to be stretched—to be taxed. The individual puts a considerable investment into its realization. Once achievement is in hand, the worker knows his or her investment has paid off. You tend to value more what you have to work hard to get.

Goals that allow for one's creative potential to blossom are also more highly valued than mundane, routine goals. If employees can be creative at work, this means they can express their unique talents and insights. When you have an opportunity to contribute in a way that is a product of you—of your personality—you tend to value the experience more highly. The work is a product of self. One's perception of self-worth is, therefore, enhanced.

Employees have needs to express themselves through work. They desire to realize their personal potential. Opportunities at work that encourage this are perceived as valuable. Allowing employees to participate in choosing their own goals, in devising their own work methods, or in solving problems themselves helps assure that work does permit creative expression and that it does afford challenge.

16. Set goals that are meaningful.

Setting goals that are challenging and that permit creative expression is not all that can be done to make work intrinsically valuable. Meaningful goals should also be set. A goal is meaningful when the accomplishment of it is worthy (as discussed here) primarily from the point of view of others. If a highly valuable output, or a valued result, is generated by the worker, then a meaningful accomplishment has taken place. Of course the worker must know that what he or she accomplishes is highly worthwhile or significant.

A goal can be challenging by requiring a substantial exercise of effort and talent but not particularly meaningful. Such a situation often exists in the field of basic research in the natural sciences. Frequently scientists work for years on projects that have no perceptible short- or long-term value. Likewise, goals can be meaningful but not challenging. An example here is the case of delivering meals to needy folks in your local community. Similarly, goals can require a great exercise of creative talent but not be too meaningful. A good example is solving the typical mechanical puzzle kids get for Christmas.

Workers can be sensitized to the meaningfulness of their work goals by showing them how critical their output is to the success of other workers in the system or to the satisfaction levels of consumers of their products outside the organization. Also, making vivid to them how costly one small mistake can be helps heighten the value they attach to the work goals for which they are responsible. Further, how much workers are paid has a lot to do with determining how meaningful workers see their work.

17. Sensitize employees to the value of performance itself.

Sometimes goals just cannot be made challenging or particularly meaningful. Neither can they be formulated to stimulate creativity. When this situation exists, it is important for employees to see the value of performance in and of itself—the value of doing well regardless of the nature of the job.

There are numerous ways to sensitize employees to the value of performance. First, you must make sure you hold people accountable for delegated assignments. This shows them you are not taking performance lightly. It's too important to go unattended. Second, you can "talk up" performance pointing out why it is important, how it affects company profits and long-run stability, and how these things are good for the employee. Third, you can hold meetings that address the performance issue head on. In these meetings the focus of discussion should be on specific ways to improve performance. Fourth, you can offer rewards for suggestions on ways to improve performance. Perhaps a suggestion box with monthly cash awards for the best suggestion will work. Fifth, you can let workers formally report periodically on how well they are doing and on problems they are encountering. All these courses of action sensitize workers to the fact that performance itself is valuable. A sense of doing well can be a key intrinsic reward.

Perhaps the best long-term strategy is for an organization to develop an internal performance-based culture. From day one, employees should be indoctrinated with the performance focus of the company. They should understand that all company activity is directed toward one thing—performance. During every performance review (and these should be relatively frequent) attention must not stray from the performance emphasis. Performance is what it is all about. Workers can reap great intrinsic satisfaction from doing well at their jobs if they see doing well as important.

18. Break goals into subgoals.

As mentioned earlier employees will value more highly and receive more satisfaction from work goals that are challenging and meaningful. But even greater aggregate satisfaction can be intrinsically experienced when goals are subdivided into intermediate stages for accomplishment. Subdividing, in effect, distributes the goal over time. It provides multiple points in time at which accomplishment can be experienced. As each subgoal is realized, the employee experiences satisfaction. Indeed, realization of one subgoal can be nearly as rewarding as achievement of a single, larger overall goal. Dividing goals into subgoals spreads out the experiencing of rewards over time preventing the intrinsic reward overload which frequently occurs after accomplishment of one large goal. An intrinsic reward overload is a phenomenon similar to the excessive reward magnitude discussed earlier. If a reward gets too large, much of its value gets lost. The value one attaches to a reward is not a linear function of the size of the reward; rather it is a function with a slope that continually declines as the reward gets larger.

Distributing the sense of accomplishment, through subgoal construction, permits longer-term elation and greater opportunity to savor accomplishment. In effect you get more satisfaction out of the same amount of work. It is like spreading the consumption of twelve gallons of ice cream over the period of a year. You could eat all twelve gallons in one or two sittings, but the aggregate value experienced would be less than when eating one gallon each month.

Another phenomenon operates here too. By realizing subgoals in a systematic process, one senses that progress toward overall goals is being made. Progress and quality are being periodically checked. Because a sense of control comes with setting and systematically realizing subgoals, a greater value may well be attached to accomplishment of the final outcome. There is greater confidence that the final outcome is a worthy one.

19. Segment work into whole units.

Excessive specialization has long been a problem in industrialized society. With specialization, each employee produces a small portion of the total or final product. The worker sees his or her contribution as trivial. What's more, specialization usually means the work has been simplified into simple and highly routine tasks. Completion of such tasks leaves one with little to "crow" about. Anyone else could do the same job fully as well.

By expanding the variety of employee tasks and redesigning the work to allow employees to produce a larger segment of the final product, if not the entire product, you give the workers a real feeling of achievement. They see they have produced something worthwhile. They can take pride in their accomplishments. They experience a positive feeling of self-competence. They may even feel more responsible for their work. This contributes to a greater sense of self-worth. If workers know they are responsible for an entire unit of a product, they see the performance which generated that product as worth more.

Just seeing the whole finished unit of a product after having produced it can create a sense of joy for any worker. Craftsmen such as cabinet makers, home builders, and picture painters experience satisfaction after each of their works is completed. When producing a whole product, you feel more a part of that product, and you see the results of your efforts as more profound.

20. Design work goals, the acccomplishment of which will yield high employee growth and development.

A basic human need is to learn and grow, to advance one's competencies, to realize one's potentials, and to become all that one is capable of becoming.

People feel that they are personally progressing, or advancing, as long as they are continuing to learn. When work is designed to provide the intrinsic reward of high personal growth, that work is seen as more valuable to the person and potentially more satisfying.

To continually provide workers with learning opportunities, work goals have to be changed and upgraded from time to time to a higher level demanding higher skill and knowledge. Whenever you can design work to encourage search and discovery behavior, you are facilitating learning. The routine, the programmed, the simplistic, the job with nothing but predictable and certain components tends to thwart growth. As workers grow, so must their jobs, if this type of reward is to have maximal value.

Many times organizations make a mistake by attempting to fit the worker to the job. Often, to more fully utilize the capacities of the human resource, it makes sense to, at least in part, adapt job responsibilities to the workers and their growth trend. Fitting the job to the person may mean some sacrifice, on occasion, of short-term organizational objectives, but this sacrifice can more than be made up for by the increased worker satisfaction and motivation derived.

By designing work that allows for worker learning and growth, the organization will increase the value of its investment in the human resource. Not only is the worker experiencing greater intrinsic reward value by achieving goals which stimulate learning, but the organization is experiencing a resource growing in value to the company.

21. Build friendship between boss and subordinate.

Many an industrious salesperson has learned how easy it is to sell products routinely to clients who are friends. The same phenomenon applies when bosses become friends with their subordinates. The employee is much more likely to listen to a boss who is a friend, to accept directions from such a boss, and to be motivated because of the friendship.

A friendship relationship usually means that whatever rewards are issued by the boss will be more highly valued than would be the case in the absence of friendship. Words of praise generally mean more coming from a friend. Promotion, wage increases, better work assignments, and the like, all carry extra meaning when awarded by someone who is a friend. Further, when employees do good work for the boss, they may well take more pride in it and value the effort more if the boss is a friend. Even when the task is a simple routine task, if you know its successful accomplishment is important to your boss, who is a friend, you value what you achieve more highly.

We do not like to let our friends down. We like to please them. Doing work for friends and performing well tends to please them. Pleasing them means pleasing ourselves. All work outcomes—intrinsic and extrinsic—carry more value if the work is done for an individual who is a true friend.

Sometimes the argument is made that bosses should not become close to their subordinates because it interferes with rational decision making with respect to the subordinates' performance. This may be true for weaker managers. But strong, knowledgeable, and capable managers will be able to build friendships with their subordinates which have a net positive effect on performance.

22. Do not oversell or overplay rewards.

We mentioned earlier the importance of communicating rewards and of "talking up" their usefulness and value to enhance subordinate perception of their value. But this can be done to excess. Just as a reward can be too large or a given type of reward can be issued (and experienced) too many times, so also can the communications preceding, accompanying, or following a reward. Managers can say so much about certain rewards the organization offers that employees get tired of hearing it. They can hear so often about a reward that, when it is finally received, the experience is anticlimatic. Indeed, the value of rewards can be so oversold that actual receipt becomes an embarrassment—a negative outcome.

Too much talk about the annual awards banquet and who will get awards can cheapen the affair just as praise given out excessively by the boss sounds ridiculous and becomes meaningless after a while. Admittedly, excessive recognition and excessive communication about rewards are not the usual problem. Insufficient recognition and communication are far more common. But the reader must be aware that there is an optimum amount. What is more, and unfortunately complicating, is the fact that the optimum amount varies greatly from individual to individual. One person may like to be reminded of the great rewards he or she gets for performance 100 times a month. Another person has heard enough after two reminders.

I am aware of one company that spends a great deal of time selling its employees on the organization's wonderful annual outing for top performers and their families. Every year the outing seems to flop for one reason or another. The actual reward does not come close to matching the flowery build-up managment gives it. Because of this, the reward is valued less than it probably would be if the company just let it happen. The point is, what we say about a reward must match the actual nature of the reward. If communications are under- or overplayed, maximal net value can be missed.

23. Make rewards exclusive.

Why is one little boy in your neighborhood so powerful? How come he can get all the other boys in the neighborhood to do anything he wishes them to do? You do a little investigation and you find out that all the neighborhood boys love to play football. Then you discover this powerful, influential kid owns a football, and it is the only football in the neighborhood. The other kids cannot afford one and do not have access to one elsewhere. This one boy is able to influence all the other kids because he controls access to a valuable asset—the football. The football is so valuable because the kids want to play football and because this football is rare. It is exclusive. It is the only one available. A football is not obtainable from any other source.

People place particular value on things that can satisfy their needs and that are limited in supply. If the organization can assemble rewards that are exclusive as well as essential, those rewards will be highly valued, and the organization will be in a position to better motivate its workers. The promotion is a type of reward the organization can offer which is not readily available to employees outside of work. Many times, money can be earned elsewhere, as can social satisfactions, a sense of security, recognition and self-realization. But the promotion reward may be exclusively the company's. Because of this, it becomes valued and sought after. Similarly, if the organization is going to offer prizes for good performance, those prizes will tend to have higher value if they are rather unique. Any company would do well to invest a little extra in developing a degree of exclusiveness in its reward repertoire.

24. Make extrinsic rewards contingent on performance.

It was mentioned earlier that challenging goals are valued highly because you have to work harder to achieve them. The same applies to extrinsic rewards. People tend to value what they have to work to get. I have seen, on a number of occasions, how differently kids, who work to earn money to buy themselves bicycles, value those bicycles than kids who are given bicycles by somebody else. I have seen more than one young married couple working and saving for a number of years to finally buy a house. How much more such couples value their houses than the young couples, from well-to-do families, who are given houses.

When people have to invest time and energy to get something, they value what they get. Does a promotion really mean anything to someone who gets it automatically? It means a lot to those persons who know they earned it—who know they excelled to achieve the promotion. Lower-income people who work for what they have are very frequently happier than well-to-do people who inherit what they have. The reason is in large measure because high value is attached to anything you have to work hard to get. Even though the reward received may be insignificant from other points of view, if your sweat earned it, you tend to appreciate it. Because of this phenomenon, the organization would do well to put a substantial portion of its major intrinsic and extrinsic rewards on a performance-contingent basis. Rewards that are made contingent on performance are valued more than rewards given regardless of the level of performance simply because their receipt depends on performance and on a serious investment of effort and skill.

25. Make employees part of a team.

Building closely knit employee work groups can affect the reward values experienced by employees in many ways. First, when you receive praise or other forms of recognition from team members, it is generally more highly valued because a true team member is likely to be fully cognizant of the real contribution of a teammate. You know the recognition is deserved.

Second, when in a team situation, you tend to see your individual productivity as valuable not only for yourself but also for the team as a whole. You become sensitive not only to how your performance affects your success but also to how your performance affects the success of others. It can be a rewarding experience to know you are really contributing to others' achievements.

Third, you can never value what you do not receive. Being a member of a cohesive team helps assure that certain social satisfactions are derived, that certain security and belongingness needs are met, and that various esteem and status needs are satisfied. Often these needs cannot be as highly satisfied by any other means. Social satisfactions come from the opportunity teamwork affords to work closely with others and to coordinate and cooperate with others in integrating efforts. A sense of job security comes from team participation because you see that you are needed. You see how your role is an essential component in the system. Also, you have other close team members to lean on to vent frustrations, ask advice, or stick up for you. Recognition comes regularly from team members as they thank you for holding up your end of the work effort, for sharing with them, and for cooperating. Without a team atmosphere, these kinds of rewards are frequently absent.

26. Increase the amount paid for rewards.

The company's investment in rewards offered employees is a prime determinant of employees' perceptions of reward value. Of course employees have to have information on what the magnitude of that investment is, or the size of the investment has no impact.

A gift shop in one of the world's largest hotels on Miami Beach provides a good example of the phenomenon at work here. Customers swarm this shop in the winter months to buy gifts of various types. The actual quality of the merchandise is not better than what can be purchased at half the price from Sears. But the shop continually attracts a high volume of business. The reason is that people like to say they bought such and such an item at this shop because the shop has a high-priced image. It is a prestigious place to do business. The price attached to an item coming from this shop adds to one's perception of the value of the item. Paying a lot gives you identity and stature. Whether the item is really worth it in pure economic terms does not matter. What counts is how much you "forked over" for it.

Employees react the same way, to a degree, as shoppers in Miami. If they know the organization invested a lot in a prize, or if considerable effort was put into arranging a promotion, or if a considerable investment of management's time and energy, and of company dollars, went into devising a quality benefits package, they will value the reward more.

27. Assure the percentage increase in rewards is adequate.

One group of employees says they value highly the $5 per hour raise they received. Another group says the $5 per hour raise is worthless. Why the difference? It may be difficult to understand until you realize that members of the first group were making $4 per hour prior to the raise, and members of the second group were making $90 per hour before the raise. How much value is attached to a reward depends on the starting place. It is more the relative magnitude of the increase than the absolute magnitude that often affects perception of the reward's value.

A $5-an-hour raise for the lower-paid group permits members of this group to substantially upgrade their standard of living. The effect is highly compounded when you realize that the income tax bite from the wage increase of the second group is far higher than the bite taken out of the increase given to the first group.

To assure employees value raises and other types of rewards, attention must be given to the base from which the increase is given. Though related in concept to the phenomenon of declining marginal utility mentioned earlier, the emphasis here is on the magnitude of the reward base to which increases are added. With declining marginal utility, each unit of reward added provides less increase in satisfaction than the previous unit. Here we are recognizing that this declining utility can be offset, in certain situations, by increasing the number of units added.

28. Give things to people that have practical, multiple, and long-term uses.

All other factors being equal, practical value is a weightier factor than symbolic value when people are judging the overall worth of some object or event. Of course, an item with both practical and symbolic value would be still better. Most people in our middle-class society are practically oriented. They want something they can apply to improve the quality of their lives. Symbols of success are nice, but they are no substitute for usable items.

All other factors being equal, industrial-type items are more valued than consumer-type items when people are judging the worth of an object or event. Industrial-type items have an indirect effect on satisfaction. They are objects, events, or information bits, for example, that you can use to accomplish or produce something else that can be directly consumed. For example, a hammer has no useful value in its own right. It is only useful as a tool to produce something else like a cabinet or house which does have consumable value. Generally, industrial-type items have greater value because they are seen as providing flexibility in what is produced for ultimate consumption. Which would you value more, a $100,000 home given to you already finished in a given location, or $100,000 given to you to build your own house wherever you please?

Also, all other factors being equal, items with long-term utility tend to outshine items that are good only for immediate consumption. The prime example here is perhaps this choice of prizes: Which would you rather have? A three-week, $10,000 vacation in the South Pacific or a $10,000 new automobile? Of course your actual choice would depend on many factors, but ignoring all other factors for the moment, people tend to lean toward the automobile because of its long-term utility. The vacation is gone in three-weeks, and, though the rest and relaxation provided by the vacation would have a valuable carry-over effect, the investment is essentially lost after the three weeks. The car, on the other hand, can be consumed over a number of years. It provides longer-term satisfaction. It better distributes reward value over time. The vacation provides a reward overload at one point in time. Long-term savoring (except by way of memory or pictures) is not possible.

4

Principle 3: Employees Will Be Motivated When They Perceive a Performance-Supportive Cost Structure

Employees must sense that the costs (negative outcomes) they experience at work do not encourage low effort expenditure. Negative outcomes from work can overshadow rewards and render a high-quality reward system relatively useless for employee motivational purposes. The less the positive correlation between effort and costs or the stronger the perceived inverse relation between effort and costs, the stronger the motivation.

The classical focus in motivation theory is on positive outcomes (rewards) and how to control them. Neglected, but just as important in motivating, are the negative outcomes (costs) experienced by employees. If not controlled, these can outweigh the motivating impact of an organization's reward system.

PROPOSITION 3.1: EMPLOYEES MUST PERCEIVE THAT THE COSTS ASSOCIATED WITH HIGH EFFORT ARE LOW.

To prevent costs from encouraging low effort, management must get employees to sense that the negative outcomes associated with high effort are low. One must sense that high effort will be accompanied by relatively little stress, fatigue, fear, boredom, and the like. When one senses such, high effort becomes more palatable, and one will strive for the rewards of high effort because one senses those rewards will not be negated, or offset, by the negative outcomes (sacrifices) associated with high effort.

The following are ways to get employees to see that relatively low costs accompany high levels of effort.

1. Properly schedule work breaks.

To keep the costs associated with high effort low, work breaks can be given to workers. Work breaks allow workers to rest or to do something different for a while thus helping to reduce fatigue and boredom.

Breaks can be scheduled in different ways. They can be prearranged as to length and always taken at the same time of day, or they can be set up to be taken at different times or to be of varying length. Sometimes workers may be given a number of options for when to take breaks or allowed to take breaks whenever they see fit—providing, of course, production is not excessively disrupted.

Permitting workers to break at their choice has some real advantages because it allows workers to adapt break times to their own needs and changing moods. Of course limits have to be placed on how much total time for breaks is permitted as well as when breaks are taken if the worker's efforts must be carefully integrated with the efforts of others. But regardless of how break decisions are made, a sufficient number of breaks should be taken at properly spaced intervals depending on the nature of the job.

It is important to make sure workers use breaks for rest and relaxation. Sometimes workers use breaks to catch up on old projects, to help out fellow workers, to carry grievances to the boss, and to do other work-related projects. The purpose of the break must not become clouded. If the worker is not getting relief from pressures or fatigue, the break is not doing what it is supposed to for cutting the perceived costs associated with high effort.

2. When possible, allow employees to adapt tasks to personal energy rhythms.

Biorhythms are a biological phenomenon experienced by all people. At times we have high energy; at times we feel down or "drained," whether we have been exerting high energy in the immediately preceding time period or not. Different people seem to have different energy rhythms. It depends primarily on physical make-up and on personality—personal characteristics—rather than on the job one is doing. Some people experience extreme highs and lows during each energy cycle. Others have relatively steady energy levels over time with only slight ups and downs. Some people have relatively long spaces of time between successive highs or lows.

If you are going to minimize the fatigue and stress you experience, it is helpful if you can adapt your work to your energy rhythms. When you are feeling strong and energetic, it makes sense to tackle tough tasks, which are those demanding concentration or intense physical exertion. When you are feeling weak and perhaps psychologically down, it makes sense to engage in simpler, less critical tasks. Allowing workers to work on assignments when they feel best about it—allowing them to sequence and schedule their own tasks— can help them better accommodate their biorhythms and reduce long-run costs.

Some companies have adopted flextime work scheduling for professionals or executives. Flextime systems allow workers to choose, within limits, the hours they work. If your best time is early morning, this is when you will tend to choose to work. If you prefer nights, you can choose nights. If you want to leave in the middle of the day, but come back after supper, fine. Numerous employees find such systems do cut the costs perceived to be associated with high effort. Under such systems, they are encouraged to exert greater total effort.

3. Instruct employees in proper diet and exercise.

The evidence is in, and the evidence is clear. Employees who eat properly and exercise properly have more energy. They get tired less quickly. They are able to handle factors that produce stress with relative ease. They become less anxious at work. Even boredom diminishes.

Workshops should be set up for employees to dramatize the importance of proper diet and proper exercise and to instruct workers in practical ways to prepare proper diets and to engage in proper exercise. Workers should be taught which foods contribute the most to good health and which should be avoided or consumed in minimal amounts. They should be taught about calories, nutrients, artificial food additives, fibers, and fats. They should be taught how the quantity and rate of food intake affect health, how the mix and kinds of foods ingested affect health, how the scheduling of food intake affects health, and how the quality of the particular food consumed affects health.

When it comes to exercise, employees need to know the exercises that are most appropriate for different jobs. Weight lifting might be good for one who must frequently lift heavy items. Aerobic exercise might be best for one who frequently must ascend flights of stairs. Employees need to know what different kinds of exercises will and will not do for them. They need to know how to properly execute exercises, and how often and how long to engage in a given exercise each exercise session. They also need to know how to progress in exercise routines—how to "work up" as their bodies become more and more capable. The latest research shows that generally employees should choose a variety of exercises, incorporating recreational sports, for best overall fitness.

4. Provide quality food and exercise opportunities.

You can go one giant step beyond simply instructing workers in proper diet and exercise. Organizations are beginning to realize that they can, at reasonable cost, provide proper foods on site. Instead of having workers bring their lunches, which are often not the most nutritious, companies can build cafeterias and provide different workers with different diets as called for by workers' dietitians or physicians. Different menus can be planned for workers with different physical (and emotional) fitness needs. Also the quantities of food received by workers can be properly regulated. Usually these food-providing systems can be easily sold to workers once they understand the great benefits of such systems to personal health. Usually companies can keep the cost of food very reasonable so that cost is not viewed as a deterrent for these systems.

Organizations are also beginning to realize the value of providing workers with physical fitness opportunities. Some companies offer exercise classes during hours preceding or following the workday, or during a midday work break. A number of companies are building their own gyms and weight-lifting rooms, and constructing softball fields, cross-country skiing trails, and jogging facilities. Sound costly? It is. But, as with investing in on-site food services, investing in exercise facilities pays off. Workers develop more stamina and more strength. They come to see higher effort as accompanied by less fatigue, stress, and physical ailments. The increased performance and production that come from the increased effort employees are willing to exert usually more than compensate for the cost of providing exercise opportunities.

5. Design work to minimize mental and physical fatigue.

Streamlining procedures, arranging the workplace to allow ease of maneuvering, building machines that require relatively little continuous, strenuous effort, and designing jobs that are not too emotionally or mentally demanding are some work design options that help workers see that less negative outcome is experienced with high effort. They perceive that more productive effort can be exerted without encountering high fatigue, stress, or other problems. They see that they can sustain a given level of effort longer, or that they can exert a greater level of effort in a given span of time.

Mental and emotional fatigue usually come from quite different sources than does physical fatigue. Work that involves dealing with highly complex problems or work that requires a high level of interpersonal coordination, cooperation, or counseling, for example, can tire one quickly if attention is not given to carefully designing the work to avoid excessive stumbling blocks. Work that yields uncertain outcomes can also be psychologically wearing. Serious attention should be given to minimizing these uncertainties. Designing work with fewer trial-and-error responsibilities can help here. Definitive duties with prescribed means and predictable outcomes tend to cause employees to see high effort as less mentally and emotionally exhausting.

Physical fatigue can be reduced by allowing workers to engage in smooth, fluid movements. One should not have to stretch too far, punch too hard, lift too much, change direction too often, engage in continuous stop-and-start behavior, strain too much to see or hear, or be forced into random behavior patterns. Whether at the desk or on the production floor, work design to keep fatigue at a minimum is an admirable objective for keeping the perceived costs of high effort down.

6. Assure adequate task variety.

Excessive task variety interferes with the workers' ability to perform their assignments well and with efficiency, as discussed earlier, but too little task variety must be avoided too. Too little variety means that the worker is doing just a few tasks, each with a substantial degree of repetition. And few tasks, each with a short cycle time and, therefore, high frequency of repetition, lead to boredom as well as to a sense of meaninglessness in one's job. One will attempt avoidance of high effort which means rapid repetition and the onset of boredom.

Performing few tasks with high repetitiveness does, of course, have considerable benefit in terms of the efficiency with which one can perform. One learns his or her job well and can avoid excessive effort spent on task transitions and task start-up and shut-down. But these advantages have to be balanced against the disadvantages of boredom and meaninglessness.

It is difficult to say that a given variety of tasks is too great or too small. The optimal degree will depend on many factors, not the least of which is the personality of the individual. Some people prefer relatively large task varieties and have the ability to successfully execute a large variety of tasks. Others will actually prefer a relatively small variety of tasks—a job scope they feel more comfortable and confident with. Complicating the decision on what variety is optimal is the fact that what is optimal at one point in time is not likely to be optimal at another point in time. People's needs and skills change. The effect of task variety on motivation will not be constant. This means that job designs must be changed, periodically, to maximize motivation.

7. Provide adequate annual vacation time.

Giving employees vacations is not just a benefit for the employee. The organization profits from employee vacations too. When employees use vacations to rest, relax, recuperate, and rejuvenate, the organization's investment in those employees is secured. If employees do not have vacations, or too short vacations, boredom, frustration, fatigue, and stress can mount to unacceptable levels. Employees know this and will cut back on effort to avoid such extreme costs.

The human resource is unique among resources. The value of an organization's investment in this resource can grow at a tremendous rate. But that investment will not likely grow at a maximum pace if vacation time—for mental and physical regrouping—is insufficient or inappropriately scheduled. Scheduling is particularly critical. Often two weeks total annual vacation can rejuvenate the human resource as well as four weeks if the days taken are properly spaced throughout the year or properly timed to immediately follow highly demanding periods on the job. Companies, generally, may be too lax in not influencing vacation schedules more.

The type of vacation one takes also has much to do with the impact of the vacation on rejuvenating the worker. Usually the company will not see it as ethical to tamper with one's usage of away-from-work vacation time, but companies could probably do more in this area by creating incentives for pursuing certain kinds of vacations. Instead of letting the employee "slip" into two weeks of highly competitive golf for a vacation, the company might provide the employee with tickets for a trip to an island resort where relaxation and avoidance of stress will more likely occur.

8. Lay out the work to allow for sufficient physical movement.

If you are stuck in one physical location for many hours in succession, you can "go through the roof" with boredom, stress, and fatigue. Even though you perform fifty different tasks per half day, have a clear set of reasonably challenging tasks, and have the finest equipment, tools, and work layout in the world, you will not be content standing or sitting in one spot, or staying in one small space for an extended period of time. The need for movement is basic. People need a change of scenery, and people need to move their bodies in a variety of ways. No movement can be more tiring than applying energy to physical movement—at least up to a point.

Some organizations purposely build some inefficiency into procedural and layout designs to allow employees an opportunity to physically move. One example is in the area of office design. Efficiency experts tell us to locate file drawers and other equipment so that workers can simply pivot in their chairs and gain access. But such designs do not allow the workers to get out of their chairs. By positioning file cabinets across the room, it may take a little longer to get to them, but the physical movement necessitated by the "distant" file location may be more than worthwhile as a trade-off. Another example is in the use of elevators. Some companies no longer are installing elevators, for general employee use, in buildings that have only two or three floors. Forcing employees to walk up and down stairs gets their blood circulating and can, over time, ease fatigue and stress instead of increasing it.

9. Teach stress management techniques to employees.

One straight-to-the-point approach for reducing worker stress is to teach employees how to cope with stress or how to prevent stress. If employees know the techniques, they are not so likely to try to avoid high effort because of perceived stress. They know how to limit those stress-related costs.

Employees can be taught ways to relax on the job using stretching and breathing techniques. They can be taught meditation techniques to use on or off the job. They can be taught the benefits of such physically relaxing devices as steam baths and massages.

Employees can also learn biofeedback techniques which permit them to monitor physiological indicators of stress such as the rate of perspiring, the pulse rate, and nervous responses. Once they learn how to interpret these measures, they can learn to control the underlying variables and their cause—stress.

Scores of possible means actually exist for dealing with stress because stress has scores of possible determinants. As mentioned earlier, diet and exercise can have a significant impact in controlling stress. Aerobic exercise, off the job, tends to make people more relaxed on the job. Diets that avoid such foods as sugars and caffeine tend to reduce stress levels. In addition to diet and exercise, daydreaming, reading, social conversation, laughing, storytelling, work breaks, vacations, self-hypnosis, and better scheduling of work activities all have their place in controlling stress. Employees must be taught what variables in their lives can be altered to positively impact on stress. With full knowledge here, workers are likely to perceive that they can avoid the high negative outcomes that would otherwise be the expected outcomes from high effort.

10. Orally downplay the costs of high effort.

Managers can simply tell employees that the costs of high effort are not all that high. After all, we are talking about perception here. Employees avoid high effort because they *think* high costs will be encountered. In fact, high costs may not be experienced at high effort. Once employees try exerting high effort, they may find that in reality high costs are not experienced at high effort. It seems perfectly ethical for managers to try to persuade employees of the small negative outcomes associated with high effort, at least to the point where employees give high effort a try to see what they actually experience for costs.

Downplaying the negatively valued outcomes associated with high effort serves to motivate just as talking up the value of positive outcomes can motivate. Managers can develop and present arguments to employees as to why stress, fatigue, boredom, fear, and anxiety should not be significantly greater at higher effort than at low effort. Sometimes such messages not only can get employees to attempt high effort levels but also can result in a real long-term lowering of the costs perceived to accompany the exertion of high effort. It is all in the mind. You may be tired, but someone may be able to convince you that you are not. You may be bored, but someone with the right argument may convince you that you are not bored. This may be mind control and rejected by some readers, but the fact is that mere persuasion can work. What we sense is as much a product of our frame of mind as it is of actual stimuli from the design of the job. Fear, a cost, is but a state of mind. Stress is largely a state of mind. Boredom is a state of mind. Even fatigue can be, in part, a state of mind. So simple persuasion can help.

11. Minimize workplace hazards.

When you sense that the workplace is dangerous, you are likely to go cautiously about your tasks for fear of injury. You avoid high effort directed entirely toward performance because you know you need energy for keeping alert and avoiding personal injury or harm. When dangerous obstacles are always present in the work setting, a portion of your effort is directed toward being careful not to "bump" into those obstacles. You also try to avoid fatigue that comes with high effort because you know you are not as sharp when you are tired, and the risk of accident goes up.

The physical work environment must be properly designed to prevent accidents and to alert workers of sources of danger. Areas of the plant where accidents are likely should have posted within them easy-to-read signs stating the danger and, perhaps, how to protect against it. Potentially injurious equipment should be encased in protective cages whenever possible. Walkways should be properly marked and roped off or built with railings to help prevent workers from wandering into dangerous areas.

Protective clothing should be provided when such helps protect against hazards in the workplace. Goggles, breathing masks, steel-toed shoes, insulated gloves, and hard hats may be called for. Certainly, readily accessible first aid equipment should be in place.

On top of these mechanisms which screen out the danger, employees need to be trained in how to avoid danger. With proper indoctrination, employees can learn how hazards can be avoided without devoting excessive effort to the process. We do not want workers to perceive that hazard avoidance takes an excessively high level of effort. Proper training can help on this.

12. Use job rotation.

Some companies use job rotation schemes on a wide scale. With job rotation, the designs of actual jobs are left unchanged, but employees are given an opportunity to experience a greater variety of tasks by moving from job to job, usually in a cyclical pattern, over time. For example, the employee starts with job A in week number one, moves to job B in the second week, takes on job C in the third week, and in the fourth week starts a repetition of the cycle by going to job A again.

The advantages of job rotation are many. First, the company profits by having a number of workers trained on each of a number of different jobs. This means that when somebody is sick, somebody else who has rotated through the job performed by the absent worker can take over.

Second, job rotation means that no one worker will be stuck with a particularly undesirable job. With rotation, each worker in the rotating system will stay on a given job for a relatively short period of time. Each worker will have to perform that one undesirable job for a while, but can look forward to a definite point in time when he or she will be moved to more palatable work. Often workers are willing to exert high effort on an undesirable job as long as they know it is short term.

Third, rotation gives workers that all-important sense of the total operation. They often feel more valuable to the company and understand better how the total system of jobs is integrated. They become much more sensitive to the demands on fellow workers and perceive that all-important work load balance. The perception of balanced work loads means workers do not feel cheated by having to endure the tough tasks while their peers have it easy. High effort becomes more acceptable because workers do not see it as singularly abusive. Everyone else faces the same situation.

Fourth, job rotation relieves costs associated with high effort such as fatigue and boredom. With rotation, workers get a change of scenery periodically and a chance to use different physical and mental skills. Over the long run, this can help prevent burnout. It should be recognized, however, that rapid job change can increase stress. This is particularly true if the worker is constantly having to spend time and energy learning the new work and interacting with different people.

13. Periodically change task sequencing.

Monotonous routines or boring work can be relieved, to a degree, simply by altering the ordering of the tasks or by leaving the choice of task sequencing up to the workers themselves. This cannot always be done, but where jobs are done relatively independent of one another, there may be relatively great flexibility in just what sequence things are done.

Leaving task sequencing up to the workers means they can adjust what they engage in at specific times to their individual moods and sense of priority. On some days workers may wish to tackle tough tasks first, or to do all tasks required in a given physical location first. On other days workers may prefer to start out with easy tasks and perhaps do a few tasks in location A, then move to location B, then come back to A. Such opportunity for flexibility can go far toward relieving fatigue and boredom.

If management controls task sequencing, periodic alteration of task sequences is desirable if the production process permits such. When management controls the character of task sequences and the timing of task sequence change, it is generally not as beneficial to the relief of fatigue and boredom as when the worker controls these things, but frequently workers will prefer that management bear the responsibility for this. Having management control sequencing means the worker is relieved of the burden of having to make decisions here. Further, it can introduce the exciting element of surprise into work assignments. Not knowing what will have to be done next can be stimulating. It can reduce the blandness and dullness which "creeps in" when workers see only the same old routine lying ahead of them. Employees are more willing to exert effort if that effort is not perceived to be accompanied by increased boredom.

14. Introduce pleasant visual and auditory stimuli to the work environment.

The stress, fatigue, and boredom you might associate with high effort can be reduced by introducing into the work system pleasant sounds and visual effects. Soft music piped into the office can be soothing and relaxing and can serve as the focus of one's attention during highly repetitive tasks. Such tasks often do not require much thought, so it is okay for the mind to wander to the sound of music.

Loud noises and startling sounds should be screened out of the work environment. Wall soundproofing and physical facility layout, which positions sources of loud noise in relatively isolated areas, can help here. It may be necessary to provide employees with ear plugs or headphones to screen out excessive noise.

Proper colors and proper decor in the workplace can be soothing and comforting. Soft pastels, a variety of colors, and a well-decorated workplace—possibly with plants, paintings, and ornaments—generally add to the potential of the workplace in minimizing stress and in sustaining high effort.

It may make a real difference to some workers if they have an opportunity to gaze out a window—to see the sunlight once in a while. Studies show that stress mounts up quicker and to higher levels when workers are closeted in interior rooms that provide no opportunity to look out. An occasional glance out the window can relax; it is a diversion, a break. It helps some workers develop a broader perspective on life so that they do not become "stressed out" by the relatively narrow-focused job demands of the day. When you look only at your desk all day long, you see life as simply a pile of papers and tasks that need to be done. A look out the window makes one quickly realize there is more to life.

15. Minimize task uncertainty.

One of the most crucial factors in stress development is the degree of control you exert over your world of work. When you feel you are on top of things—that you decide what you will do, when, where, and with whom—you tend to feel good about yourself and your work. When you know that your work is a product of your own decisions, not somebody else's, you sense you are in control. The alternative is uncertainty about your assignments, which is what occurs when the job is not highly structured and when others tend to tell you what to do with little or no warning.

Uncertainty is something few people like although there is the element of surprise which some people welcome under the right circumstances. Uncertainty in task assignment means you cannot prepare well for assignments. It means you may be caught with an assignment you cannot do very well or do not want to do. It means you may not be able to engage in certain tasks you have planned to do. It means you may have too little to do or too much to do. In general, uncertainty means pressure that would not otherwise exist.

When you experience an uncertain task set, you may tend to reduce effort expenditure because the higher the effort, the greater the volume of unexpected tasks you see as being thrust your way. There is no sense to hustle too much because the boss will find something else for you to do. More effort simply means heavier engagement in an environment of uncertainty.

Uncertainty and the accompanying loss of control generate stress which one can, in part, avoid by cutting back effort. To prevent this effort cutback, management would do well to provide well-developed job descriptions which spell out to employees the task areas in which they are expected to perform. These should be supplemented with sufficient delegation of decision-making powers and authority to permit significant self-control opportunity in the workplace.

16. Assure the demands of jobs do not differ from the capacities of the individuals performing those jobs.

Job designs must be matched to the ability levels of the persons performing the jobs. You must not design work independent of considerations of who will do the work. If the worker's abilities are low, and you cannot find somebody else, you will want to modify the required task assignments so that the worker can perform them reasonably well. If the employee's abilities are high, you will want to upgrade the job to take account of this outstanding asset. You do not want someone underqualified or overqualified. Both situations can create stress for the worker.

Since individuals' abilities generally improve over time, with learning, job content should be altered periodically to keep the design in line with ability change. Not always can companies transfer or promote workers as their growth makes them eligible for more demanding assignments. Alteration of given jobs will be required.

Workers who are underburdened may experience stress because they feel their contributions to the company are not significant or that their talents are not being used. They may even sense guilt. Workers who are overburdened often develop a sense of incompetence, of inability to keep up, or of inability to achieve. It is extremely important to set realistic job goals to prevent a sense of overburdening or inability to achieve. Both overburdening and underburdening can lead to early burnout for the worker. Both can lead the worker to think high effort carries high costs. The underburdened worker may see high effort as simply generating useless output. The overburdened worker docs not see effort—no matter how much is exerted—as leading to accomplishment, only failure.

17. Assure that informal production norms are not too low.

In most organizations, groups of workers develop their own concepts of how much is a reasonable level of production. These informal production norms may or may not coincide with what the organization establishes for formal production quotas.

Informal production norms can be extremely powerful in controlling employee production. If employees in a group feel close to one another, psychologically, if they value being members of the group, or if they have a real team spirit, these norms can far outweigh formal organizational production quotas in their influence on behavior. Employees do not want to violate informal norms because they do not want to be rejected by their peers. Approval from fellow workers can be more important than approval from management.

When informal group norms are lower than formal group quotas, the worker perceives that the higher effort required by the organization has a very real direct cost associated with it. The higher effort means breaking group norms and, as a consequence, rejection by peers. Workers do not want this so they shy away from the higher effort.

To avoid such problems, management might involve workers in setting formal production quotas to help assure they are acceptable quotas. Management's voice must, of course, impact in this process to assure quotas are, in fact, set high enough. To assure quotas are set in line with company objectives during a participative decision process, management should identify and work through those workers who are informal leaders—workers respected and trusted by their peers. If management can convince these workers of what quotas should be adopted, it is likely other workers will follow suit.

18. Make sure employees do not have to give up something in order to exert high effort.

Employees will perceive that high effort carries high cost if the exertion of high effort means they must sacrifice something they value. For example, you may have an image you are trying to protect—you wish to be known as the "guy who gets things done without having to resort to high effort." You know how to get others to do the work for you, perhaps. Or you may feel that high effort will take you away from your friends. You sense you will lose some of your buddies because the high effort takes you down a path that involves far less frequent on-the-job contact. Or you may feel that high effort will force you into a promotion which you do not want because you like your present job. Perhaps, too, you perceive the high effort as leading to public recognition; but what you want is anonymity.

It depends greatly on the individual, but sometimes one can perceive significant losses from high effort, and such losses can exceed any rewards, or gain, provided by management. We are not talking about losses due to time and energy taken away from other off-the-job goal systems. These are losses too, but a special major category which is reserved for discussion in a later chapter. Here we are referring to direct losses that are caused by the high on-the-job effort rather than losses that occur because of allocating high effort to the job instead of to other goal systems.

19. Periodically alter the pace of work.

On many jobs workers have little choice about the pace at which they work. For example, the assembly line forces one to keep up with a predetermined rate. On such jobs, too fast a pace can lead to high fatigue. The worker sometimes responds to such demands by cutting back effort devoted to quality. That is, to avoid the high fatigue associated with high effort, the worker sacrifices quality since the quantity to be produced is fixed.

A practical remedy for this problem is to periodically alter the rate of flow of work. Simple pace changes can relieve tension and diminish how tired one gets. The organization may still average a certain desired quantity of output, but during certain hours the rate of production is purposely set below the average, and during other hours the rate is set higher than the average. Change of pace is less monotonous and less tiring than constant rate flow. One can actually go at a faster-than-normal pace for a period of time with little excess fatigue and monotony if that faster pace is followed by a slower pace. Actually the slower pace of working has a rejuvenating effect similar to the effect of work breaks. Altering the work pace is like a person walking for a while and then sprinting for a while instead of constantly jogging. You can cover the same total distance in the same time but may experience less overall fatigue by varying the pace. This may not work for everyone, however. It has much to do with types and levels of physical conditioning. But it is a possibility worth studying.

20. Cultivate a social system that will promote the venting of frustrations.

People are willing to exert high effort and to experience temporary anxieties, frustrations, and stresses if they know they have avenues for relieving these internal states. Training workers in stress management techniques is one avenue, as discussed earlier, that holds excellent promise. An equally promising way of helping employees relieve these states, once developed, is to assure employees are members of well-integrated social systems—in other words, that they work with others they like, trust, and feel comfortable with.

When workers are members of such systems, they can use these systems to vent pent-up emotions. They can complain about their work demands to their fellow workers. They can use their fellow workers for on-the-job social exchange which gets their minds off their work. They can relieve high, internal negative states simply by talking out their problems with their fellow workers. Sometimes it helps to scream when somebody else is there to listen—somebody other than the boss! If workers take their problems to the boss every time they have a problem, they soon may experience greater stress, as the boss may not appreciate such an extra burden. Fortunately, the informal social groups in an organization give the worker an avenue for frustration and stress venting that generally does not "back fire" by increasing the frustration and stress. Fellow workers are understanding, more sympathetic, and more likely to agree. Bosses often are critical of someone who comes to the office with frequent problems and complaints. Such response by the boss only adds to what may already be a very difficult situation.

21. Minimize fallout from mistakes.

High effort sometimes means risk. You cannot succeed without trying, so the saying goes, but trying may mean failure. Employees often shy away from high effort because of the possibility they will be worse off having tried and failed than not having tried at all.

It is up to managers to create a mistake-tolerating work environment. Managers must make it clear to employees that taking risks is desirable practice and that it is understood that a certain percentage of the time mistakes will be made. Management must assure workers that mistakes come with the territory and that they are expected. Management must further assure workers that penalties will not be forthcoming as a result of mistakes from high effort.

Any organization would do well to focus on mistakes in a positive way. Find out why they happen and help the employee avoid them, but do not create a fear of making mistakes and do not create such an intolerant climate that workers fear admitting mistakes. If workers have such fears, the organization's problems will constantly be covered up by workers who do not want management to know that they are making wrong decisions or putting together products in the wrong way, for example.

The most creative and progressive organizations see mistakes as a natural phenomenon associated with moving ahead. They actually view mistakes as a prerequisite for doing things right. Development of such an atmosphere in an organization goes far toward minimizing one's perception of the possible costs associated with high effort.

22. Instruct workers in how to deal with the fear of failure.

Even though the organization develops a tolerance for mistakes, employees will see undesirable consequences associated with those mistakes. The organization may not penalize for mistakes, but employees penalize themselves. They see themselves as unsuccessful. It is, therefore, important for employers to help employees deal with failure and to help employees avoid seeing temporary lack of achievement or one-time efforts as failures.

I once asked a vacuum cleaner salesman, who visited my home at 1:00 on a Saturday afternoon, how many more houses he was going to visit that day. The salesman said, "I'm through. No more." I asked, "Why?" The salesman replied, "I can't stand one more rejection." The salesman was saying that he would not exert any more effort because he did not want to experience any more failures that day. This phenomenon is common.

To help people overcome their fear of failure, management can take time to help them build their self-confidence. People who think they have all the required ability are not likely to see themselves as failures simply because some objective is not accomplished. Management can also take time to explain to workers that failure is an inherent part of the job. There will be successes, and there will be failures. You have to play the percentages. In time, the percentage of failures may well diminish as the person gets better at what he or she does. Further, management can show workers that they are not alone and that others have had their share of failures. In fact, many of the finest employees the company has known have experienced many failures at some point in their work lives.

23. Show workers that prefection is not essential.

Workers often exert high effort to achieve perfection. Attempting perfection brings high stress—an inordinate amount of self-imposed pressure that does not result in the perfect accomplishment. For the perfectionist, perfection cannot be achieved. The high effort is doomed to produce lack of achievement. It is up to management to show workers that what their high efforts generate is good enough and that perfection is not required. Workers must see the importance of high effort but must not worry because they have not performed perfectly.

After workers experience the high costs associated with trying to be perfect, they will often choose to avoid high effort in the future. They drop out. They give up. Not only does high effort result in imperfection in the short run, it also results in refusal to exert any effort long term.

The best thing managers can do is to show workers that what they accomplish with high effort is worthy, that they are successful for having exerted the effort, and that a perfect level of accomplishment is not what the company needs anyway. Employees must get the idea that "good enough" is perfectly all right. No one has the time or energy to perform all assigned tasks perfectly. Workers must distribute their limited effort capacities across many tasks. If any one task were to be done to perfection, enough time and energy would not remain for allocation to the other tasks. Somehow, employees must be persuaded to avoid putting out little effort because they sense high effort as leading to failure to achieve perfection.

24. Do not put constraints on effort.

Some of us do not exert high effort because we see high effort as violating certain constraints, or breaking the rules, and for that there may be penalty. Some companies require one-hour lunch breaks between the morning and afternoon work sessions. Some companies do not allow workers to come to work before normal work hours or to leave after hours or to work during weekends and holidays. As mentioned earlier, time off is good, but workers should have some flexibility to engage in higher effort expenditure if they perceive such to be in their best interest.

Some companies insist that workers draw materials from inventory only at certain times or they do maintenance on equipment during certain prescribed days of the week. Such rules should be seriously reviewed because they may be preventing high effort expenditure. Employees avoid violating the rules and exerting higher effort because they know they will be "called on the carpet" for doing so. If workers are given flexibility on these matters, they will frequently fill their slack time with organizationally relevant tasks instead of self-interest pursuits. You do not want to arbitrarily ban engagement by the worker in organizationally relevant tasks.

Too often arbitrary task boundaries and rules prevent workers from helping other workers or working at other jobs while they take a break. Union contracts often disallow such behavior. If the worker tries to vault job boundaries and to exert higher effort, he is punished. Adopting such a system means the worker's effort potential may not be realized.

25. Assure an adequate level of humor is generated at work.

High effort with humor can be totally void of stress, strains, and frustrations. Humor is highly therapeutic. A task that casts the worker in a high pressure situation and that normally generates high stress for the worker can become a relatively uncostly experience with the introduction of real humor—humor that generates real gut-felt laughter.

Humor in the workplace gets us to take things less seriously. It does not interfere with effort. Rather, it encourages effort because it helps offset the negative outcomes of boredom, stress, fatigue, and fear that may accompany high effort.

Any work group should have somebody (or several people) in it who can tell a good joke or behave in a humorous way to stimulate laughter among the workers. Companies do not realize how valuable such people are. Many more grievances would be filed if it were not for these laughter generators. These people relieve the emotional and psychological pressures that employees impose on themselves.

I once had a job that was the most difficult, boring, and fatiguing of my life. It involved working alone in the transference of birch pulpwood from trucks to railroad cars. Each stick had to be hand-carried from the truck to the freight car. One day the boss told me a friend of mine could work with me. We had to unload twice as many trucks now, but now I had somebody else to talk to. My friend and I each carried the sticks, individually, from the trucks to the freight cars. The physical demands of the job were not diminished. But because my friend kept me laughing during the work, what had been a miserable job became a most enjoyable job. Stress, fatigue, boredom—all became nearly nonexistent.

26. Assure employees' high effort does not damage others or create undesirable opposing forces.

Workers may avoid high effort when they sense that such effort might cause hardship for others, make others look bad, or generate jealousies, ill will, or extreme competitiveness from others. If you think that your accomplishments might prevent rewards going to a fellow worker (perhaps you will get the promotion and a deserving fellow worker will not), you may decide that it is not worth it. You may feel your fellow worker really deserves the promotion more. Your efforts would only lead to an undesirable outcome for your fellow worker that overshadows the desirable outcome you would receive.

If your high effort is likely to make others jealous and you see this as interfering with future working relationships, you may decide that the effort is not worth the cost. Better to preserve good relations to permit future production than to excel now and generate interpersonal friction. Similarly, you may feel that high effort now will be emulated by your chief competitors in the organization and that those competitors are likely to adopt some not-so-ethical tactics to undermine your future efforts. If you see things this way, you probably will decide to avoid the high effort. The costs associated with it are too formidable to make the net benefits of high effort outweigh the net benefits of low effort.

Most of us do not want to cause damage to others in order to realize benefits for ourselves. Neither do we want to generate forces that may make long-run performance more difficult. We avoid effort levels that are likely to cause these things to happen.

27. Reduce blockages, barriers, and conflicts encountered at high effort.

In organizations it is common for one exerting high effort to encounter more roadblocks, more disagreements, more arguments, and more rejections than one who meanders along without great effort. The faster you move and the harder you drive, the greater the frequency of encountering certain kinds of stumbling blocks. Barriers can crop up at every turn as your high effort departs from the norm and challenges the modus operandi.

Employees may exert high effort for a while until they get tired of banging their heads against the wall—until they see that the barriers are too strong to break through. But, in time, one is likely to give up if no progress is made. If management wants employees to sustain high effort, blockages, barriers, and sources of conflict must be monitored and minimized. A major role that a manager can play involves reducing stumbling blocks for aggressive employees within his or her department. If these blocks are not reduced, the employee calculates that the high effort will only be a costly, frustrating experience.

A case in point is where the employee develops a plan to, say, increase sales through a variety of promotion techniques. To get the go-ahead, this employee has to win not only the approval of the immediate superior but also the approval of the vice president of marketing, the approval (by democratic majority vote) of the president's executive committee on revenue-generating strategies, and the approval of the organization's controller. With such a chain of approval, too much opportunity exists for effort to be thwarted. This plan should go to no more than one approving group, after it has cleared the immediate superior, and should never have to pass through a majority vote where politics runs rampant.

28. Encourage off-the-job habits that are nonfatiguing and non-stress inducing.

Your on-the-job fatigue and stress are very much a product of off-the-job habits and lifestyles. If you drink (alcohol), you are likely to experience more stress and fatigue for given levels of on-the-job effort than if you do not drink. If you take other recreational drugs or if you are on certain prescriptions arranged by your doctor, you can similarly experience greater fatigue or stress, depending on just what kinds of chemicals you are ingesting.

Off-the-job activities that tire you cause you to sense greater on-the-job fatigue at high effort levels. Getting too little sleep, partying too frequently, or engaging in excessive recreation can cause you to perceive high on-the-job effort expenditure as carrying with it unacceptable levels of fatigue and stress.

Off-the-job family problems, financial problems, and personal health problems, among others, can consume so much energy that workers see high on-the-job effort as pushing fatigue and stress to the limit. The costs are so high that they perceive it best to avoid the high effort. Not that the high effort is not possible—it may well be possible—but it is not judged by workers to be in their best interest because of the high costs associated with it. Managers should advise workers on how to manage off-the-job engagements to prevent a build-up of stress and fatigue that will carry over to the job, adding to the stress and fatigue that is a function of the nature of the job.

PROPOSITION 3.2: EMPLOYEES MUST PERCEIVE THAT THE COSTS ASSOCIATED WITH LOW EFFORT ARE HIGH.

To prevent costs from encouraging low effort, management must get employees to sense that the negative outcomes (penalties) experienced at low effort levels are high. Penalties can be designed by management to make costs inversely contingent on effort and performance. These cause the employee to exert high effort because the employee wishes to avoid the higher costs (penalties) encountered as a result of lower effort. Employees must sense they will pay a price for low effort.

Some costs associated with low effort will be experienced independent of any planned management action. These can be extrinsic or intrinsic. Costs such as disrespect, peer group ostracism, loss of informal influence ability, and dislearning are examples. When these costs are not likely to be sufficient to prevent low effort, however, management can add a penalty structure.

The following are ways to get employees to see that relatively high costs will be experienced if low effort occurs.

1. Show employees you believe in them and that you have high expectations for them.

People do not want others to be disappointed in them. They usually strive hard to fulfill the expectations others hold for them. If somebody believes in you—in your skills, your abilities, your capacity for doing good work—you want those favorable beliefs to be confirmed. You calculate that exerting low effort is not likely to allow you to show your stuff. Low effort will result in your failing to fulfill those expectations. This sense of not living up to expectations is a sense of failure, or a cost. You try to avoid such costs by exerting sufficient effort to meet expectations.

Those who hold expectations of you are not just your boss and fellow employees. A powerful source of expectations is people outside the organization—your friends, your relatives, your immediate family. Sometimes the high performance expectations that a spouse or parent holds of you are far more powerful in their impact on your motivation, as an employee, than any rewards or penalties that the organization can impose. This is why it makes good sense when hiring workers to check into possible sources of their on-the-job motivation that lie away from work.

Other strong expectations of you can come from former teachers, guidance counselors, neighbors, coaches, or former employers. If you have developed a record of success, people expect you to succeed in the future. You will likely exert energy sufficient to assure this success.

2. Prepare performance-penalty schedules and communicate them.

If you are to exert high effort and performance to avoid penalties, you will have to know that penalties do, in fact, exist and what those penalties are. You do not usually worry about penalties that you do not know about or penalties that are not clear, unplanned, or uncertain. You do not usually worry a great deal about penalties which you think have a high probability of never being implemented.

To sensitize employees to the organization's penalty structure and thus to give that structure some motivational clout, the organization should prepare, in writing, schedules which show just what penalties can be expected for different levels of sub-par performance. Whereas a reward schedule stimulates high effort expenditure by pulling the worker into high effort domains, a penalty schedule stimulates high effort by pushing or repelling the worker away from low effort.

Of course it is critical that such schedules, once prepared, be carefully communicated. A fine schedule tucked away in the files of the personnel office does little good.

Many kinds of penalties can be used by an organization and built into a penalty schedule. You have to be careful here though to distinguish penalty from reward decrease. Reward decreases would show up on the reward schedule. Common penalties are criticism, demotion, undesirable work assignments, poor perform-ance write-ups for the file, suspension, loss of normal privileges, or tighter supervision. Not getting a promotion is not receiving a reward rather than a form of penalty. Admittedly, distinguishing reward decrease from penalty can be a difficult process complicated by the fact that whether a course of action is a reward decrease or a penalty depends somewhat on perspective. But the key point, regardless, is to make both desirable and undersirable outcomes a clear function of effort and performance.

3. Initiate penalties at a sufficiently high level of effort.

One of the key points brought out by the effort–net return model of employee motivation is that while the absolute level of the employee's perceived reward function is not crucial to motivation, the absolute level of the perceived penalty function is. Figure 10 illustrates the point. With the relatively low penalty function #1, the employee's level of motivation will be at X_1. By boosting the

Figure 10
The Effect of Penalty Function "Location" on Motivation

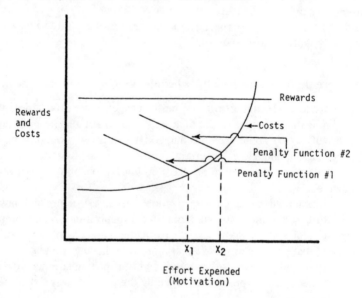

function to penalty function #2, the point of maximum satisfaction is experienced by exerting effort up to point X_2. What is really important here is where the penalty function is first encountered as effort drops off. If penalties are to motivate, they must be experienced at a sufficiently high effort level. Waiting until employees' effort drops below average before you penalize does not keep motivation high.

Even though penalties may be of extremely large magnitude—of extreme negative value—those penalties are worthless for motivation if not implemented until effort and performance have deteriorated to a low level. This means managers should not think of penalties as something to be applied only in cases of bad performance, but rather should view them as ways to assure high performance.

4. Match penalties to people's need structures.

Just as with rewards, penalties should be adapted to individual needs. For penalties to work, they must actually be seen as significant negative outcomes. One person's view on the negative value of a penalty will differ from another's.

Managers should study their employees and find out the kinds of penalties that would have the greatest impact with each employee. Ideally, penalty schedules should be individualized. This is not always practical, however, because of the high costs of administration of such systems. But managers should adapt penalties to each unique person whenever possible as long as the perceived equity of penalties is preserved.

Criticism is a penalty that works with many people. It is seen as a significant kind of negative outcome, and most people try to avoid a performance level that will bring on such an outcome. But criticism does not hurt everyone. Some employees just do not see it as a significant negative outcome, perhaps because of their upbringing in an environment where being critical was normal daily routine, or perhaps they actually see criticism as a positive force that allows them to improve and to personally or professionally grow.

Management may think the employee is being penalized when he or she is demoted, but again how the demotion is valued (negatively) depends on the individual. One may actually not mind a demotion because, though it means a cutback in status and power, perhaps these things are not highly valued by the individual. The new job may mean less pressure, less stress, and fewer negative outcomes than experienced on the present job. The point is that management has to be careful here. What management thinks is a serious penalty may be seen as fully worth incurring.

5. Talk up the use of penalties.

Talk of penalty can work just as well as the penalty itself—meaning that it is what employees think they will experience as a result of low performance that counts, not what they actually do experience. Organizations do not want employees to ever actually experience penalties, only to be aware they exist and, therefore, to try hard to avoid them.

Managers can make penalty structures vivid by talking in meetings about the kinds of penalties the company has developed, about why the penalties have been developed, and about how effectively they work. Citing examples of past employees who have been released, suspended, put into intensive remedial training programs, or required to participate in attitude improvement programs can make clear and serve as proof to employees that the company means business when it comes to performance. It says that penalties as well as rewards will be implemented to achieve desired levels of effort expenditure and performance.

The reason for talking up penalties is essentially to sensitize the employee to the kinds of penalties to expect and to assure employee understanding of how penalties are implemented or of what can cause penalties to be issued. It is done to be fair. Usually employees will accept penalties as legitimate and be influenced by them if they see them as ethical and fairly administered. If one thinks penalties are unjust or not applied objectively, the impact of the penalty can be lost. This may be one good reason for not tying all penalties to individual needs. Different penalties for different people may be seen as critically unjust and result in considerable employee relations problems.

6. Engage in negative value training and increase employee fear of failure.

Nonperformance means failure. People do not like failure. Convincing the employee that nonperformance is not right, that nonperformance is the mark of an incapable person, that low performance means goals will not be achieved, and that low performance may destroy future opportunities in the company can intensify the negative values attached to low performance. Further, pointing out that low performance brings into question such variables as one's loyalty to the organization, respect for authority, and sense of duty to society can help build employee fear of low performance and failure. Of course, these courses of action must be executed with tact or all your employees may quit! But the point is that you can do negative value training just as you can engage in the positive value training discussed in an earlier section of this book.

When you get the employee to see given negative outcomes as carrying higher negative value, these outcomes become more powerful forces pushing employees away from low effort expenditure. But not only can you build up the negative value attached to extrinsic outcomes such as criticism, demotion, and suspension, you can also point out to employees that intrinsic negative outcomes such as dislearning and disachievement will occur with low performance. Emphasis on building perception of the negative values attached to all types of outcomes resulting from low performance increases one's desire to avoid low performance. It creates a real fear of failure. When people have a real fear of failure, they will exert considerable effort to do whatever it takes to avoid performance levels that are judged indicative of failure.

7. Assure high informal group productivity norms and high group cohesion.

Employees will not violate norms that develop in their work teams and informal employee social groups because they do not want to be frowned on or rejected by their peers. Peer acceptance is extremely important to most workers, particularly when groups are cohesive and when membership means a lot to the workers.

Management, by winning the support of informal group leaders, can influence the establishing of informal group productivity norms. If informal group leaders believe in what management is trying to accomplish, they will buy into the standards and goals management has in mind. Once informal leaders have adopted standards and goals desired by management, their commitment is likely to transfer to other employees who believe in these informal leaders.

If high informal group productivity norms can be established, workers will try hard to achieve those norms, because lower performance will mean the receipt of penalty (such as criticism and ostracism) from peers. Penalty from peers can be more powerful than the same kind of penalty from management, perhaps because the employee knows that the fellow worker has been directly affected by the employee's own low performance. Or an undesirable work assignment dished out by the work group can be far more disheartening than the same assignment dished out by management. Remember, the source of a reward affects its perceived value. So also does the source of penalty affect the perceived value of the penalty.

8. Build friendships with employees.

No one likes to disappoint a friend. If managers are friends of their subordinates, those subordinates are likely to strive to keep them happy. And what keeps the boss happy is performance—production. If you do not perform for the boss, your friend, you feel you have let him or her down. This sense of deficiency is a kind of penalty or negative outcome emerging as a natural result of nonperformance.

It is often said that managers should not become too close to their workers. There is little research to support this. Evidence is to the contrary. Where good manager-subordinate teams are found, mutual trust, respect, and friendship between superior and subordinate are found too. Workers will try hard to "pull through" for their friends. If the boss is a friend, workers are not likely to risk breaking that friendship through low or sloppy performance. Friendship with the boss can be a precious commodity.

Managers can develop friendships with employees by treating them as equals on the job and off, by sharing interests with them, and by inviting them to engage in social and recreational activities. Showing workers that you enjoy being with them in off-the-job situations as well as on the job helps convince workers that there is more to your relationship than just the work you have in common. Time you spend with them to help with personal problems and concerns, and time you spend with them enjoying nonwork pursuits, can be time well invested when it comes to getting workers to avoid low on-the-job effort and performance.

9. Avoid excessive use of group penalties and attend to the source of penalties.

As is the case with rewards, penalties do not work very well when applied to groups. The individual shares the penalty with numerous others. The impact on the individual is highly diluted. Application of a group penalty does not tell individuals that their personal performance is bad. The individual knows that he or she can fail to perform, but the penalty will be borne by the entire group.

With group penalties, the individual calculates a relatively high likelihood of penalty occurrence even though he or she does not deserve such and a relatively high probability of nonreceipt of penalty when such is deserved. Thus the perceived inverse correlation between personal performance and penalty is blurred and not seen as very high. This tends to negate the potential for such penalty-stimulated performance.

As with rewards, the source of penalties is critical too in determining their impact on the worker. For example, if criticism comes from the boss, a close fellow worker, or the company president, it is likely to be taken seriously. Criticism from employees in other departments, who are out of touch with the worker's actual performance, is not likely to have much impact. Also, criticism that reaches you indirectly lacks the punch that direct criticism has even though the same words are spoken. Complaints levied against a worker by someone who does not directly interact with the worker is not likely to have much impact. Penalties emanating from a legitimate, respected, knowledgeable source are accepted and have real impact in assuring high performance.

10. Publicly state employee performance goals and actual performance levels.

When work goals are published or posted for all to see, there is considerable incentive to achieve. Low effort with accompanying lack of performance will mean public goals are not realized. This can be embarrassing. Others may question your capabilities or frown on you. Some may think you are weak or incompetent. In other words, you are penalized, severely, for nonperformance. To avoid such penalty, you choose to perform.

Work goals can be verbally stated during meetings, but a better approach is to post goals (and records of progress) in an area frequented by the work force. Posted goals provide a rather enduring record of what is supposed to be achieved. Posted goals do not let workers forget. Employees cannot depend on others' awareness of their goals rapidly vanishing.

It works best when subgoals are periodically posted. Periodic posting of subgoals prevents focus on goals from being lost and keeps all those who observe the postings continually aware of what the worker is supposed to achieve.

Of course, just simply posting is really not enough. Any posting of performance goals and progress should be given priority status among postings. Large, colorful graphic displays can have the largest impact. Animated, graphic displays centrally located on bulletin boards in work areas are another important attention getter. Newsletter and front-page company newspaper write-ups on goals and progress can also work well to keep workers focused on employees' performance.

11. Properly time the application of penalties and tie penalties to specific acts.

Like rewards, the punch of a penalty depends on its timing. If you know that your low performance may not be detected until later on and that the penalty will be received long after that—perhaps never because someone may forget about it—you are not likely to see the penalty as a formidable force propelling you away from the low effort. Meaningful penalties are those received promptly after the inappropriate, or poor performance, designated as deserving of penalty.

If a worker falls asleep on the job and lets hundreds of defective items get through the production process, this specific act of nonperformance should be addressed immediately. Doing this makes it crystal clear what was wrong and that it must not happen again. Addressing the specific act tells the employee just what it is that brings on penalty. Addressing it quickly shows that nonperformance is serious and cannot be tolerated.

It is important during the annual evaluation of employee performance that overall evaluations be supplemented with evaluations of specific performance dimensions so that workers will know precisely where correction is needed. Penalties should be given for specific task performance deficiencies. Overall, the worker may deserve high rewards, but this should not hide the areas of deficiency and should not interfere with applying penalties to help correct those areas of low performance. No performance evaluation system can afford to measure performance only once a year, however. Supervisors need to keep a constant vigil on performance to apply rewards and penalties in a timely fashion. Arbitrary timing or timing that is too late is not effective.

12. Hire people with high self-respect or a keen positive self-image.

If you are one who has high self-respect, nonperformance can cause you to feel unworthy. You will avoid low effort and low performance because a sense of negative self-worth is a cost you want to escape.

All people seek to build favorable self-images. Most of us succeed, if not readily. We twist and distort the facts until we are able to concoct a favorable self-image, deserved or not. If we are not able to develop favorable self-images, we are likely to develop emotional or psychological problems, which are clearly unhealthy and something most people want to avoid.

People with positive self-images are proud of what they are capable of doing and of what they actually accomplish. These people are not likely to let performance slip. Too much performance slippage does not just cause a simple temporary decline in positive self-image for many people, but rather contributes to development of a negative self-image. That is, the performance decline leads to penalty. Not all people see it this way, but most people have positive self-images that can be shaken or rather quickly turned into negative self-images.

Most people often have periods of doubt. If one is in a period of doubt, a performance slippage may well contribute to rapidly rising negative self-imagery. A person will attempt to avoid this. After all, one's performance is usually a variable the individual can fairly well control. One would not choose low performance with feelings of negative self-worth perceived as the outcome.

13. Properly package criticism for low performance.

Criticism is to penalties like praise is to rewards. Both work on ego needs. For criticism to work well, it should be exercised in proper surroundings to have a proper impact, just as praise should be packaged properly.

When being critical of performance, managers should take the time to call workers into their offices. This gives the criticism an air of officialdom and shows that the performance deficiency is worthy of an investment of the manager's time. Simply being critical when walking past the worker on the factory floor does not give proper focus to the problem. Likewise, issuing the criticism when the manager happens to have some free time, perhaps in the lunchroom or rest area or on the way home from work, is not an effective mode for transmitting the penalty.

Neither should criticism, directed to individuals, be made in a public forum. Criticism in public may hurt more, but a focus on the reason for the criticism is lost, and instead the workers, themselves, become that which is penalized instead of the act, or behavior, which stimulated the criticism.

Further, the impact of criticism should not be weakened by a manager who smiles and tells jokes before, during, and after discussion of the deficient performance. The seriousness of the poor performance must get through to the worker. Also, criticism for poor performance on one dimension should not be wedged between volumes of praise for good performance along other task dimensions. How the criticism is presented, where, when, and under what circumstances are all important in determining the impact of the criticism. This point applies, too, to all penalties other than criticism.

14. Do not neglect correcting low performance.

Workers will never take performance seriously if no real attempt is made by management to correct low performance. For employees to perform well, they must think nonperformance is truly a problem. When management invests time and resources in improving performance, this helps convince workers that poor performance is a problem and is something undesirable for the company and, therefore, undesirable for the worker.

All too commonly, managers let deficient performance go unattended. Sometimes they assume the problem is not that serious; therefore, it is not worth attending to. Sometimes they feel performance deficiencies are temporary aberrations and will self-correct. Sometimes they just wish to avoid confrontation. But there is really no good excuse for letting any deficient performance issue go unattended and, in turn, be perceived as unimportant.

Companies need to develop diagnostic techniques to identify the real causes of performance problems. Just detecting the existence and severity of a problem is not sufficient for setting the kind and level of penalties. Often performance problems arise through no fault of the worker. In such cases workers should not be penalized for the performance deficiency. Also diagnostic measures are required to allow for developing corrective action strategies that have a good chance at succeeding. With systems in place to diagnose and constructively correct performance problems, workers may well see more vividly the need to avoid low performance.

15. Build employees' admiration for their superiors and respect for their superiors' authority.

When employees admire their boss and respect his or her authority, they are likely to be sensitive to the fact that failing to perform at the high level desired by the boss is penalizing the boss. And it is through no fault of the boss. This can be translated into a sense of personal wrong—a penalty. Most employees do not believe their actions should negatively affect others. When this happens, it is a negative outcome for the workers themselves. The greater one's admiration for the manager and respect for his or her authority, the greater the sense of wrong that emerges when the employee does not meet the performance requirements set by the manager.

It is still common for workers to accept the institution of formal authority. Most workers accept the right of their organizational superiors to set performance standards and to require performance in accordance with those standards. They see it as their obligation to exert enough effort to meet those standards. It is the proper, right, and indeed, ethical thing to do. Violating the wishes of authority is not right, and the accompanying sense of having done something wrong is a formidable form of penalty.

Admiration for the *person* in the office has the same effect. If you believe in that person—trust, respect, and like that person—when that person requests high performance, you sense an obligation to fulfill that request. Not doing so is a failure on your part to support a person who deserves support. This failure translates to a form of cost associated with low effort.

16. Develop a graduated discipline system.

For infraction of the rules, violation of policy, or low performance, graduated penalty structures generally work better than constant penalty systems. With a graduated penalty system, successive infractions, violations, and instances of low performance carry ever-increasing penalty. For example, breaking the rules once may mean a verbal warning. Twice means a written reprimand. Three times means suspension, and so on. With a graduated discipline system, if the employees do not get the message that nonperformance is bad the first time around, they are likely to get the message the next time around. Such penalty systems make clear that poor behavior, or performance, is serious business and cannot be tolerated. And such systems are usually perceived as fair (which is crucial for penalty systems) because they allow for some mistake, or failure. They permit time to learn from mistakes.

It is a good idea to write and distribute the company's graduated penalty system to all employees. Make sure that everyone knows that all employees— managers and operatives alike—are covered by the same system of penalties. To foster this understanding and to assure these graduated discipline systems are accepted, it makes sense to involve both managers and subordinates in their design.

When it comes to penalties, it may be worthwhile to have a management-operative employee committee deciding on whether to institute penalty and how much. Using a committee helps assure the penalty is justified, helps eliminate inconsistency in application of penalties to different employees, and helps prevent employees from excessive use of appeal processes. An error in granting penalties can be much more serious a mistake than an error in granting rewards.

17. Assure that performance measurement is valid.

You are not likely to have high fear of penalty from nonperformance if you think that chances of nonperformance being detected are low. If you see that performance assessment in your ogranization is a process fraught with error, inconsistency, and uncertainty, you are likely to see that there exists great opportunity to avoid ever being "spotted" for low performance, or to "talk your way out of" a low performance measurement, if such is given.

For penalty systems to work, employees must see that performance is accurately measured. Penalties issued for performance measured as poor are not appropriate if performance is actually good. Not issuing penalties because performance is measured as good, when performance is actually low, is not appropriate either. Doing things like this causes a decline in effort expenditure, not an increase. Workers should know that if performance drops below a certain level, there is no question that it will be followed by penalty—assuming a penalty system is in place and assuming the cause of the poor performance is not beyond the worker's control.

Management needs to concentrate on devising valid assessment systems. Assessment systems are most valid if they are comprehensive—that is, they must assess all aspects or dimensions of performance. They also should incorporate numbered (quantitative) scoring of performance along precisely defined criteria, should be implemented by trained personnel, should be done with multiple individuals involved in establishing the ratings (scores), and should be done frequently. Usually there is little argument that the immediate supervisor should be the key figure involved in any evaluation of an employee's performance. Others can and should often be involved, but the supervisor's ratings should generally be weighted most heavily—assuming the supervisor is the one who has the closest, most regular contact with the work activities of the employee.

18. Communicate the purpose of the organization's penalty structure.

As stated before, penalty structures, to work, must be perceived as legitimate and be seen as a valuable tool for the organization. When this does not happen, employees naturally balk at the application of penalty to them. Instead of accepting the penalty and spending their energy trying to avoid incurring the penalty again, they direct their efforts toward fighting the penalty and trying to convince those responsible for its application that it is not deserved and should be rescinded.

By explaining to the work force why the organization—and, for that matter, all organizations—has a penalty system, a degree of acceptance of the system can be garnered. It should be emphasized first that the company's penalty system is in place to help, along with rewards and other devices, assure that employee performance reaches a high level. Second, it should be pointed out that the penality system (plan) exists so that employees will be treated equitably and that penalty will not become a product of individual managers' whims and fancies or spur-of-the-moment emotions. Third, it should be stressed that the penalty system exists to protect, not only the individual, but others who may be adversely affected by the individual's low, or faulty, performance. Fourth, employees should understand that penalty systems are being used—if, in fact, this is true—because the organization guarantees a high percentage of its rewards. A high percentage of the organization's rewards are received independent of effort. The effort–net return model of motivation tells us that with guaranteed rewards there must be a penalty structure to prevent maximum satisfaction from being realized at too low a level of performance.

Certainly employees must be appreciative of the need for discipline in an organization. Order, or avoidance of chaos, only comes through disciplined individual behavior. Individual behavior must be planned, and the behavior of multiple individuals must be coordinated. Penalty structures are designed to help achieve these ends.

19. Develop a history of consistent application of penalties.

Few things management can do probably go any further toward convincing employees that low performance brings on penalty than, over time, developing a record of consistent application of penalties for poor performance. Management can have grand penalty plans, but the proof of the pudding is in the eating. Are these plans implemented? Are these plans implemented consistently over time, across different employees, and irrespective of the particular penalty agent?

Penalty on paper helps, but idle threats soon "run out of gas." Management must follow through and regularly apply penalties as deserved. When you actually see the impact of penalties on others, or are aware of the impact on others, you become more acutely tuned in to the true meaning of penalty. When you know others who have actually experienced penalty, the penalty becomes real—the true negative value associated with penalty rises to a more conscious state. As an example of this, consider when you were a child. Your parents may have told you that if you or your brother or sister go across the street one more time, you will have to stay in your room the rest of the day and tomorrow. You hear it. You understand it. But how much does it sink in? Eventually your brother, let's say, does venture across the road. Your parents catch him and deposit him in his room. Now you get the message. You see that, in fact, the penalty will materialize. Actions, here, speak far louder than words. The message for management, therefore? Develop a clear, open display of penalty in action. Employees must see low performance as bringing on penalty for sure.

20. Assure that the degree of contingency in penalty structures is adequate.

The degree of contingency in a reward curve is important for motivation. As the degree of contingency in a reward function increases, so does motivation. The degree of contingency in a penalty structure is also important, but the situation here is a little different (see Figure 11). The degree of contingency, or the slope of the penalty function, need only be steep enough to cause the point of maximum satisfaction to be at point X_1. The penalty curve is added to the

Figure 11
Degree of Penalty Contingency

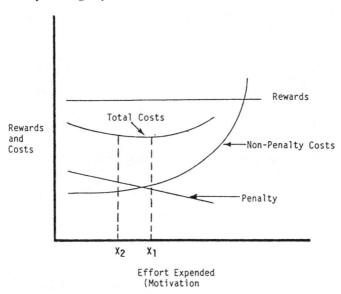

nonpenalty cost curve to get total costs. As long as total costs increase below point X_1, the employee will see that maximum satisfaction is derived at point X_1. The total cost does not have to rise any steeper. A greater slope (negative slope) does not change the point of maximum satisfaction.

You may ask why total costs have to rise (going from right to left on the graph) after a point, say X_2, just to the left of X_1. They don't! The total cost curve could be horizontal from X_2 to the vertical axis. But to keep a horizontal total cost curve in this region, the penalty curve must continue to rise to offset the decline in nonpenalty costs. The point is that it does not have to rise at as rapid a rate from X_2 to the vertical axis because the nonpenalty costs do not decline at as rapid a rate.

21. Make clear the undesirable consequences of low performance for the organization.

Some employees may get the message better that low performance hurts if you point out how low performance on the part of the individual hurts the organization. Some workers just do not see that they count for much so they wonder what is wrong with a little low performance now and then. Management must point out the disastrous results that will occur if a large number of workers thinks this way. An organization is a system of interdependent employees. Low performance by one starts a chain of low performers because others depend on the one. This point is brought up again later.

If the work force does not perform, what does it mean for the total organization? It means the organization will not be able to compete with other organizations that enjoy high levels of employee performance. It can mean loss of market share because of shortcomings of employees in the marketing area. It can mean increased per unit costs because of shortcomings in the production area. In sum, it will likely mean lower profitability. Lower profitability means the company's stock prices decline. This means growth will be stymied because of the firm's inability to attract investors. Lower profitability also will likely lead to manpower cutbacks, perhaps decreased salaries and benefits, and, for sure, longer hours—and for those not on hourly wages, longer hours with no extra compensation. Making vivid to employees how they can be affected, indirectly, because of low performance can mean more to them than direct, individualized penalties.

22. Use penalty mixes and periodically change the penalties.

No one penalty applied singularly is likely to be as effective as the application of multiple penalties. Just as multiple types of rewards have to be received by the employee to meet multiple needs, multiple penalties are valuable to assure that real negative outcome is experienced. You cannot always tell what the employee will perceive as a penalty. Using a shotgun approach may help you "hit home." For example, direct, face-to-face oral criticisim may not mean much to the workers especially if they know the boss is retiring in two weeks. But the verbal criticism coupled with a written reprimand for the file will likely have greater inpact. Better still, couple these things with suspension if the performance is deficient enough to warrant such. Using multiple penalties has greater impact, if they all hit their mark. And, with multiple penalties applied, some can miss their mark and the employee will still experience penalty.

Using multiple penalties for a given performance deficiency, in a given time period, makes sense, but to maximize effectiveness the penalty mix will generally have to be changed over time. People's needs and perceptions change; therefore, the impact of a given set of penalties will change. Often, continued use of one type of penalty will result in desensitization of the employee to that penalty. You become numb to the impact. What are a few more black marks in your file when you already have fifty of them? What is another "chewing out" when you experience three or four every day anyway?

23. Help employees develop high achievement drives.

If you have a high desire to succeed, falling short is seen as failure—as a penalty. People with high achievement drives motivate themselves to a great degree. They set goals and try hard to reach them. They know goal accomplishment is rewarding and satisfying. They also know that not reaching their goals is disappointing—even frightening—if they tend to be persons who function with extreme intensity. When goals are not reached, employees with high achievement drive usually feel that they have failed to utilize their abilities and effort capacities. They see a waste of individual effort and ability. This waste is a cost the employees see as being incurred with low effort and performance. They, therefore, attempt to avoid the low effort and performance.

It is in management's interest to help employees develop strong achievement drives. This can be done in a variety of ways. By repeatedly showing and demonstrating to employees that achievement means success for them, their families, the company, and the nation, employees soon learn to value achievement. By demonstrating to employees that life is governed by the law of survival of the fittest, their desires for achievement can be heightened. By continually using reinforcement to reward people who set goals and achieve, and to penalize people who do not set goals or do not achieve set goals, you soon instill the idea that achievement is important. Finally, a case can be presented to employees which shows that achievement, in and of itself, is highly satisfying. Achieving represents the materialization of performance and causes a sense of satisfaction. Nonperformance and nonachievement are dissatisfying.

24. Focus on areas of performance deficiency during annual performance reviews.

It is rather common for managers to hold annual or semi-annual, reviews of performance with subordinates. But too frequently these sessions turn into essentially social affairs or mutual admiration expression sessions. The manager shies away from upsetting the subordinate and making the encounter difficult when the encounter really deserves some hard scrutiny of performance. Managers sometimes do not feel comfortable pointing out performance deficiencies because they are not sure of the grounds for their low ratings of performance. They know that if challenged they could be hard pressed to produce true evidence of deficiency.

But a performance review session that overemphasizes the positive and does not show the full extent of the negative as well as the positive hurts the organization and the employee. In fact, most of the time and effort spent by manager and subordinate in the review session should be focused on performance deficiencies rather than on areas where performance is fine. The sources of deficiency must be identified, and manager and subordinate should spend considerable time deriving possible solutions to these deficiencies.

The primary role of the review should be to initiate adjustments to remedy performance problems. The review provides an uncommon opportunity to sit with the employee, to concentrate, together, on the issue of performance, and to invent strategies for overcoming weaknesses. That opportunity must not be passed up. Using the review to focus on performance deficiency tells the worker that time and effort will have to be spent on addressing performance deficiencies when such occur. This is a cost employees usually do not care to incur.

25. Make others' performance dependent on the worker's performance.

Here is a way to build into the work system some automatic costs for nonperformance. Management does not really have to get involved once work systems have been set up so that the performance of other workers is dependent on the performance of the worker of interest. If others cannot do their jobs until you have finished working with the materials, or whatever, and have passed those materials to them, or if the quality of work that others do is largely a function of the quality of your work, you will find that others will put pressure on you to perform properly.

Building integrated work systems with each employee performing in a specialized role makes each part of the system highly dependent on other parts. A serial work transformation system like an assembly line creates such an interdependence and causes workers to buoy up the "laggards" because no one else can perform well if just one person is deficient.

A parallel work system, on the other hand, allows workers to function relatively independently as each worker produces a whole product (or large portion of the product) on his or her own. The worker does not need to wait for others, does not have to coordinate with others, does not have to share with others, does not have to even communicate with others in order to get the job done. Consequently, occasions for others to pressure the worker are relatively few. Each person works independently.

26. Assure performance declines when effort declines.

Penalties should not be applied when poor performance is due to factors beyond the employee's control, but they often are because penalty agents find it difficult to isolate the causes of the poor performance. To avoid having this phenomenon occur to excess, organizations should made sure that performance is highly contingent on individual effort. If employees perceive that performance is largely independent of effort or largely a function of other variables, they will not see penalties for poor performance as effective in stimulating high effort and will not judge those penalties to be fairly administered.

Penalties only help motivation if they are instituted when low or incorrectly directed effort is exerted. Penalties, like rewards, are generally not experienced directly for effort but rather are determined by performance. This means that the effort and performance must be highly correlated in order for penalty for poor performance to stimulate effort.

This brings up an interesting issue. Perhaps rewards and penalties should be, wherever feasible, tied directly to effort instead of to the intermediate variable, performance. This would be good for motivation. The problems are measuring real effort and being able to reward if performance is not high even though the effort is. Can the company afford to reward for high effort even if performance is not high? Also, does it make sense to penalize if effort is low but performance is not? In most cases it probably makes more sense to tie rewards and penalties to performance and to assure in designing the work that performance is highly dependent on effort.

5

Principle 4: Employees Will Be Motivated When They Perceive Little "Pull" from Alternative Goal Systems

Employees must sense that goal systems in which they might participate, other than the priority work assignment goal system, hold little promise for providing much satisfaction (or for minimizing dissatisfaction) at significant effort levels in those systems. If a large portion of an employee's limited effort capacity is to be allocated to priority work assignments, other goal systems must not siphon off significant amounts of effort. One must not be drawn in too many directions to get the job done. There is only so much effort to go around!

The issue discussed in this chapter is one of direction, or the distribution, of motivation. Motivation is a vector quantity having both magnitude and direction. Motivation problems of direction are perhaps more widespread in practice than problems of effort magnitude. The real motivation problem is often one of effort distribution—not one of eliciting high effort from the employee but rather one of allocating the effort elicited. Workers frequently exert high aggregate effort but not all in a highly relevant direction. They tend to divert much of their energy from priority tasks because of strong incentive to do so. Much of this effort is organizationally irrelevant or even antirelevant.

The reader should appreciate that the discussion in this chapter is, conceptually, an alternative to discussion of the same material as an opportunity cost experienced in the on-the-job goal system. That is, one reason workers do not exert higher on-the-job effort is because to do so they must give up something. That something is the satisfaction gained (or dissatisfaction avoided) by participating in alternative goal systems.

Total effort exerted in some goal system equals effort per time period multiplied by the number of time periods spent striving for the goal. Job motivation can be increased by getting the worker to exert less time pursuing alternative systems and by getting the worker to exert less energy per time period in those systems. The prescriptions in this chapter emphasize enticing workers to spend less time in alternative systems, and to spend less effort per time period in those systems, by getting them to see that they will increase their overall satisfaction by so doing.

PROPOSITION 4:1: EMPLOYEES MUST PERCEIVE THAT NONCOMPATIBLE, AWAY-FROM-WORK PURSUITS ARE NOT TOO ATTRACTIVE.

To sense little pull away from the job, away-from-work goal systems must not be too enticing at relatively high effort levels in those systems. The less enticing the away-from-work systems such as family, clubs, and hobbies, the higher on-the-job motivation will likely be. More of one's limited effort capacity tends to become available for allocating to the job.

If away-from-work pursuits aid job accomplishment, however, such pursuits are deemed compatible and may not significantly detract from, but rather add to, job accomplishment. It is the noncompatible, away-from-work goal systems that cause the more serious effort direction problems.

The following are ways to minimize the employee's away-from-work, noncompatible effort expenditure.

1. Persuade employees to engage in compatible extracurricular pursuits.

You do not want employees spending effort in alternative goal systems instead of on the job. But it is going to happen, to a degree, because the job and its attendant satisfactions are not enough for most people. It is possible, however, for off-the-job activity to complement job activity. Effort is put into an alternative system, but the kind of activity engaged in is related to job activity. It may be that the off-the-job activity involves skills similar to those required by certain on-the-job functions, or it may be that the off-the-job tasks actually aid on-the-job task accomplishment or substitute for it. If you can persuade employees to participate in such compatible off-the-job activities, the effort exerted on those activities is not lost. It contributes to on-the-job accomplishment.

One example is the case of an employee who is the head of public relations for a firm. He or she may choose to spend considerable time working for the local Chamber of Commerce, but much of the activity for the Chamber helps with fulfilling on-the-job responsibilities. Developing lists of names for mailings or getting acquainted with other business leaders, for example, are worthwhile pursuits for the Chamber and valuable pursuits for the head of public relations in the firm. There is great compatibility here.

Another example is the case of a company marketing researcher who spends time with the local PTA developing forecasts on student enrollment. Student enrollment forecasts come from the same kind of demographic data that marketing research work inthe company uses. In such a situation, the off-the-job effort aids on-the-job performance. Even though the effort is directed to an outside pursuit, it is a company-contributing effort. Management should try to guide employees into such compatible pursuits by showing them the advantages of these (compatible) systems over other alternative systems they might choose.

2. Avoid hiring individuals with excessively time-consuming hobbies and leisure-time interests.

If workers find certain hobbies and leisure activities as highly satisfying, you are likely to witness an inordinate amount of attention, concentration, effort, and time directed to those activities. To a certain extent time spent on hobbies and leisure interests is okay. Such involvement can serve to relax one, to reduce stress, and to generally rejuvenate the worker. And if the hobbies and leisure activities are related to job activities, effort spent on them complements on-the-job work. But intense interest in off-the-job pursuits of this kind can siphon valuable energy away from the job.

It is wise to check carefully into hobbies and leisure activities before an employment commitment is made to the worker. Ask about hobbies and off-work activities. How many different interests are there? How frequently does the employee like to engage in pursuing these interests? How strong are these interests? How long-lasting, or enduring, are these interests? How could these interests interfere with job performance? How could these interests help job performance?

You do not want workers who will spend a significant portion of their workday dreaming about these off-the-job interests. Neither do you want to hire someone who will leave work early or avoid essential overtime in order to pursue such extracurricular interests. Companies too often neglect to check candidate interests in alternative goal systems assuming that if abilities and skills match job requirements and if the candidate likes the kind of work demanded by the job, all is well. But the attracting force of alternative systems must not be neglected in employee selection decisions.

3. Establish an adequate, absolute level of rewards to minimize moonlighting.

The effort–net return model of motivation shows how the absolute level of rewards has little to do with motivation. For motivation it is the degree of contingency in the reward structure that pushes motivation to a high level (see Figure 12). Moving the reward curve R up to R′ means an increase in reward magnitude and an increase in satisfaction, but no change in motivation. Effort expended stays at X_1. On the other hand, altering the slope—the degree of contingency in the reward function instead of the level of the reward function, that is, going from R to R″—does increase motivation. Effort expended goes to X_2.

Figure 12
Degree of Contingency vs. Absolute Level

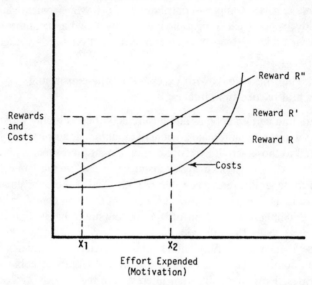

But the absolute level of rewards does affect motivation in one way. The higher the absolute level, the more satisfaction achieved on the job and the less likely the employee will be required to go outside for satisfaction. For example, if the employee's wage in the company is high enough, even though it is not contingent on effort, it can prevent one from searching out and participating in other systems to earn income. Moonlighting will be diminished. Diminished moonlighting, other factors being equal, means more effort available for on-the-job application. The level of the organization's rewards affects perception of the value of off-the-job rewards! Also, if employees earn enough on the job, they can pay others to take care of potentially demanding off-the-job pursuits. This frees up effort for the job.

4. Provide employees with help dealing with family problems.

Much employee effort is siphoned away from the job by family problems which the worker must attend to. Often persons become so consumed with family problems that the greater part of their daily attention is focused on the family, not work. Workers can be left alone to muddle through these problems, or the organization can act to provide help, advice, or counsel to permit workers to resolve the problems rapidly and thus have more time and energy for application to the job.

Organizations might, for example, provide day-care centers to help resolve problems of finding child sitters, of paying for child sitters, or of transporting their children or sitters to one place or another for a day's care. Organizations might make company lawyers available to help employees with legal problems, to help them avoid long hours locating and working with lawyers. The company's legal personnel might be used to counsel workers thinking of divorce, to help employees draw up wills, and to represent employees with insurance claims, for example. Such benefits help prevent the employee from expending high energies on these matters and thus reserve more energy for the job.

Additionally, the company's resident psychologist may provide various forms of social or psychological counseling for employees and their family members. The company doctor can do medical check-ups and advise all family members on health issues. Such benefits relieve away-from-work burdens on workers and allow them to direct more effort to the job.

5. Discourage excessive involvement in non–work-related clubs and associations.

Clubs and associations take a lot of time and energy if you are to be a worthy member. Employees often seek membership and participation in too many of them. They usually do this because the job situation is not fulfilling enough. On many jobs, no matter how hard you work, you receive little recognition. You are not promoted, your salary does not change, and nobody really expresses appreciation for the work you do. By joining clubs and associations, you may be able to pursue some worthwhile community causes and to derive some satisfactions just not provided on the job. Persons can make a name for themselves, as exemplary club or association participants. They can establish webs of friendships that strict adherence only to the job role does not permit.

But these off-the-job sources of satisfaction can become so much a part of one's life that achieving success in the club or association becomes more than a sideline. It becomes central to one's life—even an obsession. When this happens, you have "lost" the employee. He or she will spend at-work time using the company photocopier to duplicate literature for the club, phoning people in the community about club matters, and sitting at the desk working on club matters instead of tending to company business.

Management must keep aware of this extracurricular involvement and not let it get out of hand. Periodic counseling sessions may be required to bring pressure to bear on employees who get carried away. It may even be in the interest of the company to establish policies on how much of such extracurricular involvement of this type is appropriate.

6. Put constraints on employees' free time.

On-the-job free time can be valuable time to allow the employee to relax, rest, and rejuvenate. But excessive free time will often not stay free for long. Employees do not stay idle. They will find things to do during free time. The organization, or course, would prefer that employees use their free time to find other ways to positively contribute to the organization. Some employee free time may, in fact, wind up being used this way. But the general tendency is for free time to be converted to time used for pursuit of satisfying self-interests which are more often than not, not highly job relevant.

Free time may be used to pursue pet away-from-work community projects, or to develop hobbies and personal business interests. It may be used to expand one's social contacts. It may be used to get involved in local politics. There is no limit to the kind of away-from-work involvement free time may lead to. Left unchecked, free time pursuits soon begin to expand to the point where maintenance of these pursuits draws excessive amounts of effort away from the job. These free-time pursuits compete with on-the-job task pursuits.

The key here is to constrain the availability of free time by building jobs that keep the employee busy with highly relevant organizational interests. If one's job is so loose as to allow for wandering, one can become lost and misdirected. One practical way to fill free time is to keep an inventory of work projects for employees. This inventory serves as a reservoir of work to be drawn on during slack periods. It prevents the worker from wondering what to do next.

7. Provide employees with advice and help on financial matters, educational concerns, vacation plans, and the like.

It was mentioned earlier how the organization can help employees avoid spending high effort on various types of problems related to their families and life off the job. But discussion there was far from exhaustive. Sometimes employee attention to the job—concentration on work—is rocked by demanding matters such as personal financial crises (large stock market losses, real estate losses). Providing help to employees through trained in-house financial experts can mean relief for the employee. Perhaps the employee's job focus will not be lost if these in-house experts take the initiative to help the employee quickly put these problems behind. When employees know that somebody else will worry about these matters for them, it frees up effort for expenditure at work.

Similarly, in-house aid can be provided employees trying to plan vacations. Sometimes employees put so much time and energy into planning vacations— into what they will do, where, when, and how—that they are not only drawn away from their jobs during the process but are totally consumed during the vacation in managing the execution of their plans. The value of the vacation as a relaxant or a stress-reducing vehicle is lost. Large companies may be able to provide expertise to help employees plan vacations—to suggest places to go that will provide the needed rest, to plan flights, to buy tickets, to get road maps, and obtain travelers checks. In-house benefits of this type can be more comprehensive than what travel agents can provide.

Help with planning educational pursuits can also come from in-house sources. Employees can often use help in evaluating different schools and in determining how to integrate education with work. The point is that if the company can, at reasonable cost, provide efficient, quality help, the employee will have more time and energy to channel into the job.

I recognize that providing employees with such extensive help benefits can be extremely expensive. But limited advice and counsel is probably quite feasible for most prosperous middle-size and large companies. And limited help may be all that is necessary to significantly reduce employee effort directed to these matters. It may take very little time from a knowledgeable expert to provide considerable help and to, thereby, facilitate considerable reduction in required off-the-job goal system time for the employee. What we have discussed here, and in the earlier section on help with family problems, just scratches the surface in terms of the kinds of in-house benefits that may motivate workers by helping prevent excessive off-the-job effort expenditure.

8. Try to make rewards in external systems less contingent on effort.

As was discussed in Chapter 3, to motivate employees with company rewards, those rewards must be dependent on employee effort expenditure. When the employee exerts more effort, this should lead to greater performance which should, in turn, lead to greater reward. If, however, you want only to provide the worker with on-the-job satisfaction—forgetting the motivation—it is only necessary to provide rewards that are sufficiently valued. They do not have to be tied to performance to satisfy.

To decrease effort expended in off-the-job goal systems, management can operate on off-the-job goal system reward structures in just the opposite way that on-the-job reward structures work. By making off-the-job goal system rewards less contingent on effort spent in those systems, more effort is freed for application to the job. Satisfaction in the off-the-job goal system can be maintained by "horizontalizing" the reward functions experienced in those off-the-job systems. Employees then see that less effort in those systems will yield as much or more satisfaction than high effort.

It is not easy for management to influence off-the-job reward structures because management typically does not have authority in those systems. A high degree of control is just not possible. But taking the time to persuade the leaders of off-the-job systems to make the rewards less contingent can pay off. At other times managers, themselves, may get involved in off-the-job systems so that they will have opportunity to directly influence the rewards in those systems.

9. Try to relax penalty structures in external systems.

On-the-job penalty structures tend to convince workers that higher effort is in their best interest. Low effort means less satisfaction because the penalties encountered at low effort are costs which detract from any rewards causing the net satisfaction experienced to be less.

The reverse is what you want to strive for with respect to off-the-job goal systems. You do not want high penalties to be experienced by the employee in response to low effort in off-the-job systems. You want low effort to be perfectly acceptable. You want the employees to feel as good about low effort exerted in off-the-job systems as they do about high effort. Actually you want the employee to be more satisfied with low effort so a large portion of one's effort potential will be freed for application to the job.

Again, it is difficult for the manager to do much about penalties in off-the-job systems. But, as with rewards, a manager may be able to orally persuade leaders of outside systems to relax penalty structures. Or if managers can, themselves, become influential members of outside systems, they can perhaps get the authorities in those systems to remove or make less potent the penalty structures in those systems. You may say this is sabotage—that managers are hurting the outside system to benefit their company. And you may be right! The ethics of such approaches are indeed questionable.

10. Help workers locate within a reasonable commuting distance of their place of work.

Effort equals energy per time period multiplied by the number of time periods spent exerting energy. Effort on the job is more likely to be low if employee time spent on the job is low. When employees live long distances from work, the likelihood of time being taken away from the job for commutes is higher than when employees live close by. Traffic problems can cause one to be late to work as well to leave work early to avoid traffic on the way home. Automobile breakdowns and accidents can cause workers to be late, not to show for work at all, or to spend a portion of their day getting their vehicles repaired. Bad weather can cause the long-distance commuter to give up altogether and not to bother coming in. In fact, the long-distance commute magnifies the effects of any at-home problems and often puts just enough extra pressure on the worker to cause absenteeism when such would not occur if the worker were located closer.

Not only can the long distance take time away from work, but after you have traveled through hectic traffic for fifty miles or so, your energy can be sapped. There is little left for intense application at work.

Companies must strive to find living accommodations for employees close by. This solves the commuting problem plus makes employees available for extra duty when they are needed. Living close by may also result in workers' more readily volunteering for extra assignments because they do not see these assignments as interfering with travel to and from their residences.

11. Hire workers with good health and help them maintain good health.

How good health can reduce stress experienced on the job was discussed in Chapter 4. But good health contrbutes to motivation in other ways. Workers with good health will find fewer excuses to stay home. They will call in sick less frequently, will leave work less often because of ill health, and will be absent for doctor and dentist appointments less often. In short, they will have more effort for application to the job.

There are so many powerful reasons for assuring your work force has good health. It is paramount to screen candidates for employment to determine their states of health. Even though workers may not be employed in physically demanding jobs, they must have quality health if the organization is to reap maximum effort from them. Too few companies look at the full spectrum of candidates' physical and emotional health. And because of this, they get stuck with employees whose performance is deficient.

Once employees are hired, organizations must give attention to helping those people maintain—indeed, improve—their health. Providing information on how to maintain good health, providing state-of-health monitoring services, providing good foods for workers while they work, providing in-house exercise opportunities, designing work task structures that allow for physical movement, designing work responsibilities that do not "wreck" one's emotional profile, and providing quality, safe, and pleasant work environments are all practical ways for enhancing health.

12. Encourage others to influence employees away from heavy extracurricular involvement.

It is frequently impossible, or inappropriate, to carry direct persuasion to a high level. But you may be able to convince employees to avoid high extracurricular involvement by indirect means. You may not be able to influence the employee directly yourself, but perhaps you can influence others to, in turn, influence the employee to cut back effort expended in outside systems. And we are not talking here about others who lead or manage in those outside systems in which the employee participates. This was covered in an earlier discussion.

You can talk to any other people the employee happens to listen to or respect. Perhaps you can ask the employee's medical doctor to advise the employee to reduce outside involvement. Perhaps you can discuss the case of heavy outside involvement with the employee's spouse. Spouses can often be highly influential in engineering effort redistribution for their mates. Perhaps you can work through one of the worker's peers. Convince this peer to wield a little pressure on the worker. It may be quite possible to talk to neighbors of the employee and have them confront the employee with proposals for reduction of extracurricular involvement. The point is that using a barrage of indirect social power linkages can aid the influencing task immeasurably. Multiple others may be far more powerful than you alone in persuading the employee.

13. Hire new employees who are free from alcohol or drug dependency, and help present employees avoid such dependency.

Drug dependency lures the worker's attention, concentration, interest, time, and effort away from the job. Instead of focusing on tasks, workers fantasize about the highs they will experience after work when partaking of drugs or alcohol. Instead of staying at work until 5:00, the worker may slip out early to get that hit as early as possible. Instead of exerting sustained mental and physical effort over an extended period of time, the worker cops out. The employee tends to experience greater stress with high effort, when on chemicals, and constantly searches for (and often finds) opportunities to avoid work altogether—opportunity for pursuing the habit.

Employees who are chemically dependent diminish on-the-job effort and, indeed, effort capacity by overindulgence off the job. They come to work without the desire to perform and without the ability to perform. Their off-the-job habit literally destroys on-the-job effort and performance.

Companies must carefully screen employees for chemical dependency and avoid offering jobs to those who inappropriately indulge. Companies would also do well to invest in programs designed to keep employees from becoming chemically involved and to help employees on drugs and alcohol escape from that dependency. Investment in these programs pays off. Companies need to employ whole workers with their full potentials being utilized. Chemical dependency diverts too large a portion of one's efforts to nonjob issues.

14. Influence employee perception of the value of rewards received in alternative systems.

To enhance on-the-job motivation management can, as discussed in Chapter 3, act to boost employee perception of the value of rewards received from the company. By reversing this strategy as applied to off-the-job systems, on-the-job motivation can be further enhanced. If employees place less value on off-the-job rewards, they will be less strongly drawn to the systems providing those rewards.

Managers can sometimes alter employee attitudes and beliefs about certain rewards experienced in off-the-job systems. Again, there is an ethical issue here. Just how far should management go in manipulating people's values? Is this not tantamount to brainwashing! Or is it? Whoever you are, wherever you are, and wherever you live, others are always trying to influence your values. So should management be barred from doing so?

Consider the case of an employee who is heavily involved in an outside group bent on preventing a highway from being constructed through a beautiful wilderness area. The employee's efforts to thwart construction are tireless. He or she expects to reap the rewards of accomplishment by preventing construction of the highway and a dismantling of the wilderness area. What management might do here is attempt to convince the worker that less wilderness—converting wilderness to economic growth land—is in the best interest of most of the people in the state. Management may be able to get the employee to see wilderness preservation as a less worthy outcome. People put less effort into striving for outcomes of perceived lower worth.

15. Avoid hiring employees with an excessive penchant for community volunteerism.

Some folks seem to volunteer their lives away. They enjoy helping others and providing services for the betterment of the general community free of charge. This is admirable, and most people who volunteer do so for very worthy causes reaping true personal satisfaction and a sense of worthwhileness from their efforts. If it were not for volunteerism, where would our democratic society be?

But employees who labor to fulfill those off-the-job voluntary pursuits, which become obligations as soon as you have committed, are not laboring as much as they could for the company. Volunteerism can be seen as justifying detachment from the company—a legitimate reason for neglecting work at the shop. Often community volunteers expect their company to give them time off to fulfill their voluntary obligations. They even see cheating on the company as ethically proper because of the good cause they serve.

This attitude toward volunteerism must not be allowed to get out of control. The company has its own business to conduct and needs employees directed toward company goals. Though it may be difficult to keep track of employee involvement in off-the-job voluntary pursuits, it can be done. An organization might, for example, ask employees to update their personnel files every six months with information on their voluntary associations.

16. Hire employees with self-interests intensely compatible with organizational interests.

To avoid having workers vigorously seek satisfaction from participation in away-from-work systems, the organization should carefully consider the self-interests of candidates being evaluated for jobs. These self-interests should be compared with the organization's interests. What you want is a candidate whose self-interests are congruent with organizational interests. An employee whose interests do not align well with the organization's will seek to pursue interests which are not of great benefit to the organization.

It is sometimes said that organizations like to hire people who are well rounded—people who have a variety of skills and abilities and a variety of outside interests. But the wisdom of such an approach to hiring is suspect. Unless a well-rounded person is what the job requires, such a person is likely not to find sufficient opportunity at work to achieve personal satisfaction. The person who will work out best on the job is the person who has personal interests that can be fulfilled simultaneously with fulfilling organizational interests. If the person has too many other interests not capable of being fulfilled by employment, expect that person to pursue satisfaction in away-from-work systems.

It may well be that the best employees are those who live and breathe for the company—the type that gets the great majority of their "kicks" out of their work. They are the type who care about little else in life other than achieving success through employment. For example, the person whose personal ambition is only to become a great lecturer and who likes nothing better than speaking to an audience has self-interests well matched to that professional teaching position open at the local university. The physical scientist who developed a keen interest in laser research in college would be well suited for a job in basic, high energy research in the National Aeronautics and Space Administration. The person whose greatest personal interest is in travel may be well suited to long-haul trucking. If personal interests are not compatible with job demands, those interests will be pursued away from work, and the effort associated with that pursuit is effort lost by the organization.

17. Support socioeconomic and political stabilization policies.

Unstable social, political, and economic environments cause employees to turn attention away from their jobs. They see such environments as extremely critical matters that must be addressed if the general welfare is to be maintained.

Without stable socioeconomic and political systems in place, workers sense a lack of security—job security, financial security, family security, even personal health security. The need for security is a strong need in most people. People will seek to fulfill this need by varied means. Supporting stabilization policies whether by participation in community economic development programs, participation in local government, or campaigning for political candidates who support stabilization can take a considerable amount of one's time and energy. If the company, as an entity, engages in stabilization support activity, it can relieve individual workers from having to find a great deal of time and energy to participate on their own.

Environmental stabilization means security, and security means lack of worry. Lack of worry means more attention to, and more concentration on, job matters. Instead of workers' minds being occupied with the environmental risks that exist for them and their families, and how they are going to minimize these risks, workers can focus on their jobs. Instead of giving constant attention to such matters as hunting for new jobs (because old ones are being closed out), moving residence, changing investment portfolios (because of economic climate change), and the like, employees can attend to matters of employment and give more of their efforts to the company. In countries that experience relatively great social, political, and economic upheaval, the phenomenon is abundantly evident. Workers do not function very well for their companies because of larger social, political, and economic issues siphoning off their energies.

18. Avoid hiring workers with excessive interest in community politics.

Some have suggested that politics is a disease not unlike alcoholism, obsessive gambling, or addiction to drugs. Once you catch the political bug, it is like a virus; you cannot do much to make it go away. It may be latent for a while, but it breaks out when given a chance.

People who enjoy politics may well be valuable contributors to the community. Someone has to participate in our democratic society to make it run. Someone has to govern. Someone has to address and resolve the larger community and intercommunity problems—the problems of life beyond corporate walls. But organizations have to be careful not to load up with a bundle of local politicians. The demands of political life are enormous—almost without bounds. There is always more, much more, you can do in politics. You can always spend another day on the campaign trail. You can always spend another day preparing arguments for debate within local government chambers. You can always spend another day marketing your proposals for change or defending yourself against critics from the political opposition. Political activity can be so consuming that you have little energy and desire left for focus on the job.

Organizations are to be commended for having employees who are willing and able to contribute to the community and for not putting up large barriers against such contributions. But we are talking excesses here. Some employees simply use their employing organizations as forums around which to build and launch politically active lives. Employment success is quite secondary to political achievement. It is this type of candidate that organizations will usually want to screen out in employee selection processes.

19. Encourage workers to reduce the number of outside goal systems in which they participate.

You can help employees, themselves, take a look at what they are doing on the outside. Get them to look at the kinds of outside activities they are involved with. Get them to reflect on the number of outside activities they spend time pursuing. Ask them if they are happy with how they are spending their energies. Help them see what is going on. And help them manage their time.

To help employees manage their time relative to outside systems, you may want to get into discussions with employees about how important various outside engagements are to them, why certain engagements are more important than others, and about how they can more efficiently contribute to outside groups that demand their time. You may get employees to see, for themselves, how they are spreading themselves too thin. They may see the really important things in life are not getting the attention deserved.

You might ask employees to itemize and prioritize all the effort-using engagements that they participate in (and hope their jobs will be near the top of their lists!). Once this is done, get them to critically evaluate how they are distributing their time and energy among these goal systems. Having done this, ask them if they would not be more productive and more satisfied by dropping some of the low priority goal systems and redistributing their efforts across the remaining high priority goal systems. When you focus on these matters in direct face-to-face discussion with employees, they can often see, themselves, that a redistribution of effort would be in their best interests. Just getting employees to cut back the number of outside involvements will mean that the company will pick up additional effort released from these involvements.

20. Take any action that will ease the amount of time and effort one must spend off the job.

Mentioned earlier were various types of help employers can give employees. Help in dealing with family problems, financial matters, educational issues, and so forth, can allow workers to find more effort available to direct toward their work. The list of the kinds of help that might be provided is almost endless.

In addition to the major categories of help discussed earlier, organizations can do such things as provide transportation for employees' children. A worker may need to have children picked up from school and delivered to a sitter's home. Instead of the worker stepping out to do the delivery, or spending time each week finding transportation, the company might provide such service.

Another kind of aid organizations can give to employees is instruction in how to do around-the-house projects—for example, how to fix dripping faucets, repair the lawn mower, or fertilize the garden. When employees know how to do these things properly, they waste less energy on them, spend less time on them, and experience fewer frustrations.

Also, organizations can help workers by employing such tactics as giving out tools, equipment, and appliances, which serve as labor-saving devices around the home. Instead of giving out arbitrary prizes for service or good performance, truly useful prizes can be awarded that will help the employee reduce away-from-work effort. In order for workers to arrive at work, ready to go, on snowy mornings, it would be desirable for them to have snow blowers to remove snow from their yards instead of having to shovel it. Instead of giving out a canoe, or whatever, which will simply add to effort exerted elsewhere, arrange a prize that will help employees reduce effort exerted elsewhere.

21. Change the employee's job to better match extracurricular involvement.

If you cannot influence one's away-from-work effort pattern to allow for more effort devoted to work, or if you cannot influence workers to engage in away-from-work pursuits that are more compatible with job demands, you can alter one's work to be more compatible with away-from-work pursuits. This achieves the same effect. Of course such a strategy is not always practical, and obviously you cannot design jobs around workers' outside interests and expect the company to reach its objectives and be profitable. But this avenue can usually be pursued to a limited degree. Certain parts of one's job may be reshaped to achieve compatibility with away-from-work pursuits and thus to allow for the company to benefit from those away-from work pursuits instead of being penalized by them.

If workers, for example, spend considerable away-from-work time volunteering to help with raising funds for their church, it may be worthwhile to get these employees involved with company fund-raising projects. The expertise gained would be transferable, and certainly much of the effort those employees spend for the church would contribute to their on-the-job fund-raising performance.

If an employee has a hobby working as an around-the-house carpenter, the organization might make use of the talent and effort that goes into the hobby by altering the employee's job to include carpentry work. If one spends time writing, editing, and publishing manuscripts in a monthly magazine of an association to which the employee belongs, it might make good sense to have this person work in the company on writing, editing, and publishing duties. Rather than have away-from-work pursuits drain energy in unconstructive ways (from the company's point of view), adapt the job so that that energy will benefit the company. Organizations typically do far too little of this.

22. Provide organization-sponsored events that substitute for outside engagements.

Employees are going to socialize, recreate, and find ways to serve their communities no matter what the organization does to encourage cutbacks in non–job-relevant activity. And they should. But it may make sense for the company to become involved in planning or providing some of these away-from-work pursuits so that employee involvement can be better controlled. The organization may be able, for example, to provide a variety of social functions for its employees. Employees who receive plenty of social need satisfaction from these functions may decide not to develop extensive, additional social outlets away from work. The organization may also be able to provide opportunities for employees to engage in such recreational activities as after-work softball, company fishing trips, or touring the local museums. Such recreational opportunities may be enough for the worker. The organization may also sponsor community service projects in which its employees can participate. Such projects may fulfill worker needs in this area so that they do not care to join other community service organizations.

When the organization is involved, as discussed here, it obtains a measure of control over the worker's degree and distribution of effort expenditure. The organization can better monitor total employee effort expenditure and adjust extracurricular opportunities as appropriate and as job demands change, requiring different amounts of effort. With control of extracurricular event timing and duration, the organization can limit effort expended on these events when necessary and expand effort expended on the events when possible. The organization gains a measure of influence over how the employee's effort will be used.

23. Do not allow job responsibilities to become too nebulous or uncertain.

This becomes a serious problem with many managerial and professional jobs where exact duties are not clearly specified. Properly written job descriptions can help prevent jobs from being unclear and uncertain in content, but too often such are not prepared because of lack of expertise in the company as to how to prepare them. With unclear and uncertain task dimensions, measurement of whether or not employees are engaging in what they are supposed to is next to impossible. So also is determination of whether or not employees are performing well.

Under conditions of ambiguity and uncertainty, workers will find great opportunity to pursue self-interests. Just as excessive free time allows for self-interest pursuit and likely eventual conflict with formal task demands, so does ambiguity and uncertainty lead to self-interest pursuit. With nebulous and uncertain jobs, employees can do about what they want, within limits of course, and nobody will know whether it is appropriate activity or not. Employees can direct attention to away-from-work activities—plan them, prepare for them, and so on. Employees can actually leave work to spend time with outside interests, and no one may sense what is happening. The lack of control management has over ill-defined jobs makes it easy for employees to devote effort away from the job.

There can be no excuse for not defining jobs with enough precision to isolate what tasks workers should be spending their time on and how long they should be spending on each of those tasks. The argument that you cannot define some jobs—the chief executive's, for example—is absolutely absurd.

24. Locate your business where opportunities to engage in attractive outside goal systems are minimal.

Employees will be forced to become absorbed in their work if there are no other places to exert effort. Of course you cannot and should not eliminate all nonjob outlets for effort, but you may be able to minimize the potential pull from outside goal systems by locating your company's work facilities in geographical areas and communities that possess a minimum of opportunities for extracurricular burdens to develop. This is contrary to the conventional wisdom which tells us to locate facilities in attractive areas. But, of course, the reason for locating in attractive areas is to make it easier for the company to attract and retain a qualified work force. From an on-the-job motivation perspective. however, it may make more sense to isolate the company—to locate it away from social and recreational opportunities or away from opportunities to participate in community affairs, for example.

Employees may exert effort on the job short of the effort level required to maximize satisfaction with respect to the job. (Refer to Figure 2 in Chapter 1.) This can happen when considerable effort is spent reaping satisfaction in other systems. If those other systems are taken away, employees may well redirect efforts previously exerted in those other systems to the job—at least up to the point at which maximum on-the-job satisfaction is realized. If employees do not do this, they have to invent other avenues for expenditure of the effort surplus which results. This may happen, and it depends on many factors.

One closing note: Keep in mind when reading here that removing alternative goal systems as well as changing the rewards and costs one experiences in these alternative systems will likely influence employee perception of on-the-job reward-cost structures. For example, eliminating an away-from-work pursuit that provides periodic recognition with plaques to hang on the wall may make the plaques offered by the organization more valuable to the employee. They are scarcer. This certainly complicates things but does help emphasize the overriding principle that away-from-work systems affect motivation in the at-work system.

PROPOSITION 4.2: EMPLOYEES MUST PERCEIVE THAT AT-WORK, NONJOB, SEMI-WORK, ANTIWORK, AND LOW PRIORITY TASK ACTIVITIES ARE NOT TOO ATTRACTIVE.

To sense little pull away from priority work, at-work alternative goal systems must not be too enticing at relatively high effort levels in those systems. The less enticing the at-work goal systems are, other than the priority work system, the more effort the employee will likely wish to allocate to priority work.

At-work, nonjob pursuits are largely self-interest pursuits. Semi-work pursuits are not task assignments, but rather are engagements which may peripherally benefit task accomplishment, such as on-the-job socializing and interstation travel. Antiwork pursuits are activities such as contributing to work slowdowns and stoppages, or activities which involve developing and exercising countervailing social power. Low priority tasks are those that are the least important tasks in the employee's task repertoire. All of these activities can represent a formidable draw on one's time and energy if control of them is lacking.

The following are ways to minimize the employee's at-work, nonjob, semi-work, antiwork, and low priority task effort expenditure.

1. Prevent work goals, and the number of different tasks assigned the employee, from mushrooming.

Remember one's effort allocation to the job is a function of the other things one allocates effort to. Likewise, within the job, one's effort allocation to a given task is a function of the effort one must allocate to other tasks. One's motivation per task can be low if too many different tasks are built into the job.

In designing jobs we have to be careful not to indiscriminately tack on tasks as the worker grows or as the company sees a need to get more done per worker. The focus of the job must not be lost. Keeping clearly in mind the overall purpose or function of the job is essential to ensure effort allocation in the right direction.

What often happens on jobs is that the job content is expanded over time. With this comes a redistributing of employee effort to a number of relatively low priority tasks. As the job keeps mushrooming, intense effort on priority, main functions is lost. The distribution of effort becomes less than optimal. The worker's motivation is drained by low priority work and the immense amount of time that must be spent on task transitioning—moving from one task to another— starting up and shutting down each different task assignment.

Management must not allow jobs to evolve to the point where the internal structure of the job requires an effort distribution that does not maximize aggregate performance. Too much to do or too great a variety of duties can result in as severe a problem as too little to do because of flaws it creates in effort distribution.

2. Avoid attaching rewards of too high value to low priority work.

A major part of the problem of employee motivation lies with the way effort is allocated within the job. Forget about away-from-work pulls and forget about how much total effort is exerted on the job, for the moment. Away-from-work pulls can be nonexistent, and the total effort spent on the job can be high, but there can still be a severe motivation problem because of flaws in the allocation of energy or the directionality of effort vectors within the job. Simply put, we do not want too much effort expended on low priority work and too little spent on high priority work.

To assure the best distribution of effort within the job, reward structures have to be built around individual duties. Rewards for effort given to high priority tasks should be more attractive than rewards for effort expended on low priority work, all other factors being equal. This means the rewards designed around high priority work should be the more valued rewards. If low priority work carries the most valued rewards, workers will naturally gravitate toward greater-than-appropriate effort expenditure on those tasks.

Management must be careful to strike the right balance in the distribution of rewards across different dimensions of the job because the nature of these rewards directly influences how effort will be allocated. I know a college professor who allocates 50 percent of his time to a job duty, writing and publication, that is the lowest priority job dimension. Teaching, advising, community service, and program development are all of higher priority. But the professor allocates half his time to writing and publishing because that is what he gets rewarded for—recognition and influence in the academic community.

3. Make reward structures for low priority work less contingent on performance.

If you get your rewards regardless of your effort, then you calculate that little effort is more in your self-interest than high effort. See Figure 13 for illustration. The reward curve you experience is horizontal—rewards are not contingent on effort. In such a situation, and being a satisfaction maximizer, you choose effort level X_1—a very low level of effort. Higher effort makes no sense because it only brings on more costs while rewards stay the same. This suggests that to get employees to expend more effort on high priority work and less on low priority work, low priority duties should have less contingent reward structures than high priority duties. The highly contingent rewards established for highly important duties will encourage high effort to be allocated to those duties. The noncontingent reward structures for the low priority work will discourage excessive effort allocation to those duties.

Adjusting the degree of contingency of different rewards applied to different duties is a major undertaking and will take considerable expertise if the company is going to do it right. But an attempt must be made in this direction. Rewards tied only to aggregate performance measures may achieve a total effort allocation of note, but do little for the internal distribution of effort.

Figure 13
Noncontingent Rewards

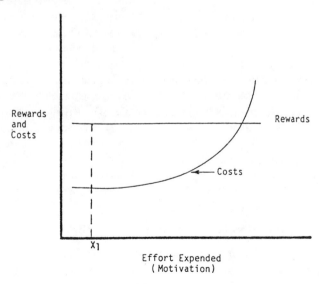

Figure 14
Motivation with Penalties

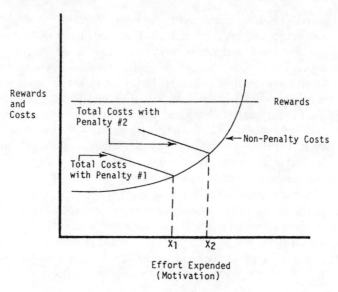

Rewards
and
Costs

Total Costs with
Penalty #2

Rewards

Non-Penalty Costs

Total Costs
with Penalty #1

X_1 X_2

Effort Expended
(Motivation)

4. Relax the penalty structures associated with low priority work.

As discussed in Chapter 4, introducing penalty functions for low effort/
performance can cause high effort to be selected as the most satisfying and,
therefore, the level of effort that will be pursued. As with reward structures,
however, penalty structures must not be designed only around aggregate
performance. If effort is to be properly distributed with sufficient focus on the
important work, penalties must be built around individual task dimensions.

To get employees to shift effort away from low priority tasks, penalty
structures for those tasks can be relaxed—that is, penalties can be instituted at a
relatively low level of effort devoted to those tasks. On the other hand, penalty
structures for high priority work can be intensified by having penalties kick in at
a relatively high level of effort (see Figure 14). The lower Total Costs with
Penalty #1 curve encourages lower effort—an amount X_1. The higher Total
Costs with Penalty #2 curve encourages higher effort—an amount X_2. Low
priority duties should have curves like #1 associated with them. High priority
duties should have cost curves relatively high in comparison, such as curve #2.

5. Focus training efforts on training for high priority work.

It was pointed out in chapters 2 and 3 that for workers to perceive a strong
correlation between effort and rewards, they must see a strong correlation

between performance and rewards coupled with a strong correlation between effort and performance. And for persons to see a strong effort-performance correlation, they must perceive that they have adequate ability to do the job. To convince workers they have adequate ability, it is logical to provide them with training. The better the training—the greater the amount and the higher the quality—the greater the perceived likelihood that effort will pay off in terms of higher performance. When workers see training as inadequate, they wonder why they should try hard. Accomplishment is not highly probable.

In light of the effect of training on motivation, it makes sense to focus training programs on developing skills for high priority work. We want to be sure workers see that high effort allocated to high priority work will pay off. Fewer of the firm's limited training dollars should be spent on training for low priority work. This, of course, makes good sense from a perspective which recognizes the direct effect of ability on employee-job performance. Here we see that it also makes good sense when considering the indirect effect of ability on employee-job performance. Assuring one has adequate ability for high performance on high priority work assures the worker will see a strong correlation between effort and performance on that high priority work. This will stimulate allocation of effort to the high priority work. When workers see they have relatively less ability for low priority assignments, this detracts from perception of a strong effort-performance correlation relative to those assignments and thus discourages high effort allocation to those assignments.

6. Focus job design improvement efforts on high priority work.

In Chapter 2 it was emphasized that workers are willing to exert effort if they see that the job design does not interfere with that effort resulting in performance. If the job is designed well, it will contribute to a high perceived effort-performance correlation.

But again we have to look at the parts of the job as well as the job as a whole. Total performance is optimized when effort is properly distributed across all tasks. We do not want to hinder motivation by having too much effort allocated to the wrong duties. By focusing job design improvement endeavors on high priority work, we allow workers to see a strong correlation between their effort and performance of that work and, therefore, stimulate high effort exertion relative to that work. By not investing in design improvement for low priority work, we tend to force the worker into seeing a weaker correlation between effort and performance relative to that low priority work and, therefore, stimulate a relatively low allocation of effort to that work.

As is the case with employee ability, job design is a direct determinant of employee job performance, and because of this, focusing design improvement efforts on high priority dimensions makes good sense. But here we are emphasizing again the effect of design improvement on motivation—in particular the distribution of motivation across all the dimensions of the job.

It is true that on more occasions than not, low priority tasks do get relatively little attention for design improvement, and this is generally good, but if low priority tasks are highly time-consuming, focusing design improvement efforts on those tasks makes a lot of sense if ways can be found to free up time which can then be reallocated to high priority work.

7. Focus performance review discussions and improvement efforts on high priority work.

Understanding and focusing on task priorities is crucial in motivation because it is these priorities that determine, to a great extent, how best limited effort should be distributed so as to maximize aggregate performance.

Nowhere can employees be better sensitized to issues of effort allocation than in the semi- or annual performance review. Managers must make clear to their subordinates what work is high priority and stress that any deficiencies relative to high priority work are the deficiencies that must be addressed and corrected. Discussions during and following these reviews should focus on diagnosing the sources of performance deficiency with respect to high priority work. Sure, low priority task deficiency has to be corrected too, but less emphasis need be placed here in helping assure limited effort is directed in the best possible way. If workers do not get around to correcting low priority task deficiencies, do not make a big deal out of it as long as high priority task deficiencies are remedied and you know the worker did not resolve the low priority deficiencies simply because of insufficient time.

Use rewards with respect to performance improvement efforts just as you use rewards for performance. When workers improve significantly on high priority task items, make sure they are recognized for it. Lessen the rewards for performance improvement on low priority task dimensions. Coaches of athletic teams do a commendable job here. At the annual players' banquet the coach will give awards to the outstanding performers and to the persons who have shown the greatest improvement. They have to be careful to assure the reward for improvement is given for improvement along priority task dimensions, though. This is a key. These systems have been known to break down when one is awarded for most improved player because of substantial improvement in ways that do not mean very much.

8. Write job descriptions that show duty priorities and expected duty time allocations.

Proper effort distribution is greatly facilitated with job descriptions which tell what that effort allocation should be like. If you want workers to avoid spending too much time on low priority items or to avoid spending large amounts of time on task items that should not require large amounts of time, then say so with a quality job description which shows the design of the work with respect to duty priorities and duty time requirements.

With proper job analysis techniques, organizations can break jobs down into numerous detailed and discrete statements of the work. Each task statement in the list can then have a number, perhaps on a one to ten scale, to indicate its relative importance. Also each task item can have a time percentage figure attached to it to indicate the relative amount of time the incumbent should spend on that item. Such descriptions add much to the value of the job description as a tool for properly preparing workers for their jobs. The job description, with such data incorporated, not only motivates workers by making clear what they are supposed to do but also motivates by aiding worker determination of how to direct effort across multiple task domains.

During performance evaluations, attention should be given to assessing how well one's efforts are aligned with planned priority and time distributions. More time spent on a low priority task than the planned time suggests something that should be carefully checked into. Less time spent on high priority items than the planned time may indicate some neglect of the high priority items. In any event, a job description with this data is a strong planning and control device for motivation.

9. Structure jobs to help prevent behavior from slipping to semi- or nonrelevancy.

Jobs have to be defined and structured. Without this, behavior quickly degenerates into behavior of questionable value or outright nonrelevancy. Employees select task pursuits that "chew-up" energy but that add little or nothing to real performance. Motivation is hurt because alternative, less relevant or irrelevant, systems are absorbing employee effort.

Structuring jobs means taking the time to plan and design them—to figure out what the employee should do, when, where, with what resources, and how. Failing to carefully structure a job means neglecting to plan one or more of these elements. Failing to thoroughly structure the job means you leave determination of one or more of these elements up to the worker. What happens when this is done? A risk that the employee will select directions in conflict with the organization develops. Employees will likely gravitate toward activity that is of self-interest but not necessarily of organizational interest. It is generally a good idea to allow employees to participate in job design but not to freely design their own jobs. Management guidance is critical to assure organizational relevancy.

In designing and structuring jobs, a tool of import is the job description. Managers and subordinates can both make good use of job descriptions which show, in writing, the details of the design of the work. The job description helps superiors and subordinates arrive at a meeting of the minds as to the areas of work activity the employee is supposed to engage in. It helps prevent job structure from arbitrarily evolving. It gives permanence and stability and helps assure that effort is properly directed across time.

10. Weight the criteria used to formally assess performance.

It was pointed out earlier that writing job descriptions and attaching numbers to the task statements in those descriptions, which show the relative importance of different tasks, is a useful way to assure proper motivation—that proper amounts of effort go to the priority tasks. Perhaps even more helpful for assuring that goal systems, alternative to the desired, do not pull too much effort is to develop performance evaluation instruments, for assessing employee performance, that display clear-cut performance criteria with attached weights. Weights on criteria show the relative importance of the individual criteria used in assessing overall performance. Weights show neither how much time should be spent nor, in absolute value terms, how important the various endeavors of the employee are, but they do show precisely how given measures of performance are being valued against other dimensions. They do show rather precisely what types of work outcomes the worker should focus on to assure the best overall performance as determined by the organization.

Well-developed evaluation instruments along with properly prepared job descriptions should be handed to new employees and fully discussed with new employees in job orientation programs. Periodically, at performance review times, the content of these instruments should be discussed along with the contents of job descriptions for the purpose of refocusing employee attention on performance expectations. Perhaps too often management does not appreciate the motivational power of these documents for defining both the direction and level of effort expenditures. Consequently, employees are not provided ready and frequent access to these documents. It is next to shameful when the organization gets out these documents only once a year for the employee to peek at during the annual review.

11. Prevent labor pool socializing abuses.

Labor pools have some great advantages over highly departmented labor systems. With a labor pool, many workers work as an organized unit to serve a variety of other workers or deparments. Instead of having a different worker in each different department, a group of workers serves all departments. With these pools, the organization can often process more work with a smaller total number of workers, can save on stocks of supplies and excessive duplication of equipment, can reduce labor training costs, can process large projects more quickly, and can continue processing priority work during times of employee absence.

Also, pools are good for helping satisfy employee social needs. People in the pool function as a team and usually are located in physical proximity to one another so that verbal exchange is frequent. But herein lies the dilemma. Pools can lead to excessive time and effort spent on socializing and on conversation of little relevance to the organization. Employees use the pool to develop and discuss personal issues and interests. Sometimes fun in the pool takes priority over getting the work done. Though this is generally not a large problem in most pooled situations, it must be reckoned with.

Social exchange can be very valuable to help ease tension, to help employees get to know one another better, and to help people better communicate. Pools can go far toward helping employees do their jobs better as they encourage helping, sharing, and learning from one another. But we are talking about excesses and abuses here. Frequently work focus can be lost in the pool in favor of a social focus. To avoid this takes quality leadership and management of the pool. Any pool should have a formally designated director whose job is to allow for the advantages of pools to be realized while simultaneously preventing the pool from degenerating into a social club. Perhaps the main thing a pool director can do is simply address socializing abuses as soon as they are detected by speaking to those involved about the problem and finding out why it is a problem.

12. Put constraints on break time amount, usage, and environment.

In Chapter 4 break time was mentioned as a vehicle for helping reduce the costs one perceives to be associated with high effort. Earlier in this chapter, idle time was discussed as a problem leading to energy expenditure on alternative, away-from-work goal systems. Here we are highlighting the problem of breaks contributing to at-work flaws in effort allocation.

Too much break time leads to employees' formulating self-interest pursuits and social contacts that can evolve into competition for the employee's efforts. For example, employees get into a discussion of baseball or local politics that they just cannot leave. Consequently, they are late in getting back to their jobs. Or employees get so relaxed during a break that they fall asleep and do not get back to the job on time. Sometimes employees get involved with eating, or reading the newspaper, and forget how long they have been on break. Thus the break time absorbs too great a portion of the employee's workday.

Sometimes break time, which is supposed to be taken for rest and personal rejuvenation, can lead to employee involvements that do just the opposite. I am familiar with a group of executives who use their lunch break to play basketball at a nearby gymnasium. The change of pace and the exercise are good for them, but the competitive atmosphere that exists during these games, and the intensity of effort exerted during these games, is so high that the executives are drained physically and emotionally when they finally return to work. More than one of these fellows has fallen asleep midway through the afternoon, and more than one of them has been unable to return to work the following day because of bruises and sprained ankles. Certainly break time used in this way is interfering with an optimal effort distribution on the job.

13. Control informal group formation and activity.

Informal employee groups will develop in any organization. Indeed, they must if the work is to get done. Everything cannot be planned in advance. Informal work groups emerge spontaneously to accomplish work that just would not be done if sole reliance was placed on formal work plans.

But informal groups other than informal work groups will spontaneously emerge within any organization. Informal employee interest groups, informal social groups, and informal power groups all develop to satisfy needs the employees have that are not ordinarily satisfied by the formal organization. These groups too can be of great benefit to the organization from the points of view of both management and subordinates. These groups cannot only satisfy basic human needs, but also can help communications and serve as a safety valve for employees venting frustrations and provide more coordinated and predictable employee behavior. It is the excesses that we are concerned about, however.

Employee memberhsip and participation in the informal group can become so important to employees that they direct too much of their limited efforts toward fulfilling informal group objectives instead of toward their formal work roles. For example, some employees become caught up in organizational politics and spend a great deal of their time in informal power groups attempting to wheel and deal throughout the organization to further their power ambitions. Another example is the case of employees who get so much recognition for demonstrating their knowledge in informal interest groups that they devote a great deal of time to these groups and thus neglect their formal roles. Through fuller structuring of jobs and better physical locationing of jobs, some control can be gained over the formation and functioning of these groups.

14. Be sure other workers have enough to do to prevent excessive on-the-job socializing.

Excessive free time, too much break time, and ill-defined jobs can all contribute to workers' directing their efforts away from priority job components. These activities not only contribute to misdirection of incumbents' efforts, they also result in effort distribution problems for other employees. If workers have idle time on their hands, they often use this time to interfere with other workers. Workers with idle time usually do not sit in their offices twiddling their thumbs. Instead, they get up and move. More often than not they go visit a fellow worker down the hall. Both visited worker and visitor become involved in social exchange which can either drag on until the idle worker decides he or she has used up enough idle time, or until the visited worker decides to refocus on the work. Usually it is the former case.

Workers with idle time have effort distribution problems, and they generate serious effort distribution problems for others as well. This is probably the greater of the two tragedies. Indeed, an idle worker can become a nemesis in many ways. He or she can invent all sorts of time-consuming, irrelevant engagements for other workers. This is what usually happens.

It is rare to find workers who are actually using idle time in a constructive, truly contributing fashion. Seldom do you find the idle worker visiting some other worker with an offer to help out in getting the other worker's work done. But management could help out here. It is in management's best interest to encourage sharing and helping behavior by educating workers not only about their own jobs, but also about the jobs of others so that they will feel as though they can contribute and that such contributions will be accepted by others. If more idle time were used in this way, real teamwork could evolve.

15. Allow employees to participate in developing their work goals.

Work goals do not have to be set entirely by management. Workers themselves will have valuable insights to bring to bear in establishing production quantity and quality goals as well as performance improvement goals. Indeed, workers themselves may well be able to provide constructive insight into job design change goals. Who knows best about the jobs than the workers?

Allowing or, better, encouraging workers to participate in formulating work-related goals helps assure that those goals are compatible or congruent with their talents and interests. Work goals that align well with personal goals are likely to draw the worker's efforts. When work goals are at odds with personal goals—when they conflict with personal goals—the worker's efforts tend to be drawn away from the work goals toward personal goals.

A good example of goal incongruence and how it might be resolved is the case of the new employee who is given a high priority task assignment which involves preparing a budget for his or her department. The employee's personal interest, however, is more oriented toward developing statistical analyses of actual revenue and expense deviations from past budgets. This statistical analysis may be important, but management may have assigned it to someone else who does not care to do it and would rather do the budget. By letting both employees take part in establishing their roles, work assignments may come out much better matched to individual interests. If such can be achieved, more effort is likely to be spent on official assignments. Motivation does not become misdirected toward personal interest pursuits.

16. Encourage workers to bring to your attention low-priority, nonjob, semi-work, or antiwork activity that begins to consume too much time and energy.

Low priority work, nonjob work, semi-work, and antiwork activities will consume large amounts of effort unless controls are implemented to prevent them from happening. Jobs change and the people occupying jobs change. With change, opportunity for greater states of disorder or entropy develop. Low priority work, nonjob activity, antiwork, and semi-work activity may well consume larger and larger amounts of energy when change becomes rapid. It is up to management to watch for this and to correct the problem as soon as it begins to emerge. Employees should be encouraged to alert management as their efforts seem to drift in relatively unimportant directions.

Most workers do like to be productive and do want to be recognized for their work-relevant performance. Therefore, most are likely to cooperate with attempts made to limit growth of energy-consuming, but irrelevant, at-work activities. If you can reward them for alerting you to the growth of irrelevant activity, this will improve the quality of your control.

An example of this is the case of an organization that recently experienced high labor turnover among managers and subordinates. Some results of the turnover were a loss of clear definition of jobs, redoing projects that had already been done a short time before, and restructuring work routines in ways that had already been proven far less efficient time and time again in past years. Many workers sensed what was happening; their efforts were being redistributed to the pursuit of irrelevant activities. The horror of it all was that no one alerted top management! Workers knew that their efforts were being diverted from highly important endeavors, but they said nothing.

17. Do not reward nonjob, antiwork, and semi-work behavior.

Nonjob behavior such as working during company time on strictly personal projects, and semi-work behavior such as interstation physical travel or on-the-job social activity, will typically occupy a considerable portion of the average employee's workday. Management, however, must find ways to limit such endeavors. Too much effort must not go to these relatively irrelevant pursuits.

To minimize the effort one spends on nonwork, semi-work, and antiwork, management can reduce the rewards one experiences for effort spent on those activities. Some of these rewards actually come, unknowingly, from management itself. For example, on occasion managers will praise employees for doing work on projects that are strictly personal interest projects. Consider the case of the employee who spends one hour each day inventing tools that have nothing to do with application to the job. The manager tells the employee what tremendous, ingenious work he or she is doing.

Semi-work behavior is often rewarding too. The employee must travel from point A to point B in the office complex. As he or she moves, many social encounters occur. The employee must walk by the open door of many other offices. The employee takes five or six times longer to reach point B because of the social rewards experienced during the travel. The employee sees time spent in travel as paying off in terms of rewards. Also the travel may lead the employee past the manager's office, and eight times out of ten the manager will see the employee and engage him or her in friendly conversation. This is a reward for not working and must be minimized.

18. Use penalties for abuse of nonjob, antiwork, and semi-work activity.

Penalties can be used to divert employees from nonwork, antiwork, and semi-work. For example, if workers are found working during company time on personal projects, they can be given a demerit or a negative write-up on the annual performance evaluation. They can be reprimanded for such nonjob activities as interdepartmental politicking or eating during times other than the lunch break. They can be advised against participating in a friendly social gathering of their peers while trying to prepare important documents or trying to do some other critical task. They can be penalized for spending too much time each day on playing games at work. Such activity literally becomes central to the work worlds of some employees. They waste so much time and energy doing this that little time and energy are left for priority task execution.

Employees must be made aware of the amount of effort that can easily be diverted to nonjob, antiwork, and semi-work if not monitored and held in check. They must be made aware also that effort directed to such activity will be monitored, and they must be aware of the penalties that will be applied if too much time is spent on this kind of activity.

I am aware of a case where a group of workers developed a habit of playing games with one another that involved hiding one another's tools and work clothing. Items were hidden in the worker's work area. If a worker could find a hidden item within five minutes, his lunch would be purchased by the other workers. If he could not, he bought lunch for one other worker. This type of thing might be fun, but five minutes cuts into production. Some sort of penalty might be the only practical way to prevent this kind of activity from becoming excessive.

19. Design workstations to prevent excessive at-work socializing.

The physical design of workstations can go far toward discouraging too much attention being given to at-work socializing. Of course we do not want to isolate workers from others. Doing this can destroy opportunity for satisfying social needs. And satisfaction of basic social needs must occur, to a large degree, through one's employment. But we do want to prevent social exchange from exploding into something so voluminous that it is more costly in terms of disruption of work flows than it is positive in terms of keeping workers happy.

Generally no-wall offices should be avoided. No-wall offices have their advantages, but they encourage a large volume of non–work-oriented conversation. Access to the employee is too easy. You walk by the employee and sometimes feel obligated to, at least, offer a greeting. And greetings are often followed with additional exchange, usually of questionable relevance.

Workstations that position workers such that their backs face in-plant travel routes or lanes of in-house pedestrian traffic lead to far less work disruption than stations that put the worker in face-to-face contact with every person who walks by. Similarly, employees whose office desks are positioned in full view from the open office door attract considerable social engagements. Better locate office desks a bit out of sight of the casual passerby.

Workstations located close to one another, for no reason from a production standpoint, contribute only to time spent in nonproductive social exchange among those manning the work stations. If these stations must be close to save on the investment in physical space, then barriers (walls, mobile partitions, rows of plants) can be erected to prevent attention being too frequently shifted to things other than work.

20. Develop rules and policies to prevent energy allocation to semi-work, antiwork, and nonjob engagements.

Organizations can develop rules and policies to guide employee behavior away from nonwork, antiwork, and semi-work. Manuals can be developed which identify typical kinds of this behavior. These manuals can be written to provide the worker with data on why such behavior must be minimized. These manuals can also be written to incorporate rules and policies designed to help employees avoid an excessive allocation of effort to nonwork, antiwork, and semi-work. Further it is in these manuals that write-ups on any penalties for violation of rules can be displayed.

It may be wise to have rules and policies in an organization that spell out limits on personal interest pursuit on company time, policies that limit the number of times you can leave your workstation, rules or policies that suggest limits for on-the-job socializing, and policies that guide organizational politics. Rules and policies of this type provide a framework for helping prevent excessive effort allocation to activities other than work assignments. Of course, the rules and policies alone may not have much clout, but when coupled with appropriate penalties, which are enforced when infractions occur, they can help. Certainly the existence of rules and policies makes it easier for workers to say no to pressures exerted by others for nonjob, antiwork, and semi-work engagements.

Sometimes publication of the rules and policies helps by simply making people aware of those factors that can cause effort to be pulled away from the job. Many employees will appreciate this because they have good intentions and want to spend their energies for the good of the company. Slippage occurs with natural ease if one is not cognizant of the sources of slippage from relevant to irrelevant systems.

21. Encourage employees to pursue organizationally relevant projects during idle time periods.

Just a little verbal persuasion can help prevent effort being wasted on organizationally irrelevant activities. Managers can encourage workers to work on special projects or assignments during slack time. If employees can be sold on the benefits of this, the company goes a long way toward preventing diversion of effort to nonproductive endeavor.

The company would do well to develop a written inventory of special projects employees might work on. When idle time comes up, employees can search the inventory to locate special assignments that they feel would best match their interests and abilities. The important element here is choice. The worker chooses what to work on. This helps assure the worker gets what he or she likes and feels competent doing. It also helps assure the organization gets good work.

The organization's reward system must fully recognize worker involvement with these special, idle-time projects. Rewards should be tied to the number of special projects taken on, the completion rate, and the qaulity of work done. These rewards should be above and beyond the rewards for regular work. The possible problem here is that aggressive workers may neglect some of their regular duties if they see special projects are more rewarding. Again, a balancing act in reward system design is important to facilitate a proper distribution of effort between regular assignments and special projects. But if the company plans it right, these special projects can provide more reward than nonwork, antiwork, and semi-work involvement, thereby discouraging that involvement, but not enough reward to interfere with regular duties.

22. Properly design inter-station travel routes.

Often workers do not stay at one workstation or office for very long; they move among offices and stations. Some workers such as salespeople and floor supervisors spend the majority of their time traveling on the highway or traveling on the plant floor. Travel can lead to high energy spent on nonwork and semi-work activity.

Long routes take time and energy. If you have to carry a load over the route, the more energy it takes per time period and very probably the longer it will take. Therefore, routes should be shortened as much as possible. Make sure that salespeople follow the shortest possible path in making their rounds. Make sure in-plant workers transporting material can follow essentially straight paths between pick-up and deposit. Make sure the floor supervisor knows how to cover all workers with a minimum of walk time.

Routes that are difficult, or that have obstacles to overcome, often take too much time and energy. If you have to wind around numerous dangerous machines, climb narrow stairs, or step over wires on the floor or holes in the floor, you will be drained of energy just in passing from one station to the next. The distance may be short but the difficulty of passage is great.

Also travel routes can zap effort by incorporating too many distractions. For example, the in-plant workers' travels may take them by the security guard (which takes five minutes' conversation), by the president's office (where the president's secretary invites you in for coffee), by the latest piece of computer equipment (which the enthusiastic computer operator must spend fifteen minutes telling you about), and through the middle of the rest/break area (where twenty or more employees are waiting to hear the latest news you bring). Travel routes should be planned to reduce this kind of pull away from the goal systems of primary interest to the organization.

23. Avoid making the work situation too frustrating, discouraging, or competitive.

When the work situation is too frustrating, discouraging, or competitive, workers may invent counteraction strategies which consume effort, the pursuit of which represent considerable effort expended in alternative goal systems.

Frustrated workers may spend much time venting their emotions. They may capture fellow workers and use up countless minutes of the day "bending the ears" of their captives relative to their frustrations. Or they may decide to go beyond mere vocalizing of these emotions and take real action to prevent frustrations from emerging in the future. In any event, effort is used up.

Discouraged workers will spend energy blaming themselves for failures and seeking ways to avoid discouragement in the future. Highly discouraged workers often need counseling. This is time- and energy-consuming for both counselor and client. It takes effort away from the job. Discouraged and frustrated workers may also decide to develop political action groups or social power groups to wield influence over those in positions of formal authority in the organization. Participation in such groups is effort-consuming.

Workers in highly competitive work situations engage in practices designed to combat the competition—to excel in comparison with the competition. Frequently effort is spent making the competition look bad by generating false or misleading rumors about the competition or by such tactics as discrediting the work of the competition, or creating stumbling blocks or bottlenecks for the competitors. In any case, the bottom line is that such competitive endeavor uses up energy in an organizationally irrelevant way. Management has to prevent such situations from getting out of hand. Management must not create conditions that spur antiproductive or organizationally destructive activity. Allowing workers to become too frustrated, discouraged, and beaten by others may generate irrelevant or antirelevant actions which consume considerable energy.

24. Tie incentives directly to how appropriately employees distribute their effort and time.

To encourage the right distribution of effort, organizations can tie rewards directly to how employees spend efforts. To do this the organization needs quality measures of time and energy utilization. One way to measure how the individual is spending effort—whether it is on high priority work, low priority work, nonwork, antiwork, or semi-work—is to do a work sampling study. With such a study, random observations are made of workers and what they are doing at the instant of each observation. If enough such observations are made (the required number can be easily calculated with statistics), an accurate determination of how long the worker spends on the different areas which consume energy can be determined. Once one's actual effort distribution is isolated, it can be compared with task item time percentages in the job description. Workers can be rewarded for how close they come to these time/ effort distribution standards.

Some organizations may want to grant direct incentives for worker avoidance of nonwork, antiwork, and semi-work. With work sampling, the worker's time on these activities can be determined and then compared with desired or acceptable amounts of time spent on non-, anti, and semi-work. If workers cut their involvement in this nontask activity, they get a reward. This type of system is analogous to a practice, growing in popularity, where organizations reward workers for not being absent or for not being injured.

Of course, tying incentives directly to usage of time is not reward for performance. But in certain cases, particularly where effort distribution issues are involved, rewards issued in direct response to effort levels may make good sense. Such can be done well with appropriately executed work sampling methodologies.

6

Application Aids: Cases, Exercises, and Instrumentation

A number of short case situations related to employee motivation are described in Part A of this chapter. Each case emphasizes different points about motivation. Following each case are questions for the reader to ponder relative to employee motivation issues depicted in the case. After the questions, a brief commentary is provided showing the use of the effort–net return model (ENR) as a framework for analysis and resolution of issues raised by the questions. This development should aid the reader in applying the propositions and prescriptions highlighted in previous chapters.

In Part B of this chapter, further application aids are provided through a number of exercises in which you can participate and a number of sample instruments you can use to help in managing employee motivation. Each exercise and instrument presented is coupled with directions for use or guidelines for interpreting data. These exercises and instruments should help you see how to apply the propositions and prescriptions discussed in earlier chapters.

A. CASES FOR APPLYING THE TENETS OF THE EFFORT–NET RETURN MODEL

The following cases are arranged to address issues in approximately the same sequence those issues were developed in preceding chapters.

a. Ability and Motivation

The ABC Company, which manufactures electronic components for military and civilian aircraft, hired a new division manager for its new product division six months ago. The individual hired was a 33-year-old, named Joe, who recently graduated from an MBA program at a prominent New England university. Joe had ten years of experience in the electronics component manufacturing business prior to coming to work for ABC. Two of those years had been in supervisory and mid-management positions. His undergraduate degree was in electrical engineering. His MBA work had focused on the study of finance.

ABC Company has been experiencing numerous and severe interpersonal relations problems between its technician group and its engineers. The technicians are largely graduates from two-year technical schools and individuals who have learned the trade through apprenticeships. The engineers are four-year college graduates. The engineers are paid about one-third more than the technicians.

The technicians tend to socialize together off the job. The engineers lead their own independent lives while away from work.

The major responsibility of the engineers is to design electrical components. The technicians have to make the parts, test them, and calibrate them. The technicians field most questions about the components that come from customers.

The technicians think they do all the work. The engineers often blame the technicians for shoddy work. The technicians are frequently overheard complaining about the engineers not really understanding how their component designs will stand up under real-world operating conditions. The engineers keep saying the technicians are narrow minded.

The problem between the two groups has developed to the point that constructive communication between the groups has broken down. Some serious technical problems are not getting solved, and neither the engineers nor the technicians seem to care.

The company hired Joe expecting him to address the problem between engineers and technicians and to get production and morale up. ABC expected Joe to spend a considerable amount of time resolving the problem. ABC had told Joe this, very clearly, when Joe first came to work. In fact, other duties had not been assigned to Joe so he would have plenty of time to address these interpersonal difficulties. It was obvious, however, after the first six months that Joe had done little or nothing about the problem. Conflict between the two groups was intensifying, but Joe was putting almost no effort into the task of remedying the conflict. ABC management had talked to Joe twice about it but little changed. Joe seemed to use most of his time on budgeting and cost control procedures.

Questions

1. In terms of the effort–net return (ENR) model, how can Joe's behavior be explained? Why did he not spend more time addressing the interpersonal difficulties here?

2. In terms of ENR, what might explain why the technicians or the engineers have not made attempts, themselves, at bridging the gap between them?

Commentary

Joe probably lacks the ability, knowledge, and skill to deal with the behavior problems apparent in this case. His formal educational background involved little study in the social sciences, organizational behavior, or human relations. He has very limited management experience too. It is likely he is aware of the conflict between engineers and technicians, but does not know what to do about it. So he does not put any effort into resolving the conflict. In ENR language, he perceives his limited knowledge and skill in the human behavior area as limiting the payoff from any effort he might put into resolving the difficulty. Consequently, he does not exert the effort needed.

Neither the technicians nor engineers have attempted to address the conflict either. Again, a plausible reason is that they do not know what to do about it so they do not try to do anything. The problem, therefore, continues because of their lack of motivation to solve it. This lack of motivation is caused by a perceived lack of ability which leads to perception of a weak effort-performance linkage.

b. Job Design and Motivation

Jerry works in a machine shop operating a lathe. He has done this for thirty years and loves his work because he can see himself creating something each time he "turns down" and shapes raw stock. He also feels proud because he knows few other people have the skill needed to meet the close tolerance limits required in machining the precision-demanding components which he makes for use in medical laboratory equipment. Jerry earns $20 per hour base pay plus a substantial incentive wage.

Jerry used to prepare blueprints for his work himself, but now he receives blueprints to follow from the Mechanical Engineering Department. These are usually well done but sometimes do not give sufficient detail. He always calls Engineering when something on the prints needs clarification. Engineering is cooperative. They send a person right over, and the problem is almost always resolved within minutes. On occasion, though, Jerry has to make an educated guess on what engineering really wants.

Sometimes Jerry's lathe breaks a belt or needs greasing. When this happens, he calls his supervisor to get authorization to requisition a new belt from the Supplies Department or calls Maintenance to send someone over with a grease gun to lubricate his machine. How long it takes for these departments to respond has become somewhat unpredictable.

Jerry has discovered that the faster he operates his lathe, the more frequently it needs new belts and greasing. On top of this, the lathe has developed a vibration for which no one can find a source.

Jerry "works down" a pile of raw materials inventory which is replenished each morning before he gets to work. Some days he depletes the pile by 1:30 P.M. if his machine does not break down or if he does not have too many interruptions.

Jerry gets a lot of praise from his boss for his good work. There are no regular, formal performance evaluations, however. He learns about the real quality of his work from customers who sometimes write him about how they appreciate his work on a part that he has machined or about how something he machined was not quite right. He gets very, very few comments about things not being right.

Lately, management has heard from other employees that Jerry is not trying as hard as he used to on the job. His effort intensity per time period has decreased, and the time he spends running his machine (when it is in running order) has declined. Management wonders what is wrong and what can be done.

Questions

1. What might be causing Jerry's apparent decline in motivation? Explain in ENR terms.
2. What would you do as a manager to improve Jerry's desire to exert high effort?

Commentary

Jerry's lack of motivation is likely due to his perception of flaws in job design. He sees that high effort will not yield high performance results for several reasons. First, there is an informational input problem. Blueprints often do not tell him everything he needs to know. He has to guess and he knows this can mean mistakes with low quality output. Second, Jerry has to endure red tape and unpredictable downtime every time his machine breaks down. It is hard to get excited about working hard when you have little control over how long you will be down. Third, Jerry has found that if he is motivated—works hard and fast—his machine breaks down more frequently. He thus realizes that increased effort during a period of time only leads to more idle time. The net change in performance from increased effort is zero. Fourth, he has become leery about the quality of his work because of the unexplained vibration in his machine. Fifth, he realizes there is no sense to be highly motivated—to exert high effort in the morning—because he will often run out of raw materials and have to sit idle in the afternoon. And sixth, Jerry receives no regular feedback from management. This job design deficiency makes it difficult for him to make sure he is doing things right. All these job design problems serve to dampen the strength of the relationship he perceives between effort and performance.

To improve Jerry's motivation, management must take action to assure the blueprints are accurate, sufficiently detailed, and presented to Jerry so that he fully understands them. Management should let Jerry, himself, replace belts and grease the machine. He knows how to do this! This will allow him to get the machine back on line much faster. The vibration problem needs to be eliminated, and the machine needs to be adjusted so it can stand a faster pace of operation without more frequent breaks. Management must assure an adequate stock of inventory to cover Jerry in the afternoon, or arrange for Jerry to be productive at other related work in the afternoon when there is an inventory outage. Finally, Jerry needs regular, quality performance feedback from management so he can stay on track with the organization's expectations.

c. Two Silver Dollars

As plant personnel manager, your boss (the plant manager) often consults with you about problems of job motivation. One day he asks your opinion on a major program he has been mulling over for several weeks:

"I think I have an idea on how we can get this plant to raise productivity. For two years now we've had some kind of psychological barrier about shipping two million dollars' worth of product in one month. Many times we have gotten close to shipping that figure, but we fall down in the final few days.

"My plan is to set up an incentive system. If in any one month the plant ships two or more million dollars of product out the door, everybody in the plant will get two silver dollars. We'll mail the dollars right to their homes so the whole family can share in their achievements. Every month our people reach two million dollars, they will get two more silver dollars. Everybody likes silver dollars and everybody likes recognition.

"But before I go ahead and announce the campaign, I want your opinion. Will my plan work?"

Questions

1. What would you tell the boss about his motivational scheme?
2. How could this scheme be modified to be more effective?

Commentary

The idea of an incentive system is good for motivating. And recognition is a fine type of reward to use to motivate. But there is a real problem with the motivational plan here. This scheme provides a group reward. The only way an individual receives the reward is if the whole labor force succeeds! A worker may well feel that no matter how hard he or she works—or how well he or she does—it will not have much impact. If others do not produce, group performance will be low, and no reward will be forthcoming. The worker sees little correlation between his individual efforts and group performance. And it is group performance that determines how much the worker will get in the way of rewards.

Also there may be questions here in workers' minds about how realistic the production quota is and about how dependent production really is on worker efforts. Perhaps workers see a significant job design constraint here—enough of a constraint to prevent vivid perception of a strong effort-performance correlation.

Another problem with the scheme is that two silver dollars is not much. It is difficult to perceive a reward as having significant value when its magnitude is minuscule. A reward of insufficient size will not motivate. Here the two dollars seem far too little in light of what is required for performance to get it. Since it is not proportional to the effort required to get it, it may be perceived as a slap in the face. Perhaps the symbolic value of two *silver* dollars will be sufficiently high to overcome the low economic value, but this is not likely.

The plan could be effectively modified by monitoring each individual's performance within the group and distributing recognition and a significant cash award to each member on the basis of individual contribution to the group effort. It could be further upgraded with an incentive system that grants greater rewards per unit produced the greater the number of units produced. Such a double incentive system can encourage production not just up to quota but well beyond quota. Also rewards, ideally, should be tailored to individuals. Some workers may not be turned on by recognition. Or some may appreciate a form of recognition other than two silver dollars. Over time, silver dollars, as a form of recognition, are likely to wear out for any given individual anyway. Other forms of recognition will have to be devised.

An idea which seems highly commendable here is getting families to share in the celebration of worker success. Sending two silver dollars home for others to see adds to the perceived value of those dollars as a recognition device. Making the granting of rewards public can give those rewards more clout. The public packaging of rewards seems quite good here.

d. Health-More Foods Corporation

Health-More Foods Corporation of Lincoln, Nebr., has been growing at a compounded rate of 30 percent for the last seven years. It entered the vitamin and health food business at a time when many people were concerned about natural foods and vitamins, and it sells high-quality products. It has captured a dominant position in its regional market; it now has about 150 employees.

Because of its growth, it has had difficulty maintaining trained clerical employees. Billing errors have been 9 percent, and accounts payable errors have been 8 percent. The new personnel director was asked to recommend corrective action. He proposed and installed a simple two-step program. First, supervisors and employees in each work unit met to discuss and set goals for improvement. Then supervisors regularly praised employees who had fewer errors than standard. Results for each work unit were charted and posted daily. Within one month the error rate for both billing and accounts payable declined to less than 1 percent and remained there.

Questions

1. Discuss the two-step program and its results in terms of the ENR model of motivation.

2. Discuss how goals motivate.

Commentary

This case shows good application of the effort–net return model. Precise targets were set for improvement; performance was accurately measured;

performance results were fed back; and reward (praise) was given in accordance with the performance level. The employees perceive here a strong effort-performance linkage and a strong performance-reward relationship. What management did to motivate worked. Errors declined to less than 1 percent. You cannot argue with that. Other types of rewards besides recognition could have been used, and a reward schedule could have been developed to show how varying degrees of achievement would be rewarded, but obviously a more elaborate system was not essential. One important lesson here: Do not invest more than you have to in motivation!

Goals motivate in numerous ways. They make work expectations clear for one thing. This helps the worker see a high contingency relation between effort and performance. Goals serve as benchmarks signaling accomplishment. You can vividly see, with goals, what constitutes accomplishment. And since accomplishment is intrinsically satisfying, goals intensify the strength of the perceived performance-reward linkage.

Goals, well formulated, help in providing feedback on progress to workers too. A worker can compare actual progress with the goal and take corrective action if a significant difference is found. Thus goals help keep the employee on track allowing him or her to feel that effort is more likely to lead to true performance.

Goals will be particularly motivational if they are both realistic and challenging. A realistic goal is needed for one to perceive that effort will, in fact, yield desired results. In this case the participative goal setting helped assure formulation of realistic goals, as well as employee understanding and acceptance of goals. This helped build perception of a particularly strong effort-performance correlation. A challenging goal, once achieved, represents a more meaningful and, therefore, more satisfying experience than does achievement of a nonchallenging goal. Such a goal strengthens the performance-reward link.

There is one other key point in this case. The public posting or charting of performance can create great incentive to do well. Who wants to look bad in the eyes of others? Who does not enjoy looking good? With public posting of workers' performance, they see more vividly a strong correlation between performance and reward (or penalty). You get respect from others for good performance; you get penalty (criticism, ostracism) for poor performance. Also, the charting provides more vivid feedback to workers on how they are doing, thus strengthening the effort-performance link. The feedback helps workers feel they will be able to correct performance when they have to and thus will more likely reach their goals.

e. The Instructor's Proposal

Jonathan Borland was the plant manager for Universal Farm Equipment, Inc., a full-time manufacturer of farm implements. The plant employed 310 factory workers who earned an average of $25 per hour, and 53 office and managerial staff who were on rather high salaries.

Borland was attending a management development course at the local university entitled "Motivation and Productivity," in which he heard the instructor extolling the virtues of the effort–net return model. The instructor claimed that the model had been successfully used by numerous companies faced with high absenteeism among employees. This comment was particularly interesting to Borland because absenteeism at Universal had been creeping steadily upward during the last five years and now stood at roughly 20 percent on Monday and Friday, and 10 percent on Tuesday, Wednesday, and Thursday. This absenteeism caused considerable difficulty in both time and money, as workers had to be rescheduled after it was clear who was not going to show up for work.

After the class, Borland approached the instructor and asked if she would be interested in designing an ENR system to reduce absenteeism at Universal. The instructor agreed. Two weeks later the two met and the instructor described her proposal: Every Monday, the names of all employees who had a perfect attendance record for the past week would be put into a bowl and one name drawn. The individual whose name was drawn would receive a $200 cash bonus. In addition, at the end of each month, the names of all those who had a perfect attendance record for the preceding month would be placed in a bowl and a name drawn. This time, however, the winner would receive a color television valued at $600. And finally, those who had perfect attendance for six months would be eligible for a drawing for which the prize was a trip to Florida for two with all expenses paid.

Questions

1. Analyze the instructor's proposed course of action. What are its strong points? What are its weak points?
2. What part of the ENR model does this course of action address?

Commentary

Here the performance dimension under scrutiny is attendance. The company is trying to motivate high attendance. The plan calls for putting a potential of 310 plus 53 names in a bowl each week—363 names in total. One name will be drawn each week from the 363. The one drawn will get $200 cash. But to motivate good performance (attendance), employees must see a strong positive correlation between performance and reward. If they perform, they need to know the reward will be forthcoming. This system does not provide that. You can have perfect attendance quite often, but the odds are slim you will get any reward. The employee perceives this vividly in this case. Performance has a high chance of not paying off. The employee sees a performance-reward curve very low in slope. The only positive feature of the system is that the reward cannot be received if one does not perform—that is, your name does not go in the bowl if you are absent.

Other flaws in the system are the failure to tie the reward to individual needs—in other words, cash for everybody whether they need it or not—and the failure to provide a cash bonus of significant magnitude. Two hundred dollars is not much when considering many of these workers make $25 per hour. Just how valuable will they see this reward if it is not of significant size and not well matched to their most dominant needs?

The prize for six months of perfect attendance looks pretty good. Probably the number of workers who turn out to be eligible for this would constitute a smaller pool. One would, therefore, calculate a greater probability of getting the reward. And the reward is of substantial size. But to have perfect attendance over a six-month period might mean employees would incur significant costs (negative outcomes). For example, employees would have to avoid being absent even when the absence might be highly worthwhile from the employee's point of view. Employees might well sense that the expected value of the prize is just not worth the large sacrifices required to be eligible for it. Perceived costs outweigh the perceived expected rewards.

This proposed course of action attempts to get people to see that performance will bring reward. But it is deficient in its accomplishment of this. Further the plan does nothing to address the perceived effort-performance link, perceived costs, or pulls from alternative goal systems. (The previous section, The Instructor's Proposal, was adapted from Gray and Starke, *Organizational Behavior: Concepts and Applications,* Merrill Publishing Co., 1977.)

f. Recognition: How Much and When?

Managing a trade association, thought Anthony Califano, was great work. Sure, there were times when he became frustrated, but, overall, the good aspects of the job outweighed the bad. Tony was the executive secretary of a League of Credit Unions in the Southwest. He and his staff of twelve were responsible for administering to the needs of 135 credit unions. They provided advice on problem solving to members requesting help. They carried on lobbying activities for passage of favored legislation by the state legislature and testified against bills unfavorable to the League members. In addition, the League staff carried on a series of informational and training progams, including arranging the annual meetings of League members.

Tony was an easy boss. A deeply moral man, he almost invariably identified the good in people and overlooked their shortcomings. Gossip was not in his vocabulary. It was reported several years ago that Tony had expressed a "dog-gone-it" when agitated. That was the known extent of his temper, at least as recorded in the annals of the League offices.

Tony Califano constantly praised the work of his staff, both to them personally and to others. If a secretary typed a letter for him, it was "beautifully done." A report submitted by a subordinate would never receive less than a "great work." The custodian always produced an "immaculate" job with floors so clean "we could eat off them." People always "looked great." Tomorrow would be a "fantastic" day.

The annual meetings involved more of the same. Without exception, he spent the first ten minutes of his address to members listing the virtues of his staff. The tributes were profuse. He covered every member of his staff with praise. His assistants could recite from memory the glowing comments. Occasionally they were embarrassed with the extensiveness of his public pronouncements of their organizational value. "No one can be that good," one of his staff whispered to another after listening to Tony lay it on. Still, Tony was sincere in his belief of having an outstanding group of employees. Over time, though, productivity started down.

Questions

1. What is your opinion about employee recognition? Can it be overdone? What is the correct amount of recognition? How do you determine the right amount to give?
2. Would you consider the average employee suffers from the problem of too much recognition or praise? Explain.
3. Give counsel to Tony about other strategies for motivating.

Commentary

Any reward, praise included, can be overdone. Too much of a good thing is quite possible. If praise is given all the time, regardless of whether it is deserved or not, it loses its meaning and will not be appreciated. A reward can be over-used, oversold, or overplayed. And when a reward is issued irrespective of performance, much poor work becomes rewarded. Too much recognition can mean employees will perceive diminished value per unit of recognition.

The correct amount of recognition to give depends on circumstances. A manager has to look at how strong the esteem and status needs of each of his or her subordinates are. The right amount for one person may not be right for another. The amount of recognition required to motivate must also be determined by measuring the degree, or level, of performance and by matching to the priority of the task dimension along which performance occurs. One should get high recognition for high performance and less recognition for low performance. And one should get higher recognition for good performance of a high priority task than for good performance of a less important task. Califano did not recognize these basic tenets of motivation. After a while, employees began to see that regardless of their kind and level of performance they got praised profusely.

Most employees certainly do not receive too much praise. Few real-world bosses are like Califano. In fact, too little recognition is all too common and causes employee satisfaction to often be low. Praise is an inexpensive motivational tool, and it helps satisfy a type of need that is strong, if not dominant, in many of today's employees. The effective use of praise and other forms of recognition can represent a formidable component in a manager's power arsenal. It can go far toward boosting employee effort expenditure. But it does not work, for motivating, without proper timing and without a proper tying to performance.

Califano's reliance on the spoken word for motivating is excessive. He needs more motivational tools and he needs to back up his words with evidence that he is really willing to invest in rewards. Prizes, desirable work assignments, certificates of award, time off, cash bonuses, and the like would show workers that Tony really means what he says.

Whatever rewards are used, though, they must be given equitably as well as on a performance-contingent basis. If workers get rewards they think are not deserved, those rewards will not satisfy or motivate. If workers think fellow employees are getting undeserved rewards, it will also hurt their satisfaction and motivation.

g. Incentives at Karma Records

Joe Karma has owned and operated Karma Records since its founding in 1979. Joe has often been heard to say, "I believe in paying people for what they do, not for how many hours they work." This management philosophy was expressed through a variety of incentive plans that Joe designed himself. Although he was firmly committed to the use of incentives, he hired a management consulting team to make recommendations about his compensation progam.

To help the consultants, Joe wrote down the major features of each incentive program. His notes were as follows:

1. Executives do not own any stock. But they each get $1,000 for each dollar the stock price goes up from the previous year.
2. Every time sales go up 10 percent, all the hourly employees get a day off with pay or can work one day at double-time rates.
3. Production workers get paid 18 cents for each record they press and 3 cents for each record they package.
4. Sales personnel get a $50 savings bond each time a new record store or department store starts stocking Karma records.

Questions

1. What problems do you see with the incentives for (a) executives, (b) hourly workers, (c) production workers, (d) salespeople?

2. If you were a member of the consulting team, how would you alter the incentives proposed for each group?

Commentary

The $1,000 that executives receive if the stock price goes up a dollar is a reward that is contingent on the performance of the company as a whole. It is hard for individual executives to see a high correlation between individual effort and company performance and, therefore, difficult to see a strong positive correlation between individual effort and the $1,000 reward. Thus the $1,000 reward is not going to be highly motivational. Also, stock price depends on factors other than company performance—market forces beyond executive control. This causes executives to perceive even greater weakness in the relationship between their individual efforts and the reward. There are just too many moderating variables between executive effort and stock price.

With the 10 percent sales increases all hourly employees can take time off with pay or work one day at double-time rates. Such an incentive does little to motivate an individual employee because the employee does not sense how a 10 percent sales increase really depends on his or her individual efforts. Too many others have something to to with whether or not an increase in sales occurs. When rewards depend on group effort, one sees a weakened effort to reward linkage.

The incentive for production workers makes good sense assuming the piece rate has been set at a fair level. Workers clearly see how their production is related to reward. Higher performance brings a higher reward which can be precisely calculated. And individual performance here is easily measured so workers can tell if effort is paying off in terms of performance. A possible problem, though, is that quality may suffer if workers are rewarded only for quantity. Reward systems must reward total performance.

The sales personnel who get $50 savings bonds also face a reward system that ties rewards closely to performance. But a question exists as to just how valuable a $50 savings bond is perceived. Salespeople tend to like immediate payoffs. Long-term payoffs from savings bonds tend to lack perceived value. A reward that is not valued will not motivate no matter how closely tied to performance it is. Some people may value a $50 savings bond (with, say, a ten-year maturity date) but others may not.

A better motivation system for an executive might be one that rewards $1,000 for each, say, $50,000 improvement in profitability per month in the division of the company which is under the control of the executive. This would better relate the reward to individual performance. Or some type of reward other than money might be used. But whatever the contingent reward, it should be received close in time to the performance for which it is given. An executive should not have to wait until the end of the year to get all bonuses earned during the year.

Hourly employees should be rewarded on the basis of how well they fulfill their individual job assignments. Each hourly's performance should be evaluated with some kind of quality assessment device and rewards adjusted to the level of performance measured.

The salespeople should get an immediate cash bonus (incentive) for each new store that stocks Karma records. They should also get an incentive award which is tied to volume of record sales per store. Rewards can be used to direct effort as well as to encourage greater effort. Salespeople should be provided with incentive not only to acquire new accounts but also to build each account's business to a maximum.

h. Just How Good Am I Doctor?

Ms. Carlisle, a middle-aged woman with several university degrees, was employed by the federal government in a public health position prior to coming to Mentor County General Hospital. At Mentor she served as the County Mental Health Educator under Dr. Haller, Chief of the Mental Health Services Division. Ms. Carlisle's job involved giving lectures to schools, business firms, and clubs upon request and conducting training classes on mental health education for new teachers, social workers, and nurses. She was proud of her performance record which contained mainly superior ratings and nothing below excellent. She liked her boss, too, not only because he had given her an opportunity to use her talents, but also because he was always kind and considerate.

Performance evaluations at Mentor were made every six months, and the customary procedure was for the reports to be prepared and placed in each employee's mailbox. Employees could discuss them with their supervisors if they wished to do so; they were expected to sign them. One day Ms. Carlisle found her evaluation in her mailbox and became very upset over it. Instead of superior and excellent ratings on the scale, she found excellent and good ratings. There was no explanation given for the drop in ratings, only the statement that "Ms. Carlisle continues to do good work as in the past." Ms. Carlisle asked to see Dr. Haller immediately.

The interview between Ms. Carlisle and Dr. Haller took place that afternoon. Ms. Carlisle was quite blunt and wanted to know what was wrong with her work. Dr. Haller explained that her work was fine and he could not understand why she was upset. She pointed out the difference in this last rating compared with others he had given her in the past and asked him to explain the difference. Dr. Haller said that he thought it was a good evaluation and explained that he had changed his methods of evaluation. He refused to explain further, but assured Ms. Carlisle that her work was good and encouraged her to maintain this high standing. Ms. Carlisle did not want to sign the evaluation but later conceded, inserting "signed under protest" under her name. She then made plans for appealing the rating to the County Employees Association and the Civil Service Commission.

Questions

1. How do you account for Dr. Haller's change in methods? Could he have been influenced in some way to change his methods? Or is he using this as an excuse for giving her lower ratings?

2. What effect is Ms. Carlisle's appeal likely to have on her ratings? On Dr. Haller's evaluations in the future?

3. How will this episode affect Ms. Carlisle's future performance?

Commentary

Dr. Haller may have changed his methods. He may now be measuring Ms. Carlisle against a tighter standard. Perhaps he is comparing her with a new, exceptional employee who sets the pace for everyone else. If so, he should explain such. But it is more likely that Haller has not changed his methods and has instead slipped into the trap that poorly designed performance evaluation instruments can get you into. Many instruments do not define, for each evaluation scale, what excellent, good, fair, and poor mean. They do not contain anchored rating scales that allow you to objectively place your check mark at the right spot on each given scale. The rater has to use subjective judgment coupled with a changing notion from one time period to the next of what the rating terms mean.

With unanchored or poorly anchored scales (i.e., poor definitions of the precise meanings of each major point on each scale), it is easy to vary your ratings from one six-month rating to the next when actual performance does not vary. Performance changes show up when no real performance changes occur. This is a great weakness in a performance evaluation system. Employees see that they may perform well yet such performance may well not be recognized. Similarly, employees perceive that actual low performance may get high scores. The strength of the contingency between real performance and rewards is destroyed. Therefore, motivation is destroyed. One sees that real performance may or may not be recognized so any rewards that depend on performance may not be received when deserved or may be received when not deserved.

Haller is probably aware of the subjective nature of his evaluation so he is using "a change in methods" as an excuse for his arbitrary ratings. Ms. Carlisle's appeal probably will not get her ratings changed but will instead force Dr. Haller to give concocted explanations of why he rated her as he did. He will probably react defensively and "fudge" reasons to justify the lower ratings. This, of course, only makes things worse for both Haller and Carlisle. Haller becomes committed to lower scores—defending them—that he probably does not truly believe in, and Carlisle gets stuck with ratings she does not deserve.

The effect of an appeal may force Haller to upgrade the evaluation system for the future. It is not likely to get Haller to rate Carlisle higher in the future if her performance is indeed not deserving.

Carlisle's future performance could suffer unless the performance evaluation system is improved—unless real performance is validly measured—because Carlisle will not see a strong correlation between real performance and her rewards (her performance scores and associated recognition). Indeed, in this case, Carlisle was, in effect, penalized for good performance!

After a performance assessment is done by a manager, manager and subordinate should sit together and discuss the ratings. They should strive for consensus on what those ratings should be and should agree on what actions need to be taken to address any performance problems. This gives the employee clear understanding of direction (of expectations). This motivates.

To facilitate discussion, at least two things should be given attention. First, the ratee should be requested to self-evaluate and bring this evaluation to the discussion/review session. Comparing rater with ratee ratings can lead to more meaningful insights about performance, as rater and ratee attempt to iron out perceived differences in ratings. Second, the rater should take the time to write a rationale supporting each rating given the employee. These rationale paragraphs should focus on providing evidence of why ratings were made as they were. Doing these two things adds richness to the quality of the sit-down performance review and adds that all-important validity to the process.

Good performance must be rewarded if it is to continue. A faulty performance control system—unreliable measurement of performance, no feedback, among others—can cause more problems than no formal control system at all. Many raters of performance give rather arbitrary ratings because of lack of clear indicators of performance. You have to have clear measures of performance, have to actually spend time gathering sufficient data to make measurements, and have to give good feedback if your control system is going to work.

Whenever an employee performance control system is going to be changed, the ratee should be brought into the process to participate in formulating that change. This fosters understanding and acceptance of the change—both essential if the new system is going to elicit a willingness to perform.

i. James Bond

James Bond, an office clerk, has asked you, his supervisor, to issue a purchase order for a water bottle for his desk. He claims that his injured leg makes it difficult for him to get to the office water fountain about 50 feet away. You know that Bond does have a slight limp from a football injury ten years ago, but he moves about the office satisfactorily and has been going to the water fountain without complaint for five years. You know that Bond frequently seeks status symbols, and you judge that he really wants the water bottle to give his desk a more "executive look" than desks of the other clerks.

Questions

1. What are Bond's most dominant needs here?
2. Bond is waiting for your response. What will you do?

Commentary

One thing is for sure, you cannot always judge what people's needs are by what they say. You have to look beneath the surface and do a little diagnostic work to find the real need. Bond probably does not need water. It is likely he has a strong esteem and status need. A fancy water bottle would help fulfill this type of need. He may also have a strong social need which he perceives will be satisfied to a greater degree with a water bottle which will serve as a conversation piece, attracting employees to stop and talk.

The issue in this case is relatively simple on the surface, but just how to handle Bond's request presents a formidable challenge. You want to take care of your employees' needs—to keep them satisfied—but you cannot always do this if it means too large an expense. Water bottles cost, and room for such a device probably was not provided for in the budget. And you really do not want to issue this type of reward without tying it to performance because you want to get some motivational punch out of your rewards.

You also do not want to take action to satisfy a need that does not require satisfying. For example, you might decide to fulfill his expressed need for water by moving his desk closer to the fountain. But this would solve nothing. It would not take care of a status need and would not help satisfy a need for water if he does not have such a need.

You do not want to turn Bond off and frustrate him by outright denial or rejection of his request. This could lead to all sorts of behavior problems that are outgrowths of frustration. But you cannot just automatically grant the request either without considering not only its effect on Bond but the possible effects on other workers as well. What you do with respect to Bond will be felt by others throughout the at-work social system. Everyone might want a water bottle if you get Bond one! You have to think about the impact of your actions on the entire social system, not just on Bond.

You might suggest to Bond that he buy his own bottle (perhaps indicating to him that this is necessary because there is no money budgeted for this), but that would take much off the status impact of the reward and probably would not accomplish much other than irritating Bond. You might try satisfying his need for status with some alternative device. Perhaps a few words of praise or an invitation to top management's weekly parties would do the trick.

Assuming Bond is a valued employee, you do want to keep him satisfied and to keep his motivation up. You, therefore, should try to satisfy his status/esteem need with a contingent reward. Get him a water bottle, or something else appropriate, but only in return for performance. Point out to him that this is the way it works. Perhaps you can devise a performance-reward schedule that shows him and others how to earn a water bottle. You want to satisfy his needs but on a performance-contingent basis.

j. The Needs of Employees

A wholesale and retail flour and feed business employs four truck drivers (delivery men), two clerks to handle the retail trade at the store, a bookkeeper, and two outside salespeople. The proprietor himself actively manages the business.

A serious symptom in this company is the relatively high labor turnover. In the past year, six truck drivers and one retail clerk had to be hired to fill vacancies. The employees express dissatisfaction with the pay, hours of work, and oppressive management. Yet, in the community the owner is considered to be fair and is held in high respect—an apparent paradox in views.

One of the main difficulties as far as the employees are concerned is the lack of definite policies. For example, the truck drivers often work overtime when the roads are bad in winter. There is no payment for this overtime, and the owner usually says: "I'll give you some time off with pay during slack days in the summer." He intends to do this but sometimes does not, so the drivers feel that the pay situation does not even out. In addition, the store and plant do not always close promptly at the scheduled closing time, so that employees are neither certain when they will get home nor compensated for these little over-hour times.

The owner gave each employee an insurance policy for a Christmas present and is in the habit of making gifts regularly to employees throughout the year at various holiday periods. He does this to show the employees he is interested in them and to keep them in good humor. Yet, to his friends, he has expressed the opinion that despite his generosity and interest, "People won't work like they used to."

Questions

1. To what extent is the owner realistically and reasonably satisfying the needs of his employees?

2. How do you stand on the opinion of the owner as expressed in the last sentence of this case?

Commentary

The owner is giving out rewards arbitrarily. He is not individualizing rewards. He is not relating rewards to people's needs. For example, insurance policies do not do much for people whose needs are primarily economic or for people who need self-respect, or for people who have strong social needs. Also, the owner is neither timing rewards appropriately nor is he tying rewards to performance. Workers see little dependence of need satisfaction on their performance.

The owner promises rewards—time off next summer—but the impact of such a promised, long-term reward in stimulating effort is negligible. Workers calculate they may never get the reward, perhaps because they feel they will not be around six months from now, or they know the owner does not always come through with his promises. For rewards to motivate, their receipt must be close in time to the specific act for which they are given. And you have to trust the reward agent.

Workers will be hesitant to work overtime—to exert that extra effort with accompanying high costs—unless a substantial reward is given to them to offset those costs. High costs here include opportunity costs (workers will not be able to be home as much) and fatigue from too many hours at work. But the owner often gives no rewards for this extra effort.

The owner tries to keep satisfaction high by showing his generosity, but the high turnover indicates his rewards are not only inappropriate for motivation but also do little for satisfaction. The employees have expressed dissatisfaction with various elements of the workplace, and the few so-called generously given rewards are not enough to override these sources of discontent.

People will work as hard as they used to if they are given the proper types of rewards (i.e., rewards matched to their needs), rewards of the right magnitude, and rewards that are properly timed. These things are required for people to value rewards. Only valued rewards will get people to work hard. But what today's workers value is somewhat different from what yesterday's workers most valued.

Beyond providing valued rewards, an organization must bestow those valued rewards on a performance-contingent basis in order to elicit motivation. The workers in this case see no correlation between their performance and their rewards, thus the low motivation. The owner sees this low motivation, and his reaction is to blame it on what he believes is a flaw in the nature of today's worker.

k. It Takes Energy to Make Energy

Mike Harmon felt terrible. His 3:00 P.M. headache had already arrived, and it was only 11:20 A.M. He had been putting in twelve- to sixteen-hour workdays during the past five weeks in order to complete his segment of the blueprints for the new shopping mall that the architectural firm he worked for was designing. And apart from the work-related stresses in his life, he was experiencing a lot of personal stress as well. His father had been in the hospital during the past two weeks, recovering from a massive, near-fatal heart attack. The constant worry about his father's condition, the promise he had made his parents to help with the bills, the daily trips to the hospital sandwiched into an already overcrowded work schedule—all of these had taken their toll on Mike. It was not even noon yet, but he already felt exhausted. If he could only get some rest, some relief from all this stress.

John Ennis knocked once on the door of Mike's office and then pushed inside. "Hey, Mike, how about some lun . . ." he said, his voice trailing off as he saw Mike asleep at his desk, his head lying on the blueprint he had been scaling. John shook his friend awake. "Mike—Mike, wake up. Hey, it's lunchtime. Don't sleep on your own time when you can come back later and sleep on the company's." "Very funny," Mike said irritably. He was awake now, but his mood clearly was not good.

"Take it easy," John said. "I was just kidding. I can't even joke with you anymore. You've always been such an easy-going guy, but frankly, you've been turning into a real grouch lately."

Mike looked up at John and nodded wearily. "You're right—I am, but I can't seem to help it. I feel like I've been pushed way past the limit—getting burned out. And it's not just that I'm always tired; my nerves seem to have given out on me. Little things that never bothered me before drive me right up the wall. The sound of the phone ringing, for example, is enough to give me a headache. That mixup about the paychecks last week—remember how I overreacted to that? And I'm not just grouchy with you; everyone around here has been getting the same treatment. Just ask anyone on the office staff."

"Mike, you *are* burned out," John said sympathetically. "I know how hard you've been pushing yourself these last few weeks, and I know that worries over your father's condition have only made things worse for you."

"Well, I've got to cut back. I can't live and breathe 100 percent for this company anymore. I'll do my job, but execellence will not be my aim. My health has got to take a front seat around here."

"Wait a minute Mike. Let's forget going out to lunch today and pick up some sandwiches later. We're going to spend this noon hour in the gym doing some running."

"Are you crazy?" Mike asked. "I'm already wiped out. How do you expect me to run?"

"Very slowly at first, and without pushing yourself. But, gradually, by building up your speed and resistance a little bit more each day, you're going to put yourself back into shape. And you're going to find what I found out a few years ago—that daily exercise *gives* you more energy than it takes away. And it really helps you cope with stress."

Thinking back on the conversation a few weeks later, Mike had to admit John had been right. Although exercise had sounded at first like the last thing he needed, it had definitely helped to buffer him from the stress in his life. He was up to a mile and a half a day now, and he had already lost six pounds. His strength and stamina were better, his breathing had improved, and he was starting to see his muscle tone come back. But the real surprise had been the effect of the daily exercise sessions on his mental and emotional states. Within a week after he had started running every noon hour with John, Mike's nervousness and irritability had ended. The little annoyances that used to drive him up the wall no longer bothered him. His daily headaches no longer arrived.

"John, I hate to admit that you could be right about anything," Mike said with a grin as they rounded the lap marker in the gym, "but your paradoxical thinking has triumphed again. I feel really good. Who would have thought that by expending so much energy in exercise, I would actually have more energy available for all the rest of the things I have to do?"

"It's like Sparky Watts told us in our high school physics class. It's sort of like money: It *takes* energy to *make* energy."

"So let's see if you have made yourself enough energy to catch me on this last lap, old buddy," Mike said, surging ahead of John at a sprinter's pace. "Last one to cross the finish line buys the sandwiches."

Questions

1. It is often said that "a change is as good as a rest." Why might this be especially true of the kinds of changes that take place as a result of regular aerobic exercise?

2. What do you think would have happened to Mike if John had not convinced him to exercise?

3. What other techniques, aside from exercise, could Mike use to help reduce the stress he experiences with the high levels of effort?

Commentary

Regular aerobic exercise builds stamina and a greater capacity to withstand physically, emotionally, or mentally demanding work. It helps you experience less fatigue, stress, frustration, and boredom—the things that typically accompany high levels of effort expenditure. With aerobic exercise you build and strengthen your heart muscles and improve your circulatory system. You also benefit your nervous and digestive systems. In other words, the exercise makes you healthier. When you are healthy, you do not sense costs being as high as those associated with high effort when you have health problems. You are able to take a greater demand on your time and energy without experiencing excessive negative outcomes.

If Mike had not gotten into a physical exercise routine, he might have had a nervous breakdown, become withdrawn on the job, experienced such frustration that he was led to fits of anger or rage attacking other people, developed ulcers, had a heart attack, or burned out. Mike very likely would have taken numerous evasive actions to avoid involvement in the organization and to avoid significant positively directed effort expenditure. His energy directed to the job would have gone down.

Physical exercise is powerful in helping one cope with stress and other costs associated with high effort, but it is certainly not the only means of combating these costs. Proper diet—avoiding caffeine and excessive sugar, for example—is essential. Relaxation techniques can be used such as deep breathing, stretching, and meditation. Biofeedback techniques which allow you to monitor your stress levels and to make conscious decisions on what to do to control stress work well. Also learning to recognize and attack the sources of stress can help.

Eliminating high uncertainty in the workplace, properly scheduling work breaks, setting realistic work goals, making the work environment safe, putting the worker in control of his or her own job, providing buffer zones to house work queues can all reduce the perceived pressures associated with high effort too. Developing greater ability and skill to do the job can help further. In general, you can operate on the person or on the work design to cause changes that can cut the costs associated with high effort.

1. The Copying Machine Extortionist

One early spring afternoon you suddenly realize that you have forgotten to take care of an important chore. As coach of the Little League Panthers, it is your job to make sure that all twenty members of your team have a copy of the season baseball schedule. Noticing the copier in your office is not being used, you decide to make the necessary copies. Quickly you complete the chore and turn off the machine. As you are finishing the task, Alfie, a clerk in your department, approaches you.

He says with a sly grin, "I couldn't help but notice those Little League schedules you were running off on the company machine. Shame, shame, and you a management trainee. I tell you what, I'll bet you $25 that I don't turn you in to management."

"What are you talking about?" you reply.

"Okay, I'll run it by you again," says Alfie. "If I don't turn you in to management, you owe me $25. You must agree, $25 is a pretty cheap price to pay for protecting your honor in this company. Who wants to be accused of using the copy machine for their own business?"

Questions

1. Would you give Alfie his $25? Why or why not?
2. What would you do?

Commentary

You should not give Alfie the $25. It will only mean harsh penalty for you in the long run. These things usually get out sooner or later. Alfie is trying to motivate by threatening penalty—exposure—if you do not pay. Penalty, or the threat of penalty, often does motivate people. Many people would likely succumb to Alfie's promise of exposure for failure to give him $25. But you should never allow yourself to be blackmailed. It only leads to more blackmail later on.

What you should probably do here is tell management the circumstances and offer to pay for the copies. Perhaps you could persuade the company to, in the future, develop a policy on personal use of the copier that might incorporate one or more of these elements:

1. allow a limited number of personal copies;
2. permit copies as long as the number is recorded;
3. allow copies as long as they are approved by a supervisor;
4. allow as many copies as you wish as long as you pay for them;
5. permit any number of copies if copies are used for a worthwhile community activity; or
6. allow personal use of the copier if it does not interfere with company business.

You might also reverse the game on Alfie and threaten to expose him for blackmail if he does not get off your back. This would work if you had first made up your mind to tell management what you had done.

Penalties can motivate but they should be legitimate penalties. One will likely not be influenced by a penalty that does not appear to be just. One may balk at and disregard such a penalty, thinking that if it is implemented, he or she could fight it and get it reversed.

m. Jacob Arnold

Jacob Arnold is an engineer in a large design engineering office. Jacob comes from a rural background in which his family had low income and stern rules. To earn his college degree, he had to work to pay most of his own expenses.

Jacob is an intelligent and capable worker. His main fault is that he does not want to take risks. He hesitates to make decisions for himself, often bringing petty and routine problems to his supervisor or to other engineers for decision. Whenever he does a design job, he brings it in rough draft to his supervisor for approval before he finalizes it.

Since Jacob is a capable person, his supervisor wants to motivate him to be more independent in his work. The supervisor believes that this approach will improve Jacob's performance, relieve the supervisor from extra routine, and give Jacob more self-confidence. However, the supervisor is not sure how to go about motivating Jacob to improve his performance.

Questions

1. What are Jacob's needs?
2. In the role of the supervisor, plan how you will deal with the problem here.

Commentary

You motivate by controlling the consequences of behavior. The supervisor is unwittingly rewarding undesirable behavior here. Jacob keeps bringing in partially completed work for approval and he gets it. He brings problems to the engineers and his supervisor and gets resolution. This is rewarding. Therefore Jacob is likely to continue even though the supervisor does not want this. The supervisor must make this present behavior yield undesirable consequences for Jacob and make the new desired behavior yield desirable consequences if Jacob is going to change this practice of not making his own decisions and of constantly bringing in work for approval. The supervisor should not give approval to partially completed work and should not make decisions for Jacob that Jacob can make. Indeed, the supervisor might be well advised to offer Jacob criticism for bringing in partially completed work and for not making decisions. Undesirable behavior should bring penalty, not reward. Jacob should be praised for bringing in the finished product and for making his own decisions.

Also, the supervisor needs to build Jacob's self-esteem and confidence in his own ability, and make the independent role expectation for Jacob crystal clear. Jacob apparently grew up learning to always check with an authority figure, stick to the rules, and be conservative. He did not learn to exercise initiative and to operate autonomously. He feels insecure when he has to function completely on his own without approving contact from others.

Management must make it clear to Jacob that a mistake now and then will not have disastrous consequences. Jacob must realize he does not have to worry about demotion, salary reduction or firing, for example. Management needs to reward Jacob for doing good, independent work and insist that Jacob do a whole job before he brings it in. Then assure he gets the recognition he deserves. This approach should, in time, make Jacob realize that he has the ability to do good work without constantly getting approvals and will show Jacob that real reward comes only from proper performance.

Punishment, or the threat of it, may be an excellent motivator for Jacob. Some folks understand punishment and will better direct their behaviors under the threat of punishment than under any type of reward, or positive outcome. The fear of peer group, or social group rejection, the fear of looking bad in the eyes of others, the fear of generating criticism from others, or the dislike of low self-respect can be perceived by a person as powerful incentives for avoiding poor performance. Punishment will reduce satisfaction but can spur motivation.

n. The Corporate Day-Care Center

When the idea was first expressed at the weekly staff meeting, those in attendance either smiled or laughed. What began as a brainstorming session for obtaining ideas about better utilization of the wasted space on First National Bank's main floor, turned into an animated discussion. Convert the wasted space into a day-care facility for children of the bank's employees?

There is something incongruous about a bunch of youngsters and babies in the midst of serious banking business, surrounded by a large number of the bank's customers.

Pamela Coolidge supervised eight tellers at First National Bank. She had a practice of scheduling the final hour of the working week, Friday afternoon from 4 until 5, as a staff meeting. The eight tellers gathered in the bank's employee lounge for their meeting. Not only were the sessions generally productive, they also gave the employees a chance to unwind from the week's work. In one sense, the last hour was also perceived as a reward. If you survived the previous thirty-nine hours, the fortieth was free from hassles.

During the meetings, information was exchanged about jobs and new procedures or policies. Time was also spent discussing problems experienced during the previous week. Morale was good in Pamela's group, although employee turnover continued to be a problem. Apparently, there was genuine friendship among the tellers.

Teller turnover is a common problem for many banks. Tellers are predominantly young. Many have very young children or are expecting. While some parents prefer employment over staying home, others, by necessity, take jobs separating them from their children during the working days; they need the money. Getting their children to babysitters or day-care facilities has always been a problem for many parents especially when the day-care centers are several miles from where the parents work.

As Pamela began the meeting, she explained that after covering the preliminaries they were going to take up the topic of space utilization on the first floor. As in many large banks, considerable center space is unused on the main floors. The various work areas are concentrated around the four walls. Recently, Pamela received a memo from the operations officer asking for suggestions on how to make better use of the center space. A prize of $100 would be awarded for the best suggestion—the one adopted. When the routine business was completed, the group turned to the space subject.

Pamela's employees made a number of recommendations. They ranged from the usual comments of "more greenery—foliage," to such ideas as turning a portion of the area into an exhibition space for showing paintings and crafts by community residents, adding more chairs for customers, and creating a small museum with artifacts from the period of the community's early pioneer settlement. Then Louise, the most outspoken member of the group, stated in a resolute voice, "I think we ought to convert the space into a day-care center.

"Out of the nine of us here, five have young children, and two more are expecting. We need a day-care center that is more convenient for all of us than the ones we are presently using. And there is plenty of space here. With good sound-proofing, there wouldn't be any noise, and it certainly would be a lot more convenient for us. I think we need a day-care center."

Questions

1. What do you think of Louise's idea? Pros? Cons?
2. What types of actions can management take to improve working conditions for employees? Separate your answers into two categories: (a) those things that can be done at a small cost, and (b) those that are more expensive.
3. What advantages does the bank derive from increasing employee job satisfaction and motivation? Why would the firm wish to reduce turnover for tellers?

Commentary

Louise's idea might work if it would cause employees to devote less attention and energy to finding day care, to carting children back and forth to distant day-care facilities, or to worrying about how their children are faring at day care. It might well reduce turnover because employees would have a real benefit in the in-house day-care center—convenience, confidence of quality care, knowledge of what their children are doing, and the like.

An in-house care center could, however, result in employees' taking time to see their children. Some rules restricting this kind of thing would probably have to be established, or employees might expend excessive time and effort with their children when they should be spending it at work.

Management can improve working conditions in many ways. Physical facility upgrading and social system upgrading are two avenues for improving conditions. Some of the least expensive approaches work best in terms of boosting motivation or satisfaction. For example, painting a room in pleasant colors can add much to satisfaction at low cost. Allowing workers opportunity to socialize at work, or designing work so workers can function as a team, can often boost motivation and satisfaction and does not cost big bucks either.

Reducing hazards in the workplace or arranging for workers to work together in accordance with the compatibility of their personalities can boost satisfaction, but may cost a great deal. Putting in paintings, greenery, and fountains can also boost employees' satisfaction in the workplace considerably, but the cost is often high. The point to keep in mind here is that generally worker satisfaction can be greatly affected by altering working conditions, but motivation is not affected unless you can somehow make working conditions change a function of performance.

The bank will decrease turnover, absenteeism, griping, employee drug abuse, grievance filing, tardiness, extended work breaks, rumor generation, interpersonal conflict, and so forth, by boosting satisfaction. Cutting these things saves money. Turnover is especially costly. Every turnover means additional monies spent on recruiting, selection, and training. Each time you bring in a new employee, expect a long start-up period. It takes people time to learn their jobs. Look for six months to two years' worth of frequent mistakes from new employees.

A firm needs motivated employees to get high performance and productivity. Satisfaction does not generate high performance, but motivation does. To get the bank's employees to be productive, a substantial component of the reward package must be made contingent on performance; performance must be made contingent on effort; the costs of high effort must not be too high; and off-the-job forces must not be so strong that they pull a great amount of the worker's effort away from the job. The day-care center proposed here could well reduce off-the-job pulls and thus aid on-the-job motivation.

o. Hiring Outside the Mainstream of Contemporary Thought

For quite some time a local investment company had been pursuing traditional wisdom and hiring well-rounded employees. The company looked for employees who had good educations, active social lives, well-developed hobbies, strong interests in community affairs, and strong family orientations. Top management felt that people with broad interests and abilities made the best employees.

On occasion management would delegate unusual tasks to employees, and they always looked for employees who were quite busy to give new assignments to. Again management was operating under the conventional wisdom, "If you want a job done, give it to a busy person."

A recently hired top manager set up and implemented a system to carefully measure employee performance. He found something startling. He discovered that employees with the widest ranging interests—hobbies, community involvement—had the lowest on-the-job motivation. He also discovered that the busy people given special assignments did the work fast but did not do high-quality work. He decided to prepare a report for the president describing this phenomenon, but he did not know how to explain it. Neither did he know what to recommend.

Questions

1. Explain what might be happening here. Why are these "broad interest" and "busy" people not putting out high effort?
2. What would you recommend for this company to do?

Commentary

The ENR model of motivation points out that employees distribute their total effort over many different endeavors that consume energy such that they maximize their total satisfaction. Very satisfying/attractive endeavors get relatively large portions of one's limited supply of effort. Less effort "pull" comes from endeavors, or pursuits, that are less satisfying. Employees with many interests besides the job will devote a considerable amount of energy to thinking about, and actively pursuing, those interests. They will spend time at the desk working on social club matters. They will worry about family problems instead of job issues. They will leave work early to pursue their favorite hobbies.

Busy people just have too much going to do well at any one thing. No matter who you are, you have to spread your efforts over multiple demands—multiple goal systems. A busy person often does not have the time available to devote substantial effort to an added assignment. So do not expect quality work done on that added assignment.

A company might do well to hire, instead of well-rounded people, individuals who have few outside interests, individuals who would get most of their kicks out of the job—individuals who would likely have few away-from-work interests and problems to siphon off their energies. What you may want here is the type who lives and breathes for the success of the company—people who will funnel most of their energy in the direction of their tasks because it is job task accomplishment that provides most of their satisfaction.

Instead of giving special assignments to busy people, the company might do well to try assigning to people who have time to do the assignment. Busy people look productive, but they cannot spend adequate time on a given assignment if there is not sufficient time available.

This company must recognize that part of every employee's effort capacity is directed away from the job. Action must be taken to minimize this off-the-job effort expenditure if substantial effort is to be allocated to the job. Careful screening during employee selection plus assigning tasks to the right people at the right time can help assure those to whom tasks are delegated will allocate sufficient effort to their assignments.

p. The New Performance Rating Program

Miles Johnson is supervisor of a district sales office in a town of about a half million persons. Several months ago Johnson studied various articles and pamphlets about performance rating in order to determine if he could improve the rating plan which he had for his salespeople. On the basis of his reading he did develop a new rating plan which has been in effect for six months. Recently he made the following statement about his new plan:

The new plan has definitely increased morale and productivity of my employees. Formerly I ranked my people strictly on dollar volume. The highest producer was number one, and so on down the line. The ranking was posted on the bulletin board so that each salesperson knew the ranking of all other salespeople. The purpose was to increase competition, and it did accomplish this goal, but it did not tell the whole story about their performance. For example, the top producer in sales was also the worst in delinquent accounts receivable. Some of the lower producers in sales were also found to be better in sales discount expense than some of their higher-producing colleagues. I now have a performance appraisal that recognizes a person's rank in each of ten important categories of the total job, and this new approach has given my organization a tremendous boost. My people now work for achievement of the whole job, rather than for the one measure of sales volume.

Questions

1. Has Johnson improved his performance rating program? Explain how in terms of ENR.
2. Can you recommend further improvements for Johnson to make? If so, explain them.

Commentary

Johnson has definitely improved his performance rating program. By recognizing people's achievements in all aspects of the job, he has caused employees to see the reward system as fairer and has realized a better allocation of the efforts of his people. Before, performance on only one part of the job was rewarded. This caused other essential task elements to be neglected. An overall best result was not forthcoming.

Effort allocation, or distribution, is a big part of the motivation problem. Employees will slight task areas that may be important, but that do not provide much in the way of rewards. Good job descriptions that indicate approximate percentages of time to give to each task area and that indicate the relative importance of task areas can guide workers toward an optimal distribution of effort. Also, performance evaluation that not only rates employees on all relevant responsibilities, but also weights those areas of responsibility to show their relative importance, goes far toward helping employees see the proper allocation of effort.

A weakness in Johnson's system is the emphasis it places on ranking employees. This makes it impossible for everyone to do well. Some are *forced* to the bottom even though their performances may be admirable. It is better to have objective performance standards for each employee. If an employee reaches those standards or surpasses them, he or she should be judged successful.

Systems that measure performance by forced comparison force a percentage of the work force to fail. Workers see chances are good that effort will not lead to performance (as measured), and consequently no reward will be forthcoming.

To improve this program further, Johnson might develop job descriptions that indicate approximately what percentage of the worker's day should be spent on nonwork or semi-work activities. Often employees' task-directed efforts suffer because they are pulled to nonproductive rap sessions, social exchanges, political maneuverings, and other distracting events. Often, they spend too much time on semi-work. Interstation travel, required but unimportant meetings, and the like can soak up immense blocks of time and energy. A job description that shows expected allocation of one's time to all at-work time-consuming activities can help assure that enough effort goes to where it should—to the priority task assignments.

q. Slow, GI's at Work

Eight military personnel in basic training were sent out one morning by their TI (training instructor) to paint barracks. Eight different buildings were to be painted, so one GI was assigned to each building.

At noon the PL (platoon leader) was sent out to check on how the painting was progressing. Here is what happened.

The PL visited GI #1:
> *PL:* "You're not progressing too fast."
> *GI #1: "Too hot."*

The PL visited GI #2:
> *PL:* "You're going great."
> *GI #2:* "Yeh, the TI said if we did a good job, we'd get a weekend pass."

The PL visited GI #3:
> *PL:* "You're not moving very fast."
> *GI #3:* "Why bother, they bring two gallons of paint over every four hours. If I paint any faster, I'll need five or six gallons per hour. No sense to hurry."

The PL visited GI #4:
> *PL:* "Wow, you're moving right along."
> *GI #4:* "You bet. The TI said if we didn't get this done, we would receive two demerits and have latrine duty the rest of the month."

The PL visited GI #5:
> *PL:* "You're having trouble getting in gear, aren't your? I don't understand. You were promised a quick promotion if you got this done today."
> *GI #5:* "Who wants a promotion?"

The PL visited GI #6:
> *PL:* "You're moving at a snail's pace. Didn't they tell you that you would be considered for a promotion if you finished this today? Don't you want a promotion?"

GI #6: "Oh, sure I do—very much. But what's the realistic chance of that? There are only two slots open for promotees and fifty-five of us competing for those two slots."

The PL visited GI #7:
   PL: "How come you're playing your guitar?"
   GI #7: "Hey, they don't care what we do. Supervision here is loose. They didn't tell me just what they expected accomplished or when. I figure this is a great chance to do what I want to do."

The PL visited GI #8:
   PL: "You have done almost nothing. What's the matter?"
   GI #8: "I had to spend time helping an accident victim in the street out front."

Question

Using the ENR conceptual framework, identify the specific motivational forces at work in each of the above cases.

Commentary

For GI #1: This GI is avoiding high effort because of the perceived cost associated. It is hot. High effort would be very tiring and uncomfortable in the heat. It might lead to sickness.

For GI #2: This GI is exerting high effort because he knows he will get a valued reward if he does so. He perceives a strong performance-reward contingency.

For GI #3: This GI is not motivated because of a job design problem. If he works faster, he will run out of paint sooner. Higher effort will not yield greater results. Performance is constrained by inadequate input.

For GI #4: This GI is exerting high effort because of the threat of penalty. If he does not work hard, he will be punished with two demerits and latrine duty. He is trying hard to avoid these negative outcomes.

For GI #5: This GI is not motivated even though he is promised a reward contingent on performance. He does not value the reward being offered. An unvalued reward, no matter how large or how well tied to performance, cannot motivate.

For GI #6: This soldier wants a promotion and he knows he can only get a promotion by performing, but he knows even with performance the chances of promotion are minuscule. This is because many others are competing for the limited number of slots open for promotion. He sees a high probability, therefore, of performance not paying off. The performance-reward correlation is perceived to be low.

For GI #7: This GI has not been properly directed. He is not sure what to do or how to allocate his effort. There is no supervision. There is no job description, nor similar data, to channel his efforts. When such a situation exists, one tends to pursue self-interests. When no rewards or penalties are issued relative to work tasks, one seeks the path of least resistance and does what he wants. It is more fun to play your guitar than work! We have an effort allocation problem—an at-work, off-the-job pull—which could easily be solved with better job descriptions, closer supervision, and a system of rewards and penalties.

For GI #8: This person did not exert effort on the job because his energy was drawn off the job by an accident. He did not have time for the job because the accident demanded his time. The accident was an off-the-job pull that siphoned effort away from the job, causing at-work motivation (effort) to be low.

B. EXERCISES AND INSTRUMENTS TO HELP IN MOTIVATING WITH THE EFFORT–NET RETURN MODEL

The exercises and instruments on the following pages are arranged to address motivation issues in approximately the same sequence those issues were developed in earlier chapters.

a. **How Do You Perceive Your Ability to Get the Job Done**

This instrument can be used to find out the degree to which employee ability will permit effort to lead to performance. Simply have an employee rate his/her perceptions on each of the following scales. Once completed, you can spot the low ratings which suggest how perceived ability may constrain effort expenditure. Action can then be taken to overcome these perceptual "stumbling blocks" to performance.

Questionnaire

1. How confident are you in your ability/skill to do your job?

| |_____|_____|_____|_____|
Not at all   Somewhat   Fair Degree   Quite   Highly
Confident   Confident   of Confidence   Confident   Confident

2. How strongly do you feel your personality traits support your job performance?

| |_____|_____|_____|_____|
Do not   Support   Support to a   Considerably   Highly
Support   Somewhat   Fair Degree   Support   Support

3. To what degree do you possess the technical knowledge and skill necessary to do your job well?

| |_____|_____|_____|_____|
Very Low   Some   Medium   Substantial   Very High
Degree   Degree   Degree   Degree   Degree

4. To what degree do you see that quality help is readily available to you if you need it?

| |_____|_____|_____|_____|
Very Low   Some   Medium   Substantial   Very High
Degree   Degree   Degree   Degree   Degree

5. To what degree do you feel you were properly oriented, or indoctrinated, for your job?

| |_____|_____|_____|_____|
Very Low   Some   Medium   Substantial   Very High
Degree   Degree   Degree   Degree   Degree

6. To what degree do you think your abilities match the demands of
    your job?

|_____|_____|_____|_____|
Very Low   Some   Medium   Substantial   Very High
Degree   Degree   Degree   Degree   Degree

7. How often do you receive required skills upgrading?

|_____|_____|_____|_____|
Not at   Sometimes   Half the time   Often   Always
All   When Needed

8. To what degree do you possess the conceptual skills needed to do
    your job well?

|_____|_____|_____|_____|
Very Low   Some   Medium   Substantial   Very High
Degree   Degree   Degree   Degree   Degree

9. To what degree do you possess the interpersonal skills required to
    do your job well?

|_____|_____|_____|_____|
Very Low   Some   Medium   Substantial   Very High
Degree   Degree   Degree   Degree   Degree

10. To what degree do you possess the problem solving skills required
    on your job?

|_____|_____|_____|_____|
Very Low   Some   Medium   Substantial   Very High
Degree   Degree   Degree   Degree   Degree

11. How well do you manage your time?

|_____|_____|_____|_____|
Very Poorly   Poorly   Average   Good   Very Good

12. To what degree do you possess the aptitude to do your work well?

|_____|_____|_____|_____|
Very Low   Some   Medium   Substantial   Very High
Degree   Degree   Degree   Degree   Degree

13. To what degree do you possess the physical and emotional health necessary to perform your job well?

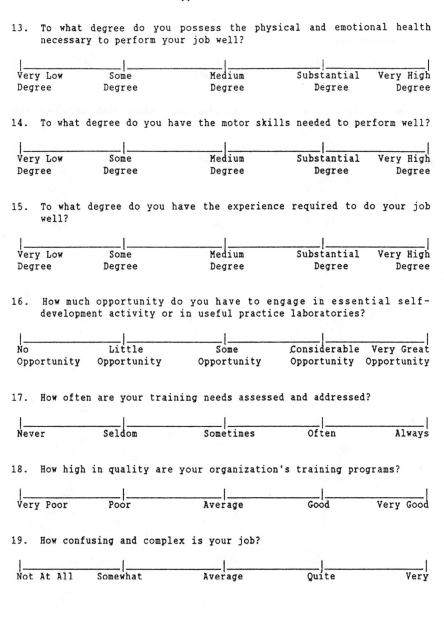

Very Low	Some	Medium	Substantial	Very High
Degree	Degree	Degree	Degree	Degree

14. To what degree do you have the motor skills needed to perform well?

Very Low	Some	Medium	Substantial	Very High
Degree	Degree	Degree	Degree	Degree

15. To what degree do you have the experience required to do your job well?

Very Low	Some	Medium	Substantial	Very High
Degree	Degree	Degree	Degree	Degree

16. How much opportunity do you have to engage in essential self-development activity or in useful practice laboratories?

No	Little	Some	Considerable	Very Great
Opportunity	Opportunity	Opportunity	Opportunity	Opportunity

17. How often are your training needs assessed and addressed?

| | | | | |
|Never|Seldom|Sometimes|Often|Always|

18. How high in quality are your organization's training programs?

| | | | | |
|Very Poor|Poor|Average|Good|Very Good|

19. How confusing and complex is your job?

| | | | | |
|Not At All|Somewhat|Average|Quite|Very|

20. How frequently do you get a chance to thoroughly prepare for new assignments?

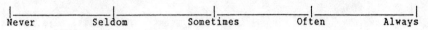

Never   Seldom   Sometimes   Often   Always

21. How compatible are your attitudes and values with required job assignments?

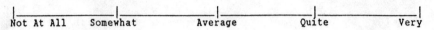

Not At All   Somewhat   Average   Quite   Very

b. A Training Needs Assessment

High ability is necessary for high motivation, but before a company invests in training to upgrade abilities a precise determination of training needs should be made. A form such as the following can be of use. Both the employee and manager can fill out one of these and their responses can be compared. Once needs have been delineated, clear learning objectives can be formulated to guide any training effort.

Training Needs Analysis Survey Form

Employee_____   Department_____

Supervisor_____   Date_____

Position: _____

Instructions: In column A, rate the skill necessary for the employee to successfully perform the job. Use the following ratings: 1--very important; 2--moderately important; 3--not important.

In column B, rate the need for training for each skill area which received a rating of 1 or 2 in column A. In assessing training needs, use the following ratings: 1--no training need; 2--moderate need for training; 3--immediate, critical training needed.

Skill Area: Clerical	(A) How important is the skill?	(B) Employee's need for training
Ability to read and comprehend rough draft material		
Typing speed		
Typing accuracy		
Proofreading skills		
Ability to use office machinery		

Skill Area: Clerical	(A) How important is the skill?	(B) Employee's need for training
Filing skills		
Ability to compose letters and memos		
Oral communications		
Ability to organize daily routine		
Human relations skills		

c. Does the Job Design Facilitate Getting Your Work Done

This instrument can be used to find out the degree to which job design will permit effort to lead to performance. Simply have an employee rate his/her perceptions on each of the following scales. Once completed you can spot the low ratings which suggest how perceived job design may constrain effort expenditure. Action can then be taken to address these perceived job design problem areas.

Questionnaire

1. To what degree do you possess the tools and equipment needed to do good work?

|_____|_____|_____|_____|
Very Low   Some   Medium   Substantial   Very High
Degree   Degree   Degree   Degree   Degree

2. How adequate are the quantity, quality, and timing of information inputs which you receive for carrying out your job?

|_____|_____|_____|_____|
Not At All   Somewhat   Average   Quite   Highly
Adequate   Adequate   Adequacy   Adequate   Adequate

3. How adequate are the quantity, quality, and timing of material inputs which you receive for carrying out your job?

|_____|_____|_____|_____|
Not At All   Somewhat   Average   Quite   Highly
Adequate   Adequate   Adequacy   Adequate   Adequate

4. Of what quality are the daily systems and procedures you follow in executing your job responsibilities?

|_____|_____|_____|_____|
Very Poor   Poor   Average   Good   Very High
Quality   Quality   Quality   Quality   Quality

5. How adequate is the feedback you receive on how well you're performing your job?

|_____|_____|_____|_____|
Not At All   Somewhat   Average   Quite   Highly
Adequate   Adequate   Adequacy   Adequate   Adequate

6. How clear to you are management's performance expectations of you?

|_____|_____|_____|_____|
Not At All   Somewhat   Fairly   Quite   Very
Clear   Clear   Clear   Clear   Clear

7. How well is your work area designed--what is the quality of the
    layout?

|_____|_____|_____|_____|
Very Poor   Poor   Fair   Good   Superior
Layout   Layout   Layout   Layout   Layout

8. Do you have adequate time to do your job well?

|_____|_____|_____|_____|
Not At All   Somewhat   Average   Quite   Highly
Adequate   Adequate   Adequacy   Adequate   Adequate

9. To what degree do unanticipated inputs to your job and interrup-
    tions interfere with your performance?

|_____|_____|_____|_____|
Very Low Degree Low   Some   Considerable   Very High
(No Inter-   Degree   Interference   Degree   Degree
ference)   (Great
                                                                Interfer-
                                                                ence)

10. To what degree are quality resources needed to do your job well
    readily available to you?

|_____|_____|_____|_____|
Not Avail-   Available To   Somewhat   Usually   Always
able   Limited Degree Available   Available   Available

11. To what degree do you possess the authority needed to get your job
    done well?

|_____|_____|_____|_____|
Very Low   Some   Medium   Substantial   Very High
Degree   Degree   Degree   Degree   Degree

12. To what degree are your tools, equipment, and facilities kept in good repair?

```
|_____|_____|_____|_____|
Very Low        Some           Medium         Substantial    Very High
Degree          Degree         Degree         Degree          Degree
```

13. How heavy is your work load?

```
|_____|_____|_____|_____|
Very Light      Light          Average        Heavy          Very Heavy
```

14. How realistic are your work goals?

```
|_____|_____|_____|_____|
Not At All      A Little        Fairly         Quite          Very
```

15. How challenging are your work goals?

```
|_____|_____|_____|_____|
Not At All      A Little        Fairly         Quite          Very
```

16. To what degree do your various work goals conflict?

```
|_____|_____|_____|_____|
Very Low        Some           Medium         Substantial    Very High
Degree          Degree         Degree         Degree          Degree
```

17. To what degree does the at-work social environment support your efforts at work?

```
|_____|_____|_____|_____|
Very Low        Some           Medium         Substantial    Very High
Degree          Degree         Degree         Degree          Degree
```

18. To what degree is your physical work environment healthy, safe, and pleasant?

```
|_____|_____|_____|_____|
Very Low        Some           Medium         Substantial    Very High
Degree          Degree         Degree         Degree          Degree
```

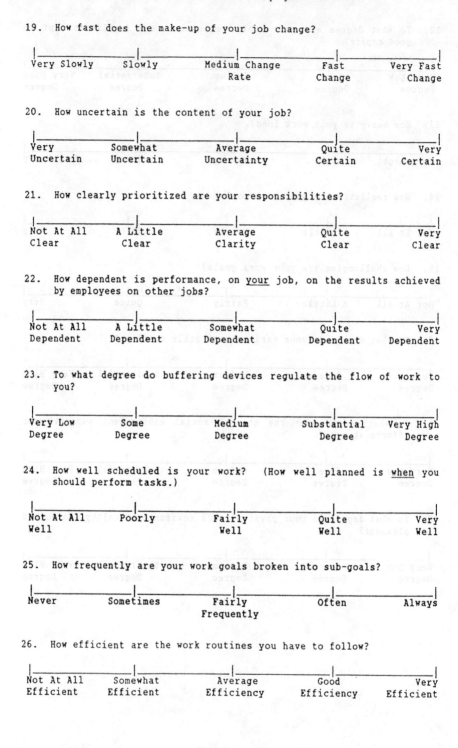

19. How fast does the make-up of your job change?

|_____|_____|_____|_____|
Very Slowly   Slowly   Medium Change   Fast   Very Fast
                             Rate   Change   Change

20. How uncertain is the content of your job?

|_____|_____|_____|_____|
Very   Somewhat   Average   Quite   Very
Uncertain   Uncertain   Uncertainty   Certain   Certain

21. How clearly prioritized are your responsibilities?

|_____|_____|_____|_____|
Not At All   A Little   Average   Quite   Very
Clear   Clear   Clarity   Clear   Clear

22. How dependent is performance, on your job, on the results achieved
     by employees on other jobs?

|_____|_____|_____|_____|
Not At All   A Little   Somewhat   Quite   Very
Dependent   Dependent   Dependent   Dependent   Dependent

23. To what degree do buffering devices regulate the flow of work to
     you?

|_____|_____|_____|_____|
Very Low   Some   Medium   Substantial   Very High
Degree   Degree   Degree   Degree   Degree

24. How well scheduled is your work? (How well planned is when you
     should perform tasks.)

|_____|_____|_____|_____|
Not At All   Poorly   Fairly   Quite   Very
Well   Well   Well   Well

25. How frequently are your work goals broken into sub-goals?

|_____|_____|_____|_____|
Never   Sometimes   Fairly   Often   Always
                               Frequently

26. How efficient are the work routines you have to follow?

|_____|_____|_____|_____|
Not At All   Somewhat   Average   Good   Very
Efficient   Efficient   Efficiency   Efficiency   Efficient

d. Developing A Performance-Reward Schedule

    Well written, published and distributed performance-reward
schedules can strengthen one's perception of the performance-reward
linkage. These schedules can be developed for any job and most any
specific duty or responsibility within a job. What you have to do is
decide different levels of rewards to be granted for different levels
of measured performance. Critical here is developing good ways of
measuring performance as well as planning the right kinds and amounts
of rewards for each different performance level. Below is a sample
performance reward schedule for one area of responsibility within a
salesperson's job.

Performance-Reward Schedule for Total Sales*

Performance Level	Reward (or Penalty)
Very poor - Fair	A. Loss of self-planning and scheduling. Base salary retained.
$100,001-120,000	B. Self-planning and scheduling permitted. Base salary.
$120,001-140,000	C. B plus $2,000 bonus.
$140,001-160,000	D. B plus $4,000 bonus.
$160,001-180,000	E. B plus $6,000 bonus, plus 2 points toward promotion.
$180,001-200,000	F. B plus $6,000 bonus, plus 4 points toward promotion.
$200,000+	G. B plus $6,000 bonus, plus 6 points toward promotion, plus 5 percent of sales above $200,001.

*Remember that such a schedule should be prepared for all performance
criteria. Here is exhibited only the schedule for the total sales
criterion.

e. A Sample Performance Evaluation Instrument

You cannot motivate employees without assessment of their performance, and without <u>valid</u> assessment. One can not perceive a strong link
between real performance and rewards if quality evidence of performance
level is not made available. Rewards received independent of
performance or received arbitrarily do not motivate. An instrument
such as the sample below can be developed for any job for the purpose
of recording performance. Once performance scores are determined,
rewards appropriate to the measured levels of performance can be
bestowed--perhaps by plan as depicted in the previous section.

Quarterly Employee Performance Evaluation for Salespersons*

Evaluator_____

Employee_____

Date_____

1. Criteria: Total Sales ($).
                           Performance Level:

|—————|—————|—————|—————|—————|—————|—————|—————|
0   1   2   3   4
($0)   ($50,000)   ($100,000) ($150,000) ($200,000+)
Very Poor   Poor   Fair   Good   Very Good

2. Criteria: Number of new clients.
                           Performance Level:

|—————|—————|—————|—————|—————|—————|—————|—————|
0   1   2   3   4
(0 clients) (4 clients) (8 clients) (12 clients) (16+ clients)
Very Poor   Poor   Fair   Good   Very Good

3. Criteria: Quality of reports (organization, completeness, and
       accuracy).
                           Performance Level:

|—————|—————|—————|—————|—————|—————|—————|—————|
0   1   2   3   4
Very Poor   Poor   Fair   Good   Very Good

4. Criteria: Number of speaking or public service engagements.
                     Performance Level:

0	1	2	3	4
(1 Engagement) Very Poor	(3 Engagements) Poor	(5 Engagements) Fair	(7 Engagements) Good	(9+ Engagements) Very Good

5. Criteria: Willingness to accept special non-recurring assignments.
                     Performance Level:

0	1	2	3	4
Very Poor	Poor	Fair	Good	Very Good

6. Criteria: Travel costs incurred.
                     Performance Level:

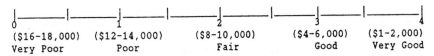

0	1	2	3	4
($16-18,000) Very Poor	($12-14,000) Poor	($8-10,000) Fair	($4-6,000) Good	($1-2,000) Very Good

7. Criteria: Quality of product demonstrations.
                     Performance Level:

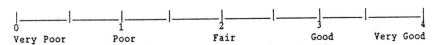

0	1	2	3	4
Very Poor	Poor	Fair	Good	Very Good

8. Criteria: Help given to new salespersons.
                     Performance Level:

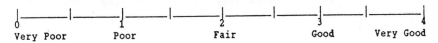

0	1	2	3	4
Very Poor	Poor	Fair	Good	Very Good

*This type of instrument can be markedly improved and performance assessment made more valid by behaviorally anchoring scales three, five, seven, and eight. Behaviorally anchoring a scale means describing the type of performance at each of the key points along the scale. The nature of each of the categories--very poor, poor, fair, good, and very good performance--along each scale should be thoroughly spelled out. The evaluator must know what is really meant by "good" performance, "poor" performance, "fair" performance, etc. Also the instrument can be improved by "attaching" a number (say 1 to 10) to each scale to indicate the scale's relative importance in contributing to an overall performance score.

f. Establishing Your Need Profile

This questionnaire can help employees' insight into their needs.
Any employee can fill out one of these. By analyzing the results you
can tell what kinds of needs are most dominant in a person and, therefore, what kinds of rewards will be most valued and motivational.
Remember you can motivate people best by rewarding their strongest
needs.

You are to circle the number on each scale that represents how
important the item being rated is to you on your present job. The
number 7 means high importance; 4 is of medium importance; 1 would be
of low importance.

Questionnaire

1. The feeling of self-esteem a person gets from being
    in my job position: 1 2 3 4 5 6 7

2. The opportunity for personal growth and development
    in my job position: 1 2 3 4 5 6 7

3. The prestige of my job inside the company (that is,
    the regard received from others in the company):   1 2 3 4 5 6 7

4. The opportunity for independent thought and action
    in my position: 1 2 3 4 5 6 7

5. The feeling of security in my job position: 1 2 3 4 5 6 7

6. The feeling of self-fulfillment a person gets from
    being in my job position, that is, the feeling of
    being able to use one's own unique capabilities,
    realizing one's potentialities: 1 2 3 4 5 6 7

7. The prestige of my job position outside the company
    (that is, the regard received from others not in the
    company):   1 2 3 4 5 6 7

8. The feeling of worthwhile accomplishment in my job: 1 2 3 4 5 6 7

9. The opportunity, in my job, to give help to other
    people: 1 2 3 4 5 6 7

10. The opportunity, in my job, for participation in the
    setting of goals: 1 2 3 4 5 6 7

11. The opportunity, in my job, for participation in the
    determination of methods and procedures: 1 2 3 4 5 6 7

12. The authority connected with my job: 1 2 3 4 5 6 7

13. The opportunity to develop close friendships in my
    job: 1 2 3 4 5 6 7

Scoring

Compute your need scores for each of the need categories, using the following scoring form. By indicating how important the different items in the questionnaire are to you, you have demonstrated the relative strengths of your needs.

1. Enter the number you circled for each question in the space next to that number.

2. Next, add up the numbers in each column to obtain your total score for each need.

3. Then divide by the number of questions used to measure that need, to obtain a raw score.

4. Finally, subtract the national mean from each raw score to obtain your adjusted score for each need. Be sure to retain the sign (+ or -).

	Security	Social	Esteem	Autonomy	Self-Realization
	5c=	9c= 13c=	1c= 3c= 7c=	4c= 10c= 11c= 12c=	2c= 6c= 8c=
Total:	____	____	____	____	____
Divided by:	1	2	3	4	3
Equals Raw Score:	____	____	____	____	____
Minus National[1] Mean:	5.33	5.36	5.28	5.92	6.35
Equals Adjusted Score:	____	____	____	____	____

[1]You are asked to subtract the national means from your own score to obtain an "adjusted" score for each category. This adjusted score tells you how strong your needs are in relation to each other. If you only looked at the raw scores, you would probably find that most people score highest on self-fulfillment and lowest on esteem or security. National means from Porter's sample of 1,916 managers. These numbers are "grand means," for all levels of management combined.

g. Matching Rewards with Needs

Following is a list of common benefits and arrangements in the work environment. Which of Maslow's five types of needs do each of these types of rewards serve to satisfy? The five categories of needs are physiological, safety and security, social/belongingness, esteem and status, and self-actualization. This exercise helps you decide the best types of rewards for given needs. Answers are upside down below.

a. Wage or salary

b. Health insurance

c. Pension fund

d. Company softball team

e. Participatory decision-making

f. Opportunities for advancement

g. Congenial co-workers

h. Bonus plan incentives

i. Annual banquet or picnic

j. Protective equipment

k. Resident physician

l. Educational benefits

m. Training seminars

n. Comfortable physical environment

o. Coffee breaks

p. The informal organization

q. On-site daycare facilities.

Answers: (a) physiological, safety and security; (b) safety and security; (c) security; (d) social, esteem and status; (e) social, esteem and status; (f) esteem and status, self-actualization; (g) social; (h) physiological, safety and security; (i) social; (j) safety and security; (k) safety and security; (l) self-actualization; (m) physiological; (n) physiological; (o) self-actualization; (p) social, social; (q) safety and security; physiological.

h. Can You Recognize the Need

Each of the following work situations stresses the denial of one of four basic needs: (1) security, (2) social, (3) self-esteem, and (4) self-actualization. Before each situation write the number of the need being denied.

This exercise helps you recognize types of needs and situations that affect satisfaction of those needs. Answers are upside down below.

____ 1. A rumor of imminent layoffs is being circulated in the company, and the employees are upset.

____ 2. A new employee felt "left out" when she was not asked to join her fellow workers for coffee.

____ 3. A machine operator developed a way to cut production time. His supervisor adopted the plan for operators on similar machines without giving him credit. The man was resentful.

____ 4. A man who had worked hard on behalf of the union wished to be elected shop steward. At the last election, he was not nominated, and he felt let down by his friends.

____ 5. A worker received $15 extra in his weekly pay check. He felt ashamed that he did not report the mistake.

____ 6. A group of employees liked to go for coffee together. The boss divided them into two groups and made them go at different times. The employees were unhappy about the ruling.

____ 7. An employee, who felt he could not work smoothly with others, wanted to take a human relations course. The course required him to leave work 15 minutes early once a week, and he offered to make up the loss by coming in 15 minutes early on those days. The supervisor denied his request, thereby causing the employee a setback in his planning.

____ 8. A store manager set a goal of a 15 percent sales increase in the next six months. He failed to attain his goal, but he did increase sales by 5 percent. He was keenly disappointed.

____ 9. A salesman is worried because he has experienced a substantial drop in sales for no apparent reason.

____10. A manager resented having to cancel, at the last minute, elaborate plans for a camping trip with his family.

Answers: (1) security; (2) social; (3) & (4) self-esteem; (5) self-actualization; (6) social; (7) & (8) self-actualization; (9) security; (10) social.

i. Planning How to Motivate

     Below are brief descriptions of several individuals. Assume that
you are their manager. Select from the following the prescription that
you feel would be most likely to motivate each person to improve
performance. Explain your reasons for selecting it. This exercise
gives you practice in developing specific motivational plans for
different individuals. There are no purely right or wrong answers
here. Just be sure you can justify your particular prescription in
light of the facts.

Prescriptions

a. An individual incentive plan.
b. Recognition for achievement.
c. A salary increase.
d. The threat of demotion or discharge.
e. Additional status (for example, a bigger office, a title, carpeting
    in the office, a secretary)
f. A group profit-sharing plan.
g. Job enrichment.
h. Additional fringe benefits.
i. More participation in management decisions.
j. More freedom of action (that is, less supervision).

Brief Descriptions

#1. Jim Hammer is a marketing representative for a large pharmaceut-
     ical firm. His job involves calling on physicians to promote the
     firm's line of prescription drugs. He is 31 years old, married,
     has one child, and holds a college degree in business administra-
     tion. He has been with the firm five years and earns $27,300
     annually.

#2. Barbara Oldeck is the head pediatrics nurse at a large public
     hospital. She is 24 years old, married, has two children, and is
     currently pursuing a master's degree. She has a reputation among
     staff physicians as an extremely competent nurse. Her yearly
     salary is $23,300.

#3. John Ekard is vice president of operations for one of the nation's
     largest fast-food franchisers. He is 49 years old, divorced, and
     has three children--two attend college, and one is married. He
     has been with the company for nine years, and he earns a salary of
     $82,500 per year. He is among a group of top-level executives in
     the company who share in company profits through a bonus system.

#4.   Dave Noe is a part-time employee for a large supermarket chain. He is 26 years old and an Air Force veteran, and he worked for the firm before entering the Air Force and has worked for it since being discharged. He is a highly valued employee, and he earns approximately $7.80 per hour. He attends a local university and at present is completing the final 15 hours for a degree in business administration.

#5.   Marie Glass is assistant director of market development for a new space industry firm. She is 32 years old, single, bright, witty, and energetic. She exemplifies the "new woman." Her annual salary is $30,000. She has just completed her master's degree.

j. What Do Workers Want

This exercise provides you with an opportunity to compare what
you, as a supervisor or manager, think employees want from their jobs
with what workers themselves say they want.

Rank the following ten job factors in order from the factor that
you think employees most want (number 1) to the factor that you think
employees least want (number 10). Then compare your answer with what
employees say they want. What employees say they want (determined from
a large national survey) are given upside down below. Any surprises?

____a. Good relationship with peers.

____b. Opportunity for promotion.

____c. Good organizational administration.

____d. Security.

____e. Good pay.

____f. Interesting work.

____g. Good working conditions.

____h. Recognition for good work.

____i. Knowing what is happening.

____j. Good relationships with supervisor.

Answers: (a) 4; (b) 6; (c) 10; (d) 1; (e) 5; (f) 7; (g) 9; (h) 2; (i) 8; (j) 3.

k. Measuring the Strength of the Perceived Performance-Reward Linkage

    and Satisfaction

     This instrument can be used to find out the degree to which one
feels that performance leads to reward. Simply have an employee rate
his/her perceptions on the first two scales in each of the following
sets. Once completed you can spot conditions contributing to low
motivation. If one values a reward highly--i.e., thinks an item is
very important--<u>and</u> sees that item as highly contingent (dependent) on
performance, then that item will motivate. If an item is not regarded
as important <u>and</u>/or is not highly dependent on performance, it will not
motivate.

     This instrument can also be used to measure one's satisfaction.
The third scale in each set does that. Once one has completed ratings
on the third scale in each set, the analyst can spot areas contributing
to low satisfaction.   Once problem areas with either motivation or
satisfaction are detected with this instrument, specific actions can be
taken to address deficiencies.

Questionnaire

1. a. How important to you is being accepted by and having good rela-
        tions with the boss?

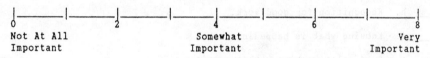

0   2   4   6   8
Not At All   Somewhat   Very
Important   Important   Important

    b. How dependent is acceptance and the quality of your relations
        with the boss on your level of effort, or job performance?

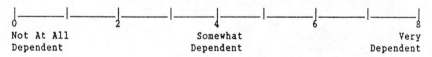

0   2   4   6   8
Not At All   Somewhat   Very
Dependent   Dependent   Dependent

    c. How satisfied are you with the present degree of acceptance and
        the quality of your relations with the boss?

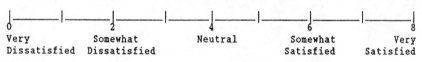

0   2   4   6   8
Very   Somewhat   Neutral   Somewhat   Very
Dissatisfied   Dissatisfied   Satisfied   Satisfied

2. a. How important to you is job security?

Not At All   Somewhat   Very
Important   Important   Important

   b. How dependent is your job security on your level of effort, or performance?

Not At All   Somewhat   Very
Dependent   Dependent   Dependent

   c. How satisfied are you with your present job security?

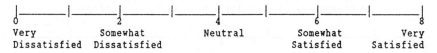

Very   Somewhat   Neutral   Somewhat   Very
Dissatisfied   Dissatisfied   Satisfied   Satisfied

3. a. How important to you is having an opportunity to learn and grow, and to develop expertise and competence, through your job?

Not At All   Somewhat   Very
Important   Important   Important

   b. How dependent is your on-the-job learning, growth, and development on your level of effort, or performance?

Not At All   Somewhat   Very
Dependent   Dependent   Dependent

c. How satisfied are you with the amount of opportunity that your job provides for you to learn, grow, and develop?

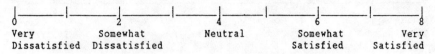

Very   Somewhat   Neutral   Somewhat   Very
Dissatisfied   Dissatisfied   Satisfied   Satisfied

4. a. How important to you is being accepted by and having good relations with co-workers?

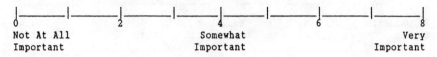

Not At All   Somewhat   Very
Important   Important   Important

b. How dependent is acceptance and the quality of your relations with co-workers on your level of effort, or performance?

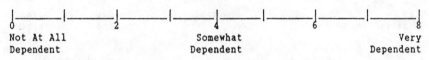

Not At All   Somewhat   Very
Dependent   Dependent   Dependent

c. How satisfied are you with the present degree of acceptance and the quality of your relations with co-workers?

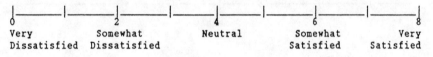

Very   Somewhat   Neutral   Somewhat   Very
Dissatisfied   Dissatisfied   Satisfied   Satisfied

5. a. How important to you is having good fringe benefits?

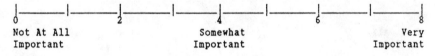

Not At All   Somewhat   Very
Important   Important   Important

b. How dependent on your level of effort, or job performance, is the quality of the "fringes" you receive?

Not At All   Somewhat   Very
Dependent   Dependent   Dependent

c. How satisfied are you with the present "fringes" you receive?

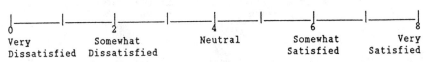

Very   Somewhat   Neutral   Somewhat   Very
Dissatisfied   Dissatisfied   Satisfied   Satisfied

6. a. How important to you is having a job with responsibility?

Not At All   Somewhat   Very
Important   Important   Important

b. How dependent on your level of effort, or job performance, is the amount of responsibility in your job?

Not At All   Somewhat   Very
Dependent   Dependent   Dependent

c. How satisfied are you with the present amount of responsibility that you have on your job?

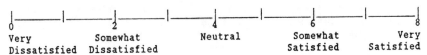

Very   Somewhat   Neutral   Somewhat   Very
Dissatisfied   Dissatisfied   Satisfied   Satisfied

7. a. How important to you is receiving recognition, praise, identity, or status for your contributions at work?

Not At All   Somewhat   Very
Important   Important   Important

b. How dependent is the amount of recognition, praise, identity, or status you receive at work on your level of effort, or job performance?

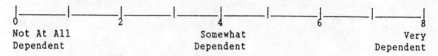

```
|————————|————————|————————|————————|————————|————————|————————|————————|
0                 2                 4                 6                 8
Not At All                    Somewhat                          Very
Dependent                     Dependent                         Dependent
```

c. How satisfied are you with the present amount of recognition, praise, identity, or status that you receive?

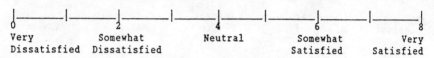

```
|————————|————————|————————|————————|————————|————————|————————|————————|
0                 2                 4                 6                 8
Very            Somewhat        Neutral         Somewhat          Very
Dissatisfied    Dissatisfied                    Satisfied         Satisfied
```

8. a. How important to you is having a sense of achievement, accomplishment, or productiveness at work?

```
|————————|————————|————————|————————|————————|————————|————————|————————|
0                 2                 4                 6                 8
Not At All                    Somewhat                          Very
Important                     Important                         Important
```

b. How dependent on your level of effort, or performance, is the degree to which you sense achievement, accomplishment, or productiveness?

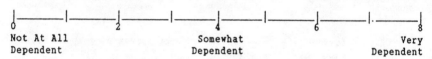

```
|————————|————————|————————|————————|————————|————————|————————|————————|
0                 2                 4                 6                 8
Not At All                    Somewhat                          Very
Dependent                     Dependent                         Dependent
```

c. How satisfied are you with your present level of achievement, accomplishment, or productiveness at work?

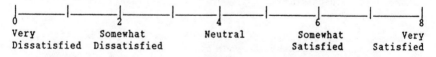

```
|————————|————————|————————|————————|————————|————————|————————|————————|
0                 2                 4                 6                 8
Very            Somewhat        Neutral         Somewhat          Very
Dissatisfied    Dissatisfied                    Satisfied         Satisfied
```

9. a. How important to you is receiving good pay?

Not At All   Somewhat   Very
Important   Important   Important

    b. How dependent on your level of effort, or performance, is the
        amount of your pay?

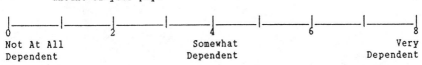

Not At All   Somewhat   Very
Dependent   Dependent   Dependent

    c. How satisfied are you with the present amount of your pay?

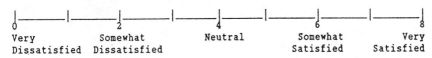

Very   Somewhat   Neutral   Somewhat   Very
Dissatisfied   Dissatisfied   Satisfied   Satisfied

10. a. How important to you is having job autonomy, or freedom, while
         you work?

Not At All   Somewhat   Very
Important   Important   Important

     b. How dependent is your job autonomy on your level of effort, or
         job performance?

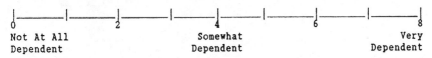

Not At All   Somewhat   Very
Dependent   Dependent   Dependent

     c. How satisfied are you with the present amount of autonomy you
         have at work?

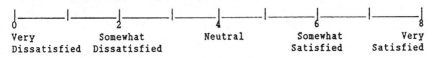

Very   Somewhat   Neutral   Somewhat   Very
Dissatisfied   Dissatisfied   Satisfied   Satisfied

11. a. How important to you is having interesting and challenging work?

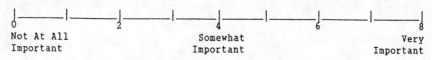

Not At All   Somewhat   Very
Important   Important   Important

b. How dependent on your level of effort, or performance, is the degree of interest and challenge you find in your job?

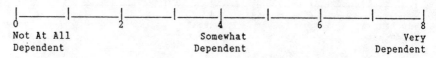

Not At All   Somewhat   Very
Dependent   Dependent   Dependent

c. How satisfied are you with how interesting and challenging your work is at present?

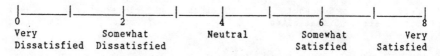

Very   Somewhat   Neutral   Somewhat   Very
Dissatisfied   Dissatisfied   Satisfied   Satisfied

12. a. How important to you is advancement, or. promotional opportunity?

Not At All   Somewhat   Very
Important   Important   Important

b. How dependent on your level of effort, or job performance, are the chances of you being promoted?

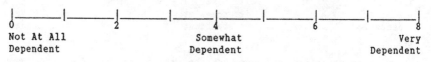

Not At All   Somewhat   Very
Dependent   Dependent   Dependent

c. How satisfied are you with your present potential for promotion?

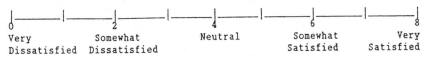

Very   Somewhat   Neutral   Somewhat   Very
Dissatisfied Dissatisfied   Satisfied   Satisfied

13. a. How important to you is having a safe and pleasant physical work environment?

Not At All   Somewhat   Very
Important   Important   Important

b. How dependent is the quality of the physical work environment on your level of effort, or performance?

Not At All   Somewhat   Very
Dependent   Dependent   Dependent

c. How satisfied are you with your present quality of your physical work environment?

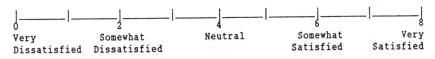

Very   Somewhat   Neutral   Somewhat   Very
Dissatisfied Dissatisfied   Satisfied   Satisfied

14. a. How important to you is being able to participate in management planning and decision making?

Not At All   Somewhat   Very
Important   Important   Important

b. How dependent on your level of effort, or performance, is the
    opportunity you are afforded to participate?

Not At All   Somewhat   Very
Dependent   Dependent   Dependent

c. How satisfied are you with the present opportunity you have to
    participate in planning and decision making?

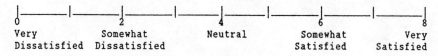

Very   Somewhat   Neutral   Somewhat   Very
Dissatisfied   Dissatisfied   Satisfied   Satisfied

15. a. How important to you is being kept informed of top level com-
         pany plans, decisions, and policy changes?

Not At All   Somewhat   Very
Important   Important   Important

b. How dependent is the amount by which you are kept informed on
    your level of effort, or job performance?

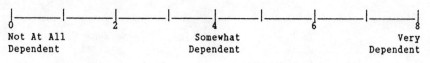

Not At All   Somewhat   Very
Dependent   Dependent   Dependent

c. How satisfied are you at present with the degree to which you
    are kept informed on top level plans, decisions, and policy
    changes?

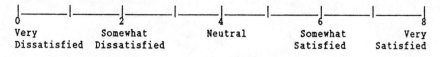

Very   Somewhat   Neutral   Somewhat   Very
Dissatisfied   Dissatisfied   Satisfied   Satisfied

16. a. How important to you is having power and influence?

Not At All   Somewhat   Very
Important   Important   Important

b. How dependent on your level of effort, or performance, is the
    amount of power and influence you are able to exercise in the
    organization?

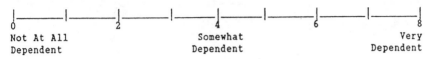

Not At All   Somewhat   Very
Dependent   Dependent   Dependent

c. How satisfied are you with the present amount of power and
    influence you are able to exercise?

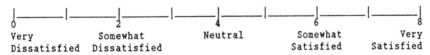

Very   Somewhat   Neutral   Somewhat   Very
Dissatisfied Dissatisfied   Satisfied   Satisfied

17. a. How important to you is having respect, or admiration, from
         your co-workers and the boss?

Not At All   Somewhat   Very
Important   Important   Important

b. How dependent is the amount of respect, or admiration, that you
    receive on your level of effort, or job performance?

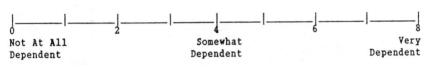

Not At All   Somewhat   Very
Dependent   Dependent   Dependent

c. How satisfied are you with the present amount of respect given
    you by co-workers and the boss?

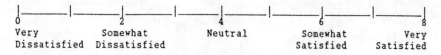

Very   Somewhat   Neutral   Somewhat   Very
Dissatisfied   Dissatisfied   Satisfied   Satisfied

18. a. How important to you is having a job with status?

Not At All   Somewhat   Very
Important   Important   Important

b. How dependent on your level of effort, or job performance, is
    the status of your job?

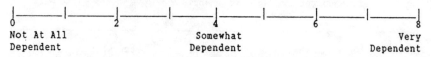

Not At All   Somewhat   Very
Dependent   Dependent   Dependent

c. How satisfied are you with the present status of your job?

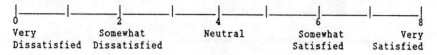

Very   Somewhat   Neutral   Somewhat   Very
Dissatisfied   Dissatisfied   Satisfied   Satisfied

19. a. How important to you is having an opportunity to provide serv-
    ice to others--to help others attain their goals?

Not At All   Somewhat   Very
Important   Important   Important

b. How dependent on your level of effort, or performance, is the
    opportunity you have to provide service to others?

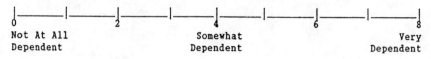

Not At All   Somewhat   Very
Dependent   Dependent   Dependent

c. How satisfied are you with the present amount of service you
    are able to give others through your work?

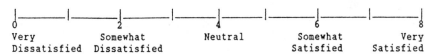

Very   Somewhat   Neutral   Somewhat   Very
Dissatisfied Dissatisfied   Satisfied   Satisfied

20. a. How important to you is performing work that you feel is really
         worthwhile, or meaningful?

Not At All   Somewhat   Very
Important   Important   Important

b. How dependent on your level of effort, or performance, is the
    feeling that you are doing something worthwhile, or meaningful?

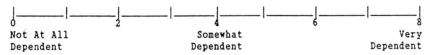

Not At All   Somewhat   Very
Dependent   Dependent   Dependent

c. How satisfied are you with the amount of worthwhileness you
    presently sense in your job?

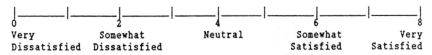

Very   Somewhat   Neutral   Somewhat   Very
Dissatisfied Dissatisfied   Satisfied   Satisfied

21. a. How important to you is working in an organization that has
         sound management and good administrative policy?

Not At All   Somewhat   Very
Important   Important   Important

b. How dependent on your level of effort, or job performance, is
    the soundness of management and the quality of administrative
    policy?

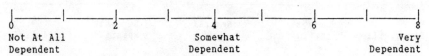

Not At All   Somewhat   Very
Dependent   Dependent   Dependent

c. How satisfied are you with the present soundness of management
    and the quality of administrative policy?

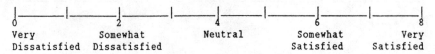

Very   Somewhat   Neutral   Somewhat   Very
Dissatisfied Dissatisfied   Satisfied   Satisfied

1. Your Personal Power Profile

To see if you can motivate others it is worthwhile to take stock
of your potential for controlling rewards available to subordinates.
You cannot reward without sufficient power which comes from your
control of things valued by the worker. Below is a sample social power
inventory. Try to develop one of these for yourself relative to motivating employees.

A Sample Power Inventory

Incentives (Rewards & Penalties)	Degree to Which the Incentives Are or Can Be Made Contingent on Performance	Degree to Which You, the Supervisor, Control the Incentives
Work associates	Low	Low
Pay	Medium	Low
Praise and recognition	High	High
Promotion	Low	Low
Demotion	Low	Low
Quality of physical work environment	Low	Low
Job content/work assignments	Medium	Low
Quality of on-the-job social relations	Medium	Low
Criticism	High	High
Quality of company's image	Low	Low
Quality of organizational communications	Low	Low
Job security	Medium	Low
Learning and growth opportunity	High	Medium
Fringe benefits	Low	Low
Job autonomy	Medium	Medium
Awards & symbols of recognition	High	High
Opportunity for worker to participate in decision making	High	Medium
Amount of authority given worker	High	Medium
Meaningfulness of work	Medium	Low
Soundness of administrative policy and practice	Low	Low
Invitations to employee social events	Medium	High
Privileges	High	Medium
Black marks on employee's record	High	High
Prizes and gifts	High	High

m.　Plotting Rewards and Costs to Determine Motivation

This exercise gives you some practice in relating data to the ENR model. Review the data below then plot it on a graph. From the graph determine how motivated the person will be, i.e., how many units of effort will maximize the unit different between rewards and costs? Your graph should look like those constructed in Chapter One. How motivated the person will be is given upside down below.

Units of Effort	Unit Value of Rewards	Unit Value of Costs
1	30	10
2	40	12
3	50	20
4	60	35
5	70	60
6	80	130

Can you determine by how much motivation will increase if the slope of the reward function is doubled and if it crosses your vertical axis at zero? What will happen to motivation if the slope of the reward function is doubled and crosses the horizontal axis at 4 units of effort?

Answers: Approximately 3 units of effort expenditure will be the effort level that will maximize satisfaction (i.e., net return). You can see this from the graph or from scrutinizing the data directly. To determine what happens to motivation when the slope is doubled carefully draw the new reward curve and then note the new effort level that maximizes satisfaction.

n. Measuring the Impact of Costs on Motivation

This instrument can be used to find out how costs may affect one's motivation. Simply have an employee rate his/her perceptions on each of the following scales. Once completed you can spot the ratings which suggest how perceived high costs associated with high effort and perceived low costs associated with low effort interfere with motivation. Action can then be taken to overcome these cost problems.

Questionnaire

To what degree do you perceive that each of the following costs are incurred when you exert high effort?

At high effort the cost at the left is perceived to be:

	High	Medium	Low
1. Fatigue	___	___	___
2. Stress	___	___	___
3. Boredom	___	___	___
4. Anxiety/tension	___	___	___
5. Fear of failure	___	___	___
6. Fear of hurting others	___	___	___
7. Frustration	___	___	___
8. Opportunity cost	___	___	___
9. Fear of the unknown	___	___	___
10. Fear of injury	___	___	___
11. Fear of peer rejection	___	___	___
12. Fear of creating or con- fronting conflict	___	___	___
13. Other costs	___	___	___

To what degree do you perceive that each of the following costs are incurred when you exert low effort?

At low effort the cost at the left is perceived to be:

	High	Medium	Low
1. Criticism from the boss	____	____	____
2. Peer rejection	____	____	____
3. Increased probability of demotion, transfer, firing	____	____	____
4. Bad performance write up for your file	____	____	____
5. Undesirable work assignments	____	____	____
6. Loss of privileges	____	____	____
7. Fear of some other type	____	____	____
8. Other costs	____	____	____

o. Measuring the "Pull" from Alternative Systems

This instrument can be used to find out how off-the-job goal
systems reduce on-the-job motivation. Simply have an employee rate
his/her perceptions on each of the following scales. Once completed
you can spot the ratings which suggest problem forces. Action can then
be planned to reduce these "pulls."

Questionnaire

1. To what degree, on average, do away-from-work forces such as family
    demands, professional interests, hobbies, community organizations
    in which you participate, etc., divert your thoughts and energies
    away from your job?

|_____|_____|_____|_____|
Very Low   Some   Medium   Substantial   Very High
Degree   Degree   Degree   Degree   Degree

2. To what degree, on average, do at-work, off-the-job factors such as
    rap sessions, socializing, job politics, self-interest pursuits,
    coffee breaks, etc., divert your thoughts and energies away from
    your job?

|_____|_____|_____|_____|
Very Low   Some   Medium   Substantial   Very High
Degree   Degree   Degree   Degree   Degree

3. To what degree do low priority duties and responsibilities,
    interruptions, etc., "siphon" your attention and efforts away from
    high priority duties/responsibilities--i.e., to what degree do low
    priority items take up more time and effort than they probably
    should?

|_____|_____|_____|_____|
Very Low   Some   Medium   Substantial   Very High
Degree   Degree   Degree   Degree   Degree

4. In general, what factors or forces draw some of your energies and
   time away from your priority work? Please list from strongest
   force to weakest.

1._____   6._____

2._____   7._____

3._____   8._____

4._____   9._____

5._____   10._____

p. A Sample Job Description

Below is a sample job description showing time percentages and priorities for duties. Such a job description can prove invaluable for giving clear direction to employees and for aiding employees in distributing their efforts to maximize aggregate performance.

Job Description

Date:_____   Job Title: Benefits Manager_____

Div. Administration_____ Dept: Personnel_____ Sect:_____

Reports to: Personnel Director_____

Supervises: N/A_____

Duties & Responsibilities	% of Time Spent	Importance
1. Maintains ERISA reporting calendars for TSA, Retirement Plan, LTD, and Life Insurance/Health Insurance.	5	8
2. Prepares and files appropriate reports to IRS, DOL, and employees, including gathering and verifying information from all insurance companies and/or other sources.	2	8
3. Maintains ERISA records for Retirement Plan. Correlates and insures accuracy of records with Trustee, Actuary, and legal counsel.	1	9
4. Calculates retirement benefits and processes forms, including Vested Terminations, Early, Normal, and Late Retirement, including Joint and Survivor and Lump sum cash-out benefits.	3	9
5. Counsels employees regarding benefits at the time of transfer in status, termination and retirement. Monitors pay period benefits reports insuring accuracy.	5	7

Duties & Responsibilities	% of Time Spent	Importance
6. Processes garnishments on employees.	5	6
7. Approves requests for Educational Assistance and makes payments, and receives reimbursements to the Hospital.	2	5
8. Administers absence control program, monitoring excused and unexcused absences, records and insures proper disciplinary action is being executed according to established policy and procedures. Maintains records and distributes reports on absenteeism to Department Heads and Personnel Director.	10	5
9. Manages salary security program, including processing of claims insuring proper reporting to insurance companies and employee understanding of life and LTD benefits and procedures.	10	6
10. Manages health insurance program including counseling employees regarding benefits and claim procedures, pays billings and insures proper payroll.	.12	8

q. A Random Observation Sheet

     Doing a random observation tally on a worker can accurately show
you where the worker's efforts are being spent. By randomly observing
what the worker is doing enough times, you can determine just how
worker effort is being distributed. Unintrusive spot checks can give
an accurate profile of actual behavior. This actual behavior can then
be compared with that prescribed by the job description and insights
developed as to what needs changing.

Random Observation Sheet

Do four random observations per day per person for four weeks.

Person Observed: _____

	Monday		Tuesday		Wednesday		Thursday		Friday	
	Time	What Observed	Time	What Observed	Time	What Observed	Time	What Observed	Time	What Observed
Week #1										
Week #2										
Week #3										
Week #4										

r. The Motivation System Audit

You can use the following questionnaire to trouble shoot your overall system of employee motivation. Answering the questions will cue you on possible areas that need more attention.

A Sample Checklist for Auditing Your Motivational System

1. Are the rewards received by your employees really valued by them?

2. Are the rewards received by your employees sufficiently contingent on performance?

3. Do deficiencies in abilities and traits prevent the employees from being high performers?

4. Do deficiencies in design of the job (work) prevent employees from being high performers?

5. Are the costs (fatigue, stress, boredom, etc.) associated with exerting high effort being minimized?

6. Are penalties being properly used to promote high effort?

7. Is the pull from off-the-job at-work and off-the-job away-from-work goal systems being minimized?

8. Are the principles of motivation being applied in worker-training programs?

9. Are you using the principles of motivation to motivate yourself?

10. Is your company screening candidates for employment with recognition of their likely on-the-job motivation after hiring?

11. Are any of the managers in your company being trapped by motivation mythology?

12. Is your company taking action to address the reasons for declining American employee motivation?

13. Does your company have well-designed performance-reward and performance-penalty schedules?

14. Do you periodically investigate ways to increase your power to motivate? For example, do you regularly look for ways to increase the arsenal of rewards that you control? (See section 1. above.)

15. Do you periodically directly asses the levels of employee motivation and satisfaction in your company and take action in response to the results of such assessment?

16. Is lack of motivation a problem? (It may or may not be.)

17. Are some workers excessively motivated, causing their performance to actually be lower than it might otherwise be?

18. How much is it costing you to motivate the workers? Is it worth it?

19. Is your reward-cost structure designed to provide a high level of satisfaction as well as motivation?

20. Do you give adequate attention to tailoring your motivational system to individuals' needs?

21. Do you give adequate attention to influencing how employees *perceive* the rewards and costs they experience in your organization? Do your employees *perceive* the motivational system as you do?

22. Does your motivational system incorporate a full measure of both intrinsic and extrinsic rewards?

23. Does your reward system recognize the major sources of satisfaction--the types of rewards that satisfy Maslow's five categories of needs (see section g. above).

24. Do you assess performance regularly and validly and issue contingent rewards immediately following these assessments?

25. Do your employees understand how to motivate themselves?

26. Is motivation of the employee indeed possible? Do you have it within your power to motivate?

27. Do you know what specific behaviors you want to motivate?

28. Do the managers in your organization understand the principles of motivation?

29. Is giving attention to performance and motivation a "daily" activity or is it a "sometimes" activity?

30. Are employee efforts being directed in the right direction?

Bibliography

Allport, G. W., P. E. Vernon, and G. Lindsey. *Study of Values.* Boston, Massachusetts: Houghton Mifflin, 1951.

Barnard, C. I. *The Functions of the Executive.* Cambridge, Massachusetts: Harvard University Press, 1938.

_____. *Organization and Management.* Cambridge, Massachusetts: Harvard University Press, 1952.

Cascio, Wayne F. *Applied Psychology in Personnel Management.* Reston, Virginia: Reston Publishing Company, Inc., 1978.

Chruden, H. J., and A. W. Sherman, Jr. *Personnel Management.* Cincinnati, Ohio: South-Western Publishing Co., 1980.

Cummings, L. L., and Donald P. Schwab. *Performance in Organization.* Glenview, Illinois: Scott, Foresman and Company, 1973.

Equal Employment Opportunity Commission. "Uniform Guidelines." *Federal Register* (1978), Vol. 43, No. 166, 38295-38309.

Garrett, Leonard J., and Milton Silver. *Production Management Analysis.* New York: Harcourt Brace Jovanovich, Inc., 1973.

Gibson, James L., John M. Ivancevich, and James H. Donnelly, Jr. *Organizations—Behavior, Structure, and Process.* Dallas, Texas: Business Publications, Inc., 1979.

Grant, Philip C. "A Model for Employee Motivation and Satisfaction." *Personnel,* September-October 1979, Vol. 56, No. 5, 51-57.

_____. "Are the Costs of High Effort Too High?" *Trade,* May 1983, Vol. 3, No. 5, 14-15, 28-31.

_____. "Do Off-the-Job Pursuits Siphon Off Effort?" *Trade,* June-July 1983, Vol. 3, No. 6, 16-17, 26-29.

_____. "Does Effort Lead to Performance?" *Trade,* April 1983, Vol. 3, No. 4, 10, 23-26.

_____. "Does Performance Lead to Reward?" *Trade,* March 1983, Vol. 3, No. 3, 18-19, 20-23.

234 Bibliography

———. "Explaining Motivation Phenomena with the Effort–Net Return Model." *Nevada Review of Business and Economics,* Spring 1982, Vol. 6, No. 1, 29-32.

———. "Exploring the Relationship between Motivation, Satisfaction and Performance." *Personnel Administrator,* July 1983, Vol. 29, No. 7, 55-69.

———. "How Much Employee Motivation Is Desirable?" *Colorado Business Review,* November 1980, Vol. 33, No. 11, 2-4.

———. "How to Manage Employee Job Performance." *Personnel Administrator,* August 1981, Vol. 26, No. 8, 59-65.

———. "How to Manage Your Own Motivation." *Trade,* May 1982, Vol. 2, No. 5, 10-12, 18, 27.

———. "Employee Motivation: The Key to Training." *Supervisory Management,* June 1989, 16-21.

———. "Key Sources of Employee Satisfaction." *Trade,* December 1982, Vol. 7, No. 6, 12-15.

———. "Motivation: The Management of Negative Outcomes." *Supervisory Management,* 1989, in process.

———. "The Missing Link in Employee Selection." *Mississippi Business Review,* February 1981, Vol. 42, No. 8, 3-10.

———. "The Pivotal Role of Job Design in Employee Motivation." Unpublished paper.

———. "The Real Motivation Problem Is One of Effort Distribution." Unpublished paper.

———. "Why Employee Motivation Has Declined in America." *Personnel Journal,* December 1982, Vol. 61, No. 12, 905-909.

Heneman, Herbert G., and Donald P. Schwab. *Perspectives on Personnel/Human Resource Management.* Homewood, Illinois: Richard D. Irwin, Inc., 1978.

Herzberg, F., B. Mausner, and B. Snyderman. *The Motivation to Work.* New York: John Wiley and Sons, 1959.

Lewin, Kurt. *The Conceptual Representation and the Measurement of Psychological Forces.* Durham, North Carolina: Duke University Press, 1938.

Lundgren, Earl F., William J. Engel, and Earl A. Cecil. *Supervision.* Columbus, Ohio: Grid Publishing, Inc., 1978.

Luthans, Fred. *Organizational Behavior.* New York: McGraw-Hill Co., 1973.

McClelland, D. C., and D. G. Winter. *Motivating Economic Achievement.* New York: Free Press, 1969.

Maslow, Abraham H. *Motivation and Personality.* New York: Harper and Row, 1954.

Miller, D. W., and Martin K. Starr. *Executive Decision and Operations Research.* Englewood Cliffs, New Jersey: Prentice-Hall, Inc., 1969.

Miner, John B. *Theories of Organizational Behavior,* Hinsdale, Illinois: The Dryden Press, 1980.

Porter, L. W. *Organizational Patterns of Managerial Job Attitudes.* New York: American Foundation for Management Research, 1964.

Skinner, B. F. *Contingencies of Reinforcement.* New York: Appleton-Crofts, 1969.

Starr, Martin K. *Production Management—Systems and Synthesis.* Englewood Cliffs, New Jersey: Prentice-Hall, Inc., 1972.

Steers, Richard M., and Lyman W. Porter. *Motivation and Work Behavior.* New York: McGraw-Hill Co., 1979.

Thierauf, Robert J., and Robert C. Klekamp. *Decision Making Through Operations Research.* New York: John Wiley and Sons, 1975.

Vroom, V. *Work and Motivation.* New York: John Wiley and Sons, 1964.

Index

Ability, 15-32, 157-59, 187-90
Achievement drive, 118
Advice, 128-29
Antiwork, 139, 149-51
Aptitude, 25
Attitudes, 31-32
Authority, 34, 61-62, 113
Away-from-work pursuits, 124-39

Behavior, nonrelevant, 145
Biorhythms, 88-89
Buffering devices, 44

Clubs and associations, 127
Coaching, 57-58
Commuting distances, 130
Conceptual skills, 20-21
Conflict, 103-4
Constraints, 101-2, 127-28, 147
Costs: downplaying, 93; measurement,
    223-24; relation to effort, 87-121;
    sacrifices, 98
Counseling, 57-58
Criticism, 112-13

Delegation, 64
Diet, 89
Discipline, 114
Drug dependency, 131-32

Effort distribution, 154-55
Effort-net return model, 2
Equipment and tools, 34-35, 45
Exercise, 89-90
Expectations, 105, 163
Experience, 25-26
External system rewards, 129
Extracurricular activity, 124-25, 131,
    136-37

Failure, 100-101
Family problems, 126-27
Fatigue, 90, 104
Fear, 100-101, 108-9
Feedback, 36-37, 163
Friendship, 80-81, 109-10

Goals, 4-5, 37-39, 45-46, 50, 61,
    76-80, 139-40, 162-63
Goals, publicly stating, 110-11
Goal systems, 123-55, 135-36, 138-39,
    180-84, 225-26
Group cohesion, 109

Hazards, 93-94
Health, 24, 89-90, 130-31
Hobbies, 125
Humor, 102

Idle time, 152-53
Incentives, 167
Informal groups, 147-48
Inputs, 33-34
Interpersonal relations skills, 21

Job dependence, 43-44
Job descriptions, 144-45, 227-28
Job design, 28, 32-46, 143-44, 159-61,
   193-96
Job rotation, 94-95

Labor pooling, 146-47
Layout, 35-36, 40, 92
Learning and growth, 58-59
Leisure-time interests, 125
Loyalty, 56-57

Methods, 35-36
Moonlighting, 125-26
Motivation: and ability, 187-90; capacity,
   9-10; definitions, 1-2; expected costs,
   2; expected rewards, 2; and job design,
   193-96; measurement, 208-20; models,
   1; strategies, 11-13; system audit,
   231-32
Motor skills, 24

Needs, 3, 67-68, 164-65, 171-74
Needs assessment, 27, 191-92, 200-207
Negative outcomes, 2
Noncontingent rewards, 6, 141
Nonperformance, 60
Norms of production, 97-98, 109

Off-the-job time, 136
Opposing forces, 103
Organizational survival, 59
Organization-sponsored events, 137
Orientation programs, 17-18

Participation, 29, 64-65, 149
Pay, 59-60
Penalties: communicating, 107-8,
   115-16; consistent application, 116;
   contingency relations, 104-21, 176-79;
   and deficient performance, 113; group,
   110; mixes, 118; and needs, 107;
   packaging, 112; scheduling, 111;

structure, 115-17, 129-30, 142; timing,
   111
Penalty function, 106-7
Penalty schedules, 105-6
Perception, 2
Perfection, 101
Performance, 5-9, 15; low, 117-18;
   value of, 78
Performance dependency, 120
Performance evaluation, 52-54, 114-15,
   146, 162-63, 169-71, 182-83, 198-99
Performance reviews, 119-20, 144, 169-70
Personality, 23-24
Policies, 152
Politics, 134-35
Positive outcomes, 2, 47-66
Power, social, 221
Practice, 26-27
Problem solving skills, 22
Procedures, 35-36
Projects, 152-53

Random observation, 229-30
Responsibilities, uncertain, 138
Reward agents, 51, 54-55
Rewards: absolute level of, 126;
   adapting, 70-71; capacity for granting,
   50-51; contingency relations, 47-66,
   129, 141, 161-63, 164, 167, 208-20;
   extrinsic, 66, 82; fairness, 68-69, 167;
   group, 55, 70, 161-62; intrinsic, 163;
   magnitude, 68, 161, 165-66; mix, 72;
   overselling, 81, 166; packaging, 75;
   publicizing, 63-64, 74-76, 162-63;
   schedules, 51-52, 62, 69, 197; sources,
   73-74; timing, 65; value of, 67-85,
   132-33, 140
Role models, 65-66
Rules, 152

Satisfaction, 2, 5-9, 181, 208-20
Self-confidence, 17
Self-development, 26
Self-image, 112, 178
Self-interests, 133-34
Semi-work, 139, 149-51
Social environment, 40-41, 57, 99-100,
   148, 151-52
Stabilization policies, 134

Standards, 37-38
Stress management, 92-93, 104, 174-76

Tasks: change, 41; integration and
   sequencing, 43, 95; priorities, 42-43;
   uncertainty, 42, 96-97, 138; variety,
   36, 91, 139-40
Teams, 82-83
Technical skill, 19-20
Time management, 22-23
Training needs, 191-92
Training programs, 19, 27, 142-43

Utility, 72-73

Vacations, 91-92
Values, 31-32, 71-72
Value training, 71-72, 108
Volunteerism, 133

Work: breaks, 88; environment, 41,
   96, 154; ethic, 56; flow, 39-40, 99;
   low priority, 140-44; scheduling, 44-45
Worker capacity, 97
Workstations, 40, 151-53

About the Author

PHILIP C. GRANT is a management consultant and Professor of Management at Husson College, Bangor, Maine. He has authored over 100 professional articles and has written five books in the management field. His last book, *Multiple Use Job Descriptions*, is also published by Quorum Books. Dr. Grant is recognized for his expertise in managing human resource performance.